A BETTER ME

GARY
BARLOW
A BETTER ME

BLINK
bringing you closer

Published by Blink Publishing
The Plaza,
535 Kings Road,
Chelsea Harbour,
London, SW10 0SZ

www.blinkpublishing.co.uk

facebook.com/blinkpublishing
twitter.com/blinkpublishing

Hardback – 978-1-911600-97-8
Trade Paperback – 978-1-911600-98-5
eBook – 978-1-911600-99-2

A CIP catalogue of this book is available from the British Library.

Designed and set by seagulls.net
Printed and bound by Clays Ltd, Elcograf S.p.A.

1 3 5 7 9 10 8 6 4 2

Blink Publishing is an imprint of Bonnier Books UK
www.bonnierbooks.co.uk

I dedicate this book to
Colin Barlow, my amazing dad,
and to Poppy, our beautiful daughter.

PROLOGUE

SEVENTEEN STONE, TWO POUNDS

'If only you knew what's in my mind.'

I've got a recording studio at the back of the house. It's got a bathroom in its farthest corner and that's where I go to be sick. Dawn goes to bed early, so if I get back from a big dinner, I go there because it is the farthest place from our bedroom that I can go. I lay a towel down to kneel on. Just the thought of laying that towel down now makes me feel sick. The first time I did it, it took me fifteen minutes to get the job done. By now it takes me thirty seconds. Fingers go down my throat and I press down. I hate being sick but it's such a relief when I've done it.

This isn't a daily thing, but it's happening more and more frequently. I'm weeks away from it becoming a real problem. It's starting to scare me because I am relying on it. My logic goes, 'I'm on this diet and we're going out on Thursday but it's all right, I can chuck it up afterwards.' It is physically traumatic, kneeling down there and making myself sick. It shakes me up. I go back to bed and lie awake next to my beautiful wife, my heart racing, throat sore, worrying and overstimulated. I can never sleep after I've done it.

How had it come to this? I was a pin-up once, a teen idol. Lead singer in a band called Take That. Gary, Howard, Jason, Mark and Robbie. You may have heard of us. From 1990 to 1996 I was never more than a few hundred metres away from screaming girls. We were Britain's first manufactured boy band and I wrote and sang pretty much every one of their hits. Robbie Williams, the youngest band member, left in 1995. A year later the rest of us went our separate ways. I was 25. It was on the news; there were helplines for the fans. Yeah, that band.

I went solo. I was told and I believed I'd be a big solo star. My first album went to number one. The fame train kept running; the goodies it brings kept coming.

The second album was a different story. It bombed. I was humiliated in a very public way. The headline 'Take That's Gary Dumped by Record Label' was in stark contrast with what was happening for my former bandmate. Robbie Williams' star was in stratospheric ascendance and he was riding a wave of credibility. He hung out with all the Cool Britannia types like Kate Moss and Oasis, while I was holed up in my massive pop star mansion, chain-smoking, getting stoned and eating huge bowls of cereal.

I can count on my fingers the people who remained in my life once I'd been dropped. It was a few rock-solid mates and my family: Dawn, Mum, Dad, my brother Ian and his wife Lisa. Everyone else legged it. I'd made a lot of money by then, and if I'd wanted I could have retired on the royalties of all my hits.

That wasn't an option. Hard graft and routine is all I know. Music is all I can do. When the label dumped me, everything I had ever known was gone and all the routine and discipline and usefulness that went with it. A record deal was the one thing I'd held so high as a teenager when I was working the North West working men's clubs. They throw them out now. You win *The X Factor* or *The Voice* and you get a record deal. A record deal was a big thing back then. Now it's gone.

Suddenly, I was sitting on my arse all day with nothing to do.

Sometimes back in the Take That days, old Nigel Martin-Smith, our manager, would say, 'You're overweight.' The worst I felt when he said that was mildly annoyed, not hurt. I could pack in an extra run and go back to looking like Jean-Claude Van Damme. Mostly, we were on stage every night and didn't have to think about food. Lulu used to tour with us and always complained she needed to go on a diet afterwards because we'd go for an Indian every night after the show. She never bothered ordering. She just watched, aghast, taking the odd mouthful as we went in like a swarm of locusts. You've just spent two hours on stage doing the sparkly shirt equivalent of running a marathon. Touring life is great: you're getting exercise, you come off stage sweating; psychologically, you're being adored every night. What an artificial and totally brilliant place. You're being looked after, anything you want you can have. Well, that's gone.

Then there was nothing. For nearly a year absolutely nothing came. The house started to feel like a prison then, the studio its torture chamber. This was a time when studios were still dark, windowless places. I sat in there, day after day, doing nothing. I can remember every detail, the grey walls and that one particular piece of the skirting board in my studio that never joined properly at the floor. I'd just stare at the walls struggling to find a chord, let alone a song. The magic, the muse, all gone. That fucking crack in the skirting board, I can see it now. 'All right, okay, come on Gaz, let's update the software or put a new wire on something.' A simple thing that normally takes me five minutes could eat up an entire day. I'd go to the piano, sit at it, I'd lie underneath it. Nothing would come.

The work dried up. One day there was a glimmer of hope: the fax woke up and started to grind out a work offer. I stood over the machine, daring to be hopeful. Did I want to play the Child Catcher in *Chitty Chitty Bang Bang* at the Liverpool Empire? No, I did not. What a waste of paper.

* * *

In the fairground of showbiz, now I am the coconut. Piers Morgan told me at the start of our career, way back when nothing could possibly go wrong, 'Gary, people like newspapers because they love to read about the misfortune of others. Remember that.'

Remember it? I am living it. Everyone lines up to have a shot.

Where once people said, 'Love your new record!' now they just come up in my face, put their heads on one side, pityingly, and say nothing. Taking the car to the garage for a service, Robbie's 'Angels' comes on and they turn it up to 11. Rummaging through the CD racks in HMV – Amazon is a distant dream at this point – they start playing Robbie's new album. People spot me across the road and shout, 'How's Robbie?' Remember that thing kids used to do at school, cough out a word behind their hands? Well, now I'm in my early thirties and I'm still getting it. Cough 'Robbie!' It's got to the point where my mum shoots across the room like a bullet from a gun if one of his songs comes on. We all feel haunted by him.

Oh I can't tell you, it is constant. Oh, it is horrible. *Horrible.* It is just consistent and humiliating stuff that I am desperate to escape.

There is one blessing: this massive pop star mansion has massive walls and a gate with no doorbell. Once they are shut, the world is a better place. At first it is days, then weeks, then months when I won't leave the grounds. Dawn takes over and behaves as if everything is normal. She shops alone, takes the kids to school.

We never eat out. I am scared to. As soon as I do, someone will remind me of all that I've lost. So then I try to remind myself of everything I still have. For all that is lost, look at what I have gained. Look at these two beautiful kids I've got now; surely they're compensation? Aren't they? Kids make everything better, don't they? The rule with kids is you've only got to say positive things, 'Oh, it's amazing having kids', 'Oh, you don't know love till you have kids', 'Kids! They say the funniest things.'

The fear of having children as a man is not something you're ever asked about. You've just got to get on with it. You wake up to that realisation, 'Oh God. Is the baby up again? It was only two hours ago.'

Dawn will say, 'It's not all about you now.'

Then there's a sinking feeling. 'Okay. I'm really being pushed down the billing now; you sit there at night with a small child that appears to need absolutely no sleep and you start listing all the things that are lost: I've got no job. Now I've gone down the pecking order again. And then another child arrives. I sobbed uncontrollably when Emily was born; I was so overwhelmed by the fact I had this little girl, a daughter. But now there are two other little lives that must come first.

You can see why women get postnatal depression. They're just thrown into your arms, these kids, and they're so all-consuming and demanding. It's understandably all about the babies, all about the women; it feels like the men are left in the corner and flung the baby when it seems like the wife's pissed off and too tired to keep her eyes open any more. It's a really big thing in a man's life too. Becoming a dad is scary, you know, and especially for a pop star – a narcissist by nature who has fought to be in the spotlight all his life. Now not only have I lost my entire life's vocation, I'm now way down the bill at home, too.

It's all too much. Dawn and I don't discuss it, but she obviously saw me unravelling and ballooning before her eyes. I know my parents are worried about me. Often during these wilderness years I'd look at my brother and envy him. If I could be Our Ian, I wouldn't have any of these worries. His life is straightforward, simple; he goes out and works hard, comes home to his kids and his missus. He has his friends, he goes out, has a laugh. I long for Our Ian's life.

I avoid any discussion of it with the people closest to me because when you leave home and you do well and you travel and make money (and you're by nature a control freak) then by default, you become like the head of the family. With that thought I want to protect them from the truth of how bad it is, so I just make it up: 'Yeah, I'm off to London next week. It'll all be fine, don't worry. I'm on top of it all.'

I am like the guy who pretends to go to the office but sits on a park bench all day with his sandwiches after being made redundant. I hide a lot from the family, from everyone, from myself.

I miss the pantomime of fame back then because when you're part of it you don't have to think. The day I joined Take That someone pressed the stop button on my personal growth. For most people, between the ages of 20 and 30 the boy becomes the man. Me, I was burped out at the back end of the nineties the same as I was at the beginning. My growth as a human being had been stunted by the strange life of a pop star. It is fun but it is not a deep existence, and especially not so when someone else – Our Nigel – is steering your entire life. For ten years I felt very little other than euphoria, ambition, and that most addictive of states: in demand. During those wonderful nineties years when record sales were through the roof, my confidence was epic to the point of being, I admit, obnoxious.

But now that sound in the background is the slow, steady hiss of my ego deflating. In a funny way, it is sort of nice, essential even, because I am feeling things for the first time. I have to gain a grip on a reality that I've never really known. Before, if I wanted to know who I was, I looked at the charts, the fans, the management, the record label, and all they ever said was, 'Legend!' Now, to cut a long story short, I am depressed, I am fat and I am emotionally 15 and suppressing it like a good Northerner. 'Just get on with it' is the Barlow way. Be stoic. So – not that I'd recommend doing this at home – I ignore the depression by simply pretending everything is fine.

Making out it's good on the outside only makes what's on the inside even more awful. Our Nigel, our manager from the TT days, comes to see me; he brings a curry round one night and you should hear the stuff I am making up. 'Oh yeah, oh I've got two big productions coming now, I've got artists, oh they're queuing up, yeah.'

The weight thing is becoming harder and harder to ignore. I am getting good at hiding behind the tall guy at weddings and christening photos (hence the lack of them in this book). I am getting too big, and I am having trouble sitting up. Even if I could have ignored it, no one is going to let me. The headlines like TAKE FAT, RELIGHT MY FRYER, BACK FOR PUD – all quite funny from a distance of fifteen years and wearing much smaller trousers.

What's great about food is there's always a good reason to eat it, hunger being last on the list for me. Lonely? Eat. Afraid? Eat. Sad? Eat. Food is soothing and numbing. Food is a big hug. Some people self-medicate with drink or drugs; I just eat and eat and eat.

I am, totally, an emotional eater but there's an added complexity. There's the fact that most of my eating at this stage is also a form of protest because I want people to stop recognising me; by eating I can make them leave me alone. So in some ways I love it. The more weight I put on, the less I hear the word 'Robbie' coughed out behind people's hands. As a fat person, I don't need the beanie in summer or the shades in winter, I can leave the house without a baseball cap pulled down to my nose. I wear my disguise under my skin. Not being recognised feels wonderful. For me, the more weight I put on, the easier life becomes. Fat, I am invisible. After all the noise and screams, finally silence.

In a way, I feel like I've been starving for years. Eating is like going 'fuck you' to the world. I just let it all go. I'd been brutally kicked out of the music business and everyone has just turned their backs on me. I don't want to be a star at all and so I am doing the utmost not to look like one. I am hell-bent on destroying that image. I've been dyeing my hair blond since 1985. I felt like a star when I had done my hair but I'm different now.

I've stopped all that. Instead, with every day and every binge, I am eating the pop star to death…

* * *

Those were indeed dark, shitty times for me, but I'm not going to pretend I spent all my time lying under a piano. I had two kids and they were amazing. Dan was starting to talk and he was hilarious and taking care of his little sister as well as his parents did. Now, in 2018, I'm so glad they can't remember those years; I was a useless dad back then. The house was split in two. The studio was a dark, desperate and unusually quiet place where I pretended to work; I'd strike a key on the piano occasionally as I tried to resurrect my corpse-like career. Next door, in the house, could not have been more different; in fact there are moments when I'd forget it all and get sucked into the magical world of young children. Dan used to take his Crayolas to the £92-a-roll wallpaper and I'd be cheering him on. I wanted to scribble all over it, too.

. Work crept back into my life in the form of a partnership with Eliot Kennedy. We had written 'Everything Changes' when we first met back in 1993. We aren't the types to mollycoddle each other, El is more northern than me. But he rang me not long after I'd been dropped. He'd seen something hideous about me in a newspaper and just thought, 'Wow, this is getting bad.' By now I'd taken to answering the phone in a funny voice so people wouldn't know it was me...

* * *

'Hello? To whom am I speaking?' I say.

'It's me, Gaz ... er, El. Mate, I hope you don't read any of this shite in the papers. Look, are you all right, lad?'

'Yes! Great! Everything's great! Yeah, brilliant.'

His voice drops an octave. 'No. Gaz. Are you all right?'

And for the first time I admit it. 'No. No, not really. I don't know what to do, El.'

He and I speak for a bit. Of all the people I know, I can count on one hand those that have bothered to call, to see how I am.

'Are you ready?' he says.

'What for?'

'Put t'kettle on, I'll be over in an hour.'

He drives across the Pennines from where he lives in Sheffield, and I register the shock when he sees me. I look older, heavier; despite my best attempts, and it's easy to clock I am unhappy. He sits with me and says, 'Gaz, you're the biggest secret weapon the music business doesn't know about. When you're ready to start making records for other people, there's a career in that. Come and be my songwriting partner.'

Back in Cheshire, slowly but surely, El gets me back into music. We sit in the studio dissecting the pop music around at the time. It has changed a lot and I realise that much of my equipment is out of date. Time to hit the shops. I have forgotten how much I used to get off on the tech side of music. We set up three studios at the back of the house and start to write.

My writing has changed. There is a new edge to it. When life took a swing at me, it also deepened the lyrical content. Anger, experience, regret, desperation: no one wants to live with that, but it doesn't half fill your toolbox with something unique to you. Writing music is like plagiarism early on; it can take a lifetime to find your own voice.

The experience of the last few years has brought a new songwriter to the studio. Hard times only make you appreciate the things we all take for granted. It's that understanding that helps you write these songs that speak to so many people, songs with a universal truth.

'Where the bloody hell's this come from?' El says.

I battled with lyrics in the nineties. I may have been living in a bubble of marvellous things, but my main inspiration would come from other people's music. Not any more. My head is starting to fill with ideas. 'Whoa! I've got to get some stuff out and down on the page.'

The blood has returned to my veins. I work for hours after El goes home; the obsession is back. Artists come to record at Delamere. Sometimes they stay. We compose, we produce, we play, we laugh. Dawn's new name for El is 'The Boyfriend'.

There's a downside to this special relationship. We both love to eat. Yes, El coaxes me out of the house, but not into fresh air and hikes. We go to a different pub for lunch every day. Not to drink, but to eat. Then we start on the Michelin gaffs, ticking them off in the guidebook. For a year or two we get really into it.

There are wake-up calls everywhere and subconsciously I know that the day is coming when I am going to have to get on top of all that because I am really eating a lot of food. In these last couple of months, things have got messy. Any excuse and El and I will be down the Chinese Delight in Delamere like a shot. After all, we've had a busy day sitting on our arses at the mixing desk. The big fizzy lagers are all lined up with a basket of prawn crackers. Then the platter. You know the one, the big oval dish with all the greasy wontons and deep-fried prawn toasts. It's like a pub fight with us all scrapping over the last spring roll. The ribs would barely touch the table and we'd be on them like dogs. Throwing the bones down like a gauntlet.

Sometimes when I eat, it's like I am unconscious. I remember a couple of times almost coming round during a meal and being suddenly painfully aware that I am eating like an animal – barely chewing and almost growling as I suck the food down. Conscious for a moment, I will be gasping inside at the painful realisation of who I am and how I feel: 'I hate myself, I hate myself.' Then I check out and continue the binge. Those are the days I go home to be sick.

Yup, I am getting quite good at making myself throw up. Deep down I know something has to change, so for the last couple of months I go batshit bingeing crazy. All kinds of addicts will relate to that madness. It can't carry on. Last days of Rome.

The main courses arrive! All with fried rice, and the essential sizzling beef thing that sets the place on fire; the sweet and sour prawns. All that shit. Just as everyone's sitting back gasping in agony, thinking they can't fit any more in, someone orders one of those banana things for pudding with ice cream, squirty cream and a neon cherry on top. And a coffee. No, make that an Irish coffee. With After Eights.

I am eating with aggression. It's like, yeah, fuck you, to myself and to the world. Weird days. I know it's a road to nowhere.

Somewhere at the back of my mind, always, I am thinking, Dawn. Poor Dawn. My beautiful, kind, funny, patient, amazing wife has got me rolling in and farting and burping, going, 'Oh, this shirt doesn't fit any more'... just being a big lummox. That isn't who she married.

Some people can carry extra weight. It suits them. It's part of their character. My dad, for example. Fit, strong, heavy. Big collars on Viyella shirts, ten potatoes at dinner. Never lost a wink of sleep.

For me, and I know for a lot of others, a body that size feels like a prison. Things you once took for granted become your enemy. Wearing clothes is an act of punishment; like someone prodding you all day, going, 'Oh, I see that doesn't fit any more.' Every mirror or reflective shop window prompts a voice inside your head to go, 'Look at the size of you!' Mobility is no longer free and unrestricted. God, I hate it. It's shit. When you wake up one day and decide 'Enough! I don't want to be inside this body any more,' it's a startling reality check.

I can't tell you what the weather is like this morning. It's enough to have to open my eyes on another day. My throat is sore because I ate so much last night, and I was so disgusted by it that I made myself sick. My head hurts. I am dehydrated. All I drink is a steady chain of caffeinated liquids, a litre of Coca-Cola and coffee, until the clock in the hall chimes six, when I start on the Southern Comfort and lemonade. I'm hung-over. I'm a committed smoker: tobacco round the clock, weed all afternoon.

The mind is awake but I don't want to open my eyes, not yet. I don't want to look at the ridiculous Regency stripe wallpaper I once found so befitting of my fame and status. I hate that wallpaper like I hate all the antiques and porcelain figurines, the expensive nicknacks and gilded Rococo swag in this mansion with the sweeping drive. I hate who I am. I'm a former pop star, and I'm fat, so fat that I must roll side to side and slowly build enough momentum to raise my lumbering carcass off the mattress and out of bed. After the grunting effort, I sit breathing heavily, looking at the floor below my stomach.

Dawn steps so lightly on the stairs that it's only Dan's toddler babble that lets me know she is coming up. She's a dancer; the girl can glide into rooms as quietly as a ghost. In pregnancy, usually it's the mum that loses control of her weight. After Dan and little Emily were born, she pretty much looked the same straight away. There's that sinking moment after Dan had drawn a picture of his mum using straight lines, when he moves on to Dad, gearing up with his big crayon to draw a massive circle.

Dawn has Em on her hip as she comes into the room to open the thick, heavy curtains that match the stupid stripy wallpaper. She is all bright and cheery, compensating for my drain-like presence slumped at the edge of the bed. Grey light fills the room but the darkness does not go away.

For the first time I admit how I feel to her.

* * *

That day was rock bottom. 'Fat Day' Dawn calls it. With my head in my hands, still puffing from the exertion of now simply getting up, I said to Dawn, 'I can't go on like this. I feel awful. Awful...'

'Why don't you go to the doctor's?' she suggested, gently, and at that moment I knew then that she knew; she knew what was up; my cunning disguise had not worked with my wife. For the first time I was present and not numbly shoving all the problems in my pockets. I was in a mess and I admitted it.

Still, it was a shock when I went to the GP and he stood me on the scales. Seventeen stone and two pounds. Then he sat me down for The Chat. It's always a bad sign, that, when the doctor sits you in a chair beside him rather than staying behind his desk.

'Hello, what's happened here? Am I dying?'

He started explaining about obesity. I hadn't even considered the word. It hit me like a bolt of lightning. I thought obesity was those people you see rolling round Blackpool on scooters.

Obese? Me? It's someone else who gets that. I was that ignorant, I thought it was something you caught, a contagious illness.

'Gary, this isn't good. For such a young guy, you're not just in the obese chart, you're well into the middle of it.' I knew so little then; I didn't realise you ate your way into obesity. I really didn't know what it was. I said, 'Right. So what can you do about it?'

He said, 'Gary, it's not a disease, it's a state.'

It dawned on me then: I am the cure. That's the thing about weight. Doesn't matter who you are, it's down to you. It's not a job for your assistant or your missus or the cleaner. You can't outsource weight loss. And I hated that.

Seventeen stone and two pounds. I know it was all on show but leaving the GP's I felt like I'd been rumbled. Argh, shit. I walked back to the car thinking about the years of steamed broccoli that lay ahead.

As I drove back from the surgery that day, I felt a mixture of things: shock, disappointment, anger, definitely embarrassment. Most of all, I had no idea what to do next. Well, I did know what I was going to do next.

I went to the McDonald's in Warrington. One last go, I thought. Let's go and finish the job off.

1

A BOY ON
A MISSION

'Hoping someone somewhere needs me'

I was born on 20 January 1971. It didn't take long for my parents to notice I was an unusually focused kid. Before I started winning the BBC *Song for Christmas* or going into battle with Phillip Jeffreys for the lead in the Frodsham High School production of *Joseph and the Amazing Technicolor Dreamcoat*, before I started working seven nights and one matinee a week in northern working men's clubs, before all of that, I was already driven.

Mum is still proud of the colouring-in competition that I won not once, but three years in a row. Year after year I had a private exhibition of my pictures up in the NatWest Bank in Frodsham.

She goes out of her way never to be boastful about any of my achievements as an adult; she keeps it very quiet. But Mum loves to tell people, 'Gary was a heck of a colourer-inner.'

I got my first keyboard when I was six or so. It was a tiny one, not much bigger than the one Schroeder played in Peanuts. Our teenage neighbour, Janice Griffiths, spent hours teaching me how to play 'Beautiful Dreamer'.

When I took up karate at seven I had to go to black belt. Not a purple belt or a brown belt, no. It had to be black. And I liked attention. I was one of those kids that's forever dancing in front of the TV looking at their reflection. I was a show-off.

My dad had this big night out once a year for Frodsham Pigeon Club. Especially notable for being the only night the wives were welcome. I begged him, 'Can I do a spot this year?' It was a proper fancy night at the Mersey View nightclub. All the greats and the not so greats had played there. The Beatles and Showaddywaddy. There I was in my little suit entertaining the pigeon fanciers of west Cheshire. This is a precocious nine-year-old's dream gig. I had this magic trick I did. I've got all the patter.

'Come on up, sir. What's your name? Where are you from? I must say you're looking very smart tonight, sir. Was that tie a gift or a bet?'

I'd hold a piece of paper over the tie. 'It really is a lovely tie, sir? Did your wife give it you for Christmas?' As I cut along the piece of paper everyone starts laughing because as well as cutting the paper, you'll never guess, I cut his tie off. Oh no, it's all gone wrong, this guy's getting mad at Colin's little lad. Oh no, the evening's ruined. Everyone's falling about laughing. This is what I do it for, I'm beaming.

I take the two pieces of tie, pretending to be flustered and apologetic, and put it in a box. I say the magic words, 'Pigeons!' Guess what? The tie is back in one piece. More cheers. Then I send him back to his seat with, 'Wasn't he great, ladies and gentlemen? Give him a round of applause.'

Christ, I must've been unbearable. Everyone's saying, 'That's not a normal nine-year-old.'

New Year's Eve we'd all go round to Janice's parents with a few other people from our street, Ashton Drive. Watching everyone dance to ABBA, ELO and *Saturday Night Fever* always stayed with me. I clocked how happy music made people. Mum's a Scouser and she loved music. I think like most people of her age from Liverpool, The Beatles runs in their blood. 'When we were young the DJs had the easiest job. They just put on a Beatles album, play it all the way through, then turn it over. We were happy. We didn't want anything else.'

Music was always on in our house. It wasn't the radio, she would choose what to listen to. She had impeccable taste in popular music: Kate Bush, ABBA, the Bee Gees, the Carpenters.

I first played music to a live audience at the Connah's Quay Labour Club Talent Show in 1982. I was eleven years old. I played whatever keyboard was in the club. I didn't win. Anyone who's watched *The X Factor* will know the best people never do. But I impressed them enough to be offered a regular gig playing at the club.

This was my second gig. This time as a musician, not a magician. I had my setlist prepared, three songs: 'Fame', 'The Girl from Ipanema' and I finished on the Blaxpoitation classic, 'Shaft'. Shaft! I was way more edgy back then.

Just before I went on stage, Mum said, 'You're going to need to talk between these songs.'

Mum cued me up with a trusty one-liner that served me well for the next six years. 'I'm gonna be quick. I've got school in the morning. I nearly didn't make it, I had a detention.'

In truth, I never had a detention. That was (my older brother) Our Ian's turf.

We had a normal, loving, stable home. I've always painted it as perfect, and it was in many ways. But it was not always happy. Consistently, throughout my childhood, I remember a need to compensate for Our Ian. He was a horrifically naughty lad. He was a bugger for fighting. Trespassing, stealing, drinking – he was the town bad boy. He was rolling his own by 12. You name it, he did it. And brought all the trouble home with him.

Mum was working at our school as a lab technician by the time I went to Frodsham High. At night I'd hide under my bed as I listened to her crying and shouting at him. Those years were hard for my mum. I was determined to be a really good boy and at the same time bring happiness into the house with my music.

That's why I worked so hard. I would never be a naughty boy. I'd make people happy.

* * *

The one good thing about having Rambo as your brother was no one ever dared touch me at school.

Ian's a world-class wind-up merchant who loves nothing more than seeing people wound up. We'd fight like brothers do but only ever had one properly bad fight. One was over 'A Whiter Shade of Pale'.

I've just had my 11th birthday, and already outgrown the Yamaha PS-2 I'd got three months before for Christmas. It's a Saturday in March 1982 and Mum and Dad announce they're going to Chester, shopping.

'Shall we bring our Gary?' Dad said to my mum.

'Yeah, but does he want anything,' says Mum, 'because if he does he's not coming. I'm not having him pestering us and spoiling the trip.'

'He doesn't want anything, he'll be fine.'

While Mum was parking the car in Chester, I marched my dad to Rushworth's Music. We walked straight through the piano section and into the glories of the electric keyboard department. I went straight up to the sales assistant – slightly bald, ponytail, skinny keyboard tie, you know the guy.

'Can I help you, young man?'

'What's the upgrade from the Yamaha PS-2?'

'Step this way, son.'

He took me to a full-sized Yamaha organ, two keyboards and bass pedals. This was more than a musical instrument, it was like a piece of furniture with a price tag to match.

Dad and I sat and watched the guy run it through its paces. He made it sing. His right hand was playing melody on the top keyboard; his left, chords on the bottom. Underneath his left foot was playing the bass notes while his right foot controlled the volume. This was proper rubbing your belly and patting your head stuff. He'd drawn a crowd. And they were all happy. At this point Mum, the smallest member of the Barlow family by now but unquestionably the head of it, comes beetling in. She knows something's up.

'Oh God, what's he up to? Colin. *Colin*?'

Dad was completely absorbed, like me. The demo ended and the whole shop thanked the guy for his performance with a round of applause.

Mum and Dad went into one of those parent scrums. Little Mum: slim, fit, ginger and *the boss*. Dad: solid, strong, the gentlest giant and usually not the boss. They are talking quietly. They weren't arguing but it was clearly a heated debate.

Dad was talking about his due holiday and how much money he could get if he sold his holiday time back to the fertiliser company he works for. Wouldn't you know, it comes to £400, about £1,500 in today's money, just enough to buy this organ.

They turned to me. Parental consensus was, 'Your dad's going to buy it.'

That was a massive turning point in my life. I learned so much on that organ. The whole foundation of everything I know I learned on that Yamaha organ. I spent every waking moment trying to master that thing.

It took me six weeks of playing the same song over and over and over. Procol Harum's 'A Whiter Shade of Pale'.

One evening as I practised before tea, Mum shouted up, 'Meal's ready!' Our Ian yelled back that he'd take his in his room. As he walked back with his tea he shouted in the direction of my bedroom, 'And shut that noise up!'

World War III broke out. He's big, Our Ian, far bigger than 12-year-old Gary. All I've got on him is a black belt in karate. He slammed the door as I hurled myself in his direction. So I kicked my way through it like Bruce Lee. Less like Bruce I went straight for Ian's neck. I'd strangle him. I had him pinned to the floor, throttling away and he reached for the only weapon he had to fight back with. His fork took a big chunk out of my face.

Still got the scar, left cheek, just below my eye. Fighting and suffering for my art at an early age, me.

* * *

When I was 15, the careers lady at school said, 'Right, Gary, what do you want to do?'

'I want to be a pop star, Miss.'

'Got anything else in mind, just in case that doesn't work out?'

'No, Miss, because it will work out.'

She didn't say much to that, but I spotted her in the Boot Inn in Boothsdale later on that week as I was playing a gig.

I'm most like my mum. She was always in control. The only time I ever saw her let my dad be boss was the first time we went on an aeroplane. Our holidays were always in Britain: Blackpool, Pwllheli, Skeggy. Generally, holidays in Britain mean rain. After one particularly wet Scottish holiday Mum went, 'That's it. We're going abroad. I'm getting on to Freddie Laker.'

Mum was the organiser. She decided what time we left for the airport. She held the passports. She had the crisps in the bag for the flight. The Wagon Wheels were safely stashed in the side pocket. That's why it was so shocking seeing her terrified of flying. She was crying. She'd held on to Dad's hand so hard she'd broken his skin and left claw marks. Mum was always the boss of the family but it was turned on its head on that flight. My dad was The Dad. And my mum was being looked after for once.

We went abroad every year after that: Ibiza, Benidorm and one year we got really adventurous and went to Crete.

When I looked down our street, it felt like everyone there was just getting by. Mum was one of the few on Ashton Drive who worked. Life for that generation was constant work, cooking, getting the packed lunches ready, all the domestic stuff as well as the nine-to-five.

Mum was constantly stretched, going off on her moped to the hospital where she worked in the labs, then rushing to get back to cook us tea. Later, when she worked at my school, I'd see her craning her neck from the staffroom to check I'd made it on time for registration. (I've never been a morning person but especially not when I was a teenager.)

My dad never took a holiday, he just always had his head down, going from one job to another. Always working. Back in the day those factories only let them out for Christmas and two set weeks in the summer. None of this lavish four-week minimum. All my dad knew was work. Even after he retired, he carried on working on the smallholding they had by then. Looking after the mowing in all my various houses was a full-time job that Dad took pretty seriously. I don't think he even thought of any of it as work. To live was to work. I've seen pictures of him picking potatoes and driving a tractor at the age of ten. He'd worked, literally, all his life.

But now we're flying to the sun. Ibiza! My dad's in charge, and he's got his arm round the queen of coping, Mum. Everyone's happy. We went abroad every summer from then on.

Dad only stopped asking, 'When are you going to get a proper trade, son?' when I passed my driving test. I was singing in a Runcorn club five nights a week at that stage and the band's drummer was a driving instructor. (Pretty much all my fellow musicians were old enough to be my dad.) This drummer got me through the test, three weeks after my 17th birthday and I started getting myself to gigs. This caused a shift in my dad's attitude towards me and my music. Something about me passing my driving test meant Dad started believing there might be something in it. I bought my first car, a Ford Fiesta. I always had some bit of gear in my ear as I drove; it was much too small for all my keyboards, so a year later I upgraded to a ten-year-old Ford Orion.

Mum was different, she always knew: she knew where I was going and what I was doing. I left school at 16 after grinding my way through a few GCSEs. Every day, I'd write music at home in my bedroom.

When Mum got home from work she'd get herself a cup of tea, drag up a kitchen chair and sit outside my bedroom. She couldn't come in, there was no room with all the equipment I was accumulating.

I was writing a song a day, and my deadline was when Mum came home from work. 'Are you ready? I've got a good one. Bit different this one.'

I'd give her the handwritten lyrics on a piece of A4 and press play. She'd often listen twice. She always loved them. Mum was my first fan. On a Thursday she might request Monday's song again. She loved 'Open Road', which I wrote when I was 16.

By the time I was 17, I'd taken the working men's clubs as far as I could. I was making £500 a week, which was a lot back then. I'd won all these crap awards. It must have meant something to me at the time, but the judging criteria was not your talent but things like how early you got booked for New Year's Eve or whether you'd attained the lofty heights of a season in Blackpool. It's not the Mercury Prize. By 17 I realised that A&R men and talent spotters aren't in these clubs. I'm working these old-fashioned places, jamming with my mates who are all these old buggers in their fifties.

Jeanie was another club act, young like me. She kept telling me, 'Gaz, you've gotta get out of these clubs. You've got to get to the next level; you're not going to find the Top 40 in Wigan's working men's club on a Saturday night, Gary.' She was practically shaking me. Together we sent all these tapes out to managers and agents in the area and within a few days I got a call back from Boss Model Agency. They called me in for a meeting; my first meeting with Nigel Martin-Smith.

★ ★ ★

Jeanie found out a lot about him. 'This guy you are going to see, he's gay. He runs a model agency. Gary, you can't go in with your flecks on.' Flecks were those pleated 'pegged' *Miami Vice* trousers with little dashes of colour in. 'Don't wear them trousers, Gary. Trust me. Just put jeans on.'

Nigel had a proper office. There was a pretty receptionist and a big room full of people on phones, always a good look. His actual office was trendy, glass desk, all that jazz. 'This is it,' I thought, '*this is it*.' It looked like I imagined the ones at EMI and Polydor did, the rooms I never got to see when I took the train down to London and sat in the record company lobbies all day hoping someone might listen to my demos. Behind his chair, above his head on the wall, was a gold disc.

A. Gold. Disc. I couldn't stop looking at it. It hung there, like the sun.

It was an artist he'd looked after who had a hit with Stock, Aitken and Waterman. That didn't matter. That's what I wanted, that was it, there. I wanted one of those.

Nigel spoke very softly and confidently. He was telling me about this group he was going to make and the way he talked it was as if they were already successful. He always had that. It's quite rare. You don't see it much. I'm far too superstitious to tell anyone something will be successful before it's happened. I told him straight off I didn't really want to be in a group. I don't fancy the idea of lugging drum kits and guitar amps about. 'No, no! There's no instruments,' and he pressed play on a New Kids on the Block video.

'Ah, right. It's like the Jackson Five,' I say. 'It's a harmony group.'

'You've got it,' he says, and presses play again, 'and I think I've got a couple of lads already.' There's Jason dancing on *The Hit Man and Her*. He pauses it. 'He is gonna be in the group, he's an amazing dancer and he's already got a fan club.'

That's impressive. Fan mail. I wanted some of that, too.

Then he gets out this model book and points at this Greek god. 'I'm thinking of this guy, too. His name's Howard.'

And that was it. That was the end of the meeting. 'I'm going to do a workshop, we'll get you in.'

As I left I asked him to do me a favour and listen to a cassette of my songs. He took the cassette as I handed it over and I knew from the way he took it, the way he looked at me, that he wasn't going to listen to it. So I held on to it and he held on to it. He pulled it and I pulled back. There was a moment, and this obnoxious 18-year-old looked him dead in the eye and said, 'No. Listen to it.'

That took him by surprise.

By the time I'd got home there was a glowing number five on the answer machine. Nigel's assistant, trying to get hold of me. I rang him and was put straight through.

'This tape, who has written these songs?'

I told him, me.

'Who wrote the words then?'

Told him again, me. 'And the music and the backing track.'

Me. Me.

'Wow! Right, you'd better come back and see me tomorrow.'

I went back the next day and he gave me the whole plan of what he was going to do. 'I've found this other kid, too. He's only young, he's not left school yet.' He handed over this tiny picture. Rob.

A week later he did this official workshop at La Cage, a gay club in Manchester. He got us all together: Mark, Rob, Jay, Howard and this other lad. This story's been told a million times, and the truth is it didn't feel like an audition to be in the biggest band in the world. For some of the lads, it felt like just another job. Howard had arrived late from a modelling job – a model! I wanna be that, too.

First off, we've all got to sing. Yeah, I swaggered straight to the top of the class for that. I was clearly the best. I should be, I'd been gigging since I was eleven. For a brief moment, I was winning. Then things took a downhill turn. They put music on.

'Let's have a look at how you move.'

The scales tipped. If you've ever stood near Jay when he's dancing, it's breathtaking. Awesome.

'I'll never be able to do that,' I think.

Jason encouraged us all to follow him, move with him. For a moment I could almost fool myself, watching him, that I was good, too. Then the concrete shoes set. I looked around. Damn it, they were all good dancers. God, I felt self-conscious.

The other lads looked brilliant, they all looked cool, all the clobber, great movers, singing, bouncing off the walls, they were full of it…

The rest is history. I made it. Not long after, Nigel came to see my mum. He said she had nothing to worry about, that I would be safe with him, and that he was going to make me a big star.

'I'm going to make your son's dreams come true.'

2

DIETS ARE SHIT ...

'Most will grow to be tall,
others will break and fall'

First, I went on my own diet. I know what to eat. Let's go. Two Weetabix with two centimetres of artificial sweeteners on top, skimmed milk. This is great this is, I'm gonna be fine. Don't worry everyone, I'm on it. Don't panic, that's Diet Coke with my Jack Daniel's. Guys, I don't eat Chinese any more, now I eat sushi. Someone had told me sushi was healthy, it's why movie stars love it. So I'm ordering a whole tray of sushi for myself.

'What's that? You want to share?'

'No, I'm having it all, 'cause I'm eating sushi, 'cause I'm on a diet.'

Of course, what I didn't know then was how much sugar there is in sushi rice. That's why you can't stop eating the bloody stuff, but I'm getting ahead of myself. Where were we? Ah yes, I'm eating my way through a huge tray of sushi, on a diet.

This first attempt was useless. I surrendered to the inevitable and bought a diet book.

The first diet was the Atkins. It's an unhealthy, horrible diet; I felt like my body was poisoned. You're going to the toilet once every two weeks, sweating bullets. Your breath smells like toxic waste but the weight's dropping off, several pounds every week. Back then I was so badly educated I couldn't have told you what a piece of protein was, or a carbohydrate. I just blindly followed the diet. Jennifer Aniston's on it, she's thin, must be good. Imagine a diet that says eat all the cream and bacon you want, but weigh your broccoli. I could read Mum's mind. She said nothing, never does, but I knew what she was thinking. 'It can't be healthy, eating all that cream and butter and steak every day. What about your veg, Gary?'

31

In four months I lost two stone on this foul torture diet and swiftly put on a stone when I finished. Back to square one, back to the diet books.

Bye bye Atkins. Hello *Slimming World*. I never went to the classes. There's no way I was gonna turn up to a Fat Fighters class. No, I went in the other direction. I'd only read the books when no one was looking. After Dawn had gone to bed I'd stay up on some 'manly' pretext like football, and crack open the diet books to sneak a read. Which diet had changed the world today?

We're quite simple, Dawn and I. We've got this enormous house, thirty rooms and this tiny room was our favourite: comfy sofa, lovely big telly and that was where we spent all our time. This is where I'd creep down and do the books.

You know you've got to lose weight but mentally you're angry, and it's not a good way to be. I literally wanted to rip these books up, stamp on them, punch the wall. I wanted to weep. 'What am I doing reading a *Slimming World*? I'm a northern bloke. I've been famous. I've written all these songs, I've got all this money. And I'm sitting here reading a *Slimming World* in the dark.'

It's pathetic. What had happened to me?

Throughout the nineties my confidence never faltered really. My focus was like a laser beam. Pop stardom and songwriting was all I wanted. Even Take That, the band that made me, were just a stepping stone to my ultimate goal of a killer singer/songwriter career. I wanted it all.

What changed with Take That, though, was I got arrogant as well as confident. Unbelievably arrogant. A few months after Rob left in July 1995, we were all sitting in a hotel in London. Everyone was just fed up with the life, but in all honesty I don't know if everyone was as ready to split as I was. As always, I was the one who said, 'Right, we're gonna do this.' I said, 'We're going to split up. The spark's gone. Let's quit while we're ahead.'

Over the years we had always wondered how it would be. 'Oh God! How are we going to go out? Are we going to go out sliding down the charts or are we going to go out at the top?'

The fact that we put an end point on it and decided to do it felt good. It felt good. It wasn't even a long conversation. It was just decided. In the week between then and when we announced it, I thought nothing of it. I was already writing a new album, my new solo album. The page has been turned. I treated the press conference as no more than a bit of promo. I got up, told Dawn, 'Oh, by the way, we've got a press conference today; we've got to tell everyone the band's split up.' I remember thinking it was a pain, an inconvenience. 'I won't be long, should be back in an hour if the traffic's not too bad.'

I had not the slightest grasp or interest in the gravity of it. I didn't even think of how our fans would react or really care about what everyone was going on to do next. I'd spent five years of my life with these guys but it was of no interest to me. All I thought was, 'Onwards! Upwards!'

When it made the news, and the helplines were launched, I wasn't bothered; I'm not even sure I noticed, if I'm being totally honest. We're talking really breathtaking levels of arrogance and entitlement here.

Once we'd announced the split we had to go and do three months of promo for the final album. Nigel promised the label we'd do that and we hauled round Europe on one of the most enjoyable trips I'd had in years, because none of it mattered any more. We were just having a laugh. Everyone was partying. We couldn't give a shit. It was great.

We were going out every night. We were literally cutting off the TV interviews short in order to go out. Every major European capital was an opportunity for a big night out and some self-promotion. I was so excited about what was next and for the new music I was going to make. I was excited just to be me.

This epic ego just wanted to move on and shed this old identity. I didn't need this any more. We enjoyed each other as a band that last few months because we knew it was over. We could see the end.

And beyond ... I was dreaming constantly of my solo career. I was shameless. So, for example, we've got to Madrid and the label takes us out for dinner and I quickly calculate who's the most important person at the table. I'm going to sit next to you. Sit down. 'Oh, hey. Listen. Get your team ready because wait until you hear what's coming next.'

Oh God! Ridiculous, I know. *Every* city. Gaz is lining everyone up to get them hyped about his solo album. Then we'd go out and get shit-faced and have a laugh. We'd sit in the corner of a nightclub, behind a velvet rope. We loved it. We didn't want to dance. We'd been dancing every fucking day for six years. I'd just be hammering the Southern Comfort and getting my money's worth from a pack of fags. Great fun. Howard and I used to sit listening to the music. 'This is a good bit.' 'Oh yeah, that's a good bit.'

I remember being out in Paris one night in a club and Prince walked in, pulled five birds and left again in about ten minutes. I don't even remember being impressed by that; in my head, it's all about the next single. If I thought anything it was, 'Does Prince know about the solo single? It's coming soon. I'll go and tell him.'

If he'd spent any longer pulling those birds, he'd have known. In my head I am the world's greatest living songwriter and a massively loved pop star. What could possibly go wrong?

Seventeen stone and two pounds, reading my *Slimming World* in the dark, I felt annoyed at everyone and everything. Some of that desperation and fury will be due to the effect of having no fat in my diet and a lot of hidden sugar in all those low-fat products. Not that I understood this then, but my blood sugar levels would have been all over the shop. Ever seen a kid have a 'hangry' meltdown or a high sugar mania? That was me. I was hungry so much of the time. And some of that anger wasn't just down to my blood sugar being all over the place. It was entirely justified.

How many diets did I do? Ten, 15, 20, I lost count. Every single one had a different theory. You're reading this book and it's saying the complete opposite to the one you read the week before. I'm looking at them both going, 'Come on, give it to me straight. Should I eat fat or not? Is a baked potato good, or is it from the dark side? You're saying peanut butter is evil; you're saying it's a healthy snack with some sliced up apple.' I know nothing, absolutely nothing about nutrition. What did I learn at school? Nothing that's helping me now.

Every single diet pushed a different kind of magic. They all contradicted each other. When you're overweight you're clutching at straws. You're on the hunt for the secret to unlocking the weight loss forever: the holy grail. If someone talks about a diet, your ears prick up – 'say that again, say that again' – it's like that next little factoid or theory could tip the balance. Someone says something and you do it, because you think, 'This is going to work.' The sound of a new diet book's spine cracking caused fresh hope. This is the one that's going to change my life. This is the silver bullet.

Silver bullshit more like.

Sometimes they had a few good tips, things worth remembering, some really simple, smart things worth knowing. Like, 'You're gonna feel hungry. That is a given. So what you need to do is, because you're not going to be eating dessert and everyone else is, finish your dinner and get up immediately and go for a walk.' I used that. It was a really good tip, that was. Though it was a bit weird, you know, Sunday lunch. I've not had any potatoes and eaten my body weight in meat, 'cos, you know, on the Atkins, that's allowed, or I've just had vegetables, trimmed the fat off my beef and said a casual no to the roast potatoes because I'm on *Slimming World*. Then the apple crumble comes out, and Daddy just gets up and says he's going for a walk. We didn't have dogs back then, either.

My eating habits were getting more eccentric with every diet I did. By 2005, Dan had coined the phrase, Daddy's Special Food, three words all my kids learned to use over the years. The more I got into the diets, the less I sat down to eat with them all. Daddy ate his Special Food earlier than the kids usually because Daddy was famished.

The thing that worked for me back then was calorie counting but oh that was crushing. With the high-fat, high-protein Atkins I could style it out. Oh, just a big juicy steak for me please, hold the chips. With calorie counting, I really felt like I was on a diet because this food was horrible. No one would choose to eat like that. I felt so obvious because you get out all this specially wrapped plastic food and everyone's like, 'Oh you're on a diet.' 'Yes I'm on a fucking diet.' It was all fat free and totally tasteless and unsatisfying, like eating cardboard.

El and the others carried on as normal, 'cause they're all right. They're not unhappy with the way they look. I'd have to mentally prepare myself for meals with the lads, thinking to myself, 'Right, Gaz, you're in the pub, choose carefully. What does the book say...?' 'Lager, Gaz?' 'Not today, ta.' 'You what?' 'Right, chicken no skin no potatoes,' and you try to do it quietly but they've clocked it, bellowing across the table. 'Why, do you not want onion rings? You what!?'

'No, no, I'm all right. Think I'll just have a salad.'

'What? What's wrong with him? Salad? Are you gay? Come on lad, get some onion rings!'

'No, no, no.'

'Oh, right, you're on a diet, aren't you?'

'No, I'm not. I'm not on a diet. Can I just have chicken, without the skin please?'

'Without the skin? What are you doing? That's the best bit!'

'Why can you not eat the skin?'

'Okay. I'm on a fucking diet, all right and I don't know why I can't eat it, it's just because the book said I can't.'

'I'm sure you can eat that!'

And then people are telling you their own theories... 'What you wanna do is eat a grapefruit before every meal, or just eat less and exercise more lad; have you tried the Caveman Diet?'

It went on and on. If you didn't before, you sure as hell feel like an outsider now. You're the fat bloke on a diet eating a shit meal that everybody's looking at going, 'Poor him having to eat that.'

* * *

Secret diets, secret ambitions, I've been here before. My last years at school I had a double life. Typical Frodsham lad by day, laughing and joking in classrooms all day with my mates, underachieving academically; by night, dreaming of one day becoming a pop star and working till the early hours on the club circuit. Of course by the time I was almost leaving school I was working so much there was no escaping it. But, I would never dream of going, 'Hey! Guess what I did last night? I was Bob Monkhouse's support act.'

Our Ian, when he left school, turned a corner. He went on a YTS, which was a kind of apprenticeship that was meant to lead to a job, but the guy didn't take him on, so he told us, 'All I can do is make my own business.' And that's what he did and he worked his arse off and now he's a successful builder. He's done well. He has got a brilliant life. Given what he was like as a teenager, Our Ian has pulled it back, big time.

One of the problems with the diet books was they gave you little idea of what to do when the regime stopped. You'd read 200 pages on the diet and then two on what to do when you go back to normal eating.

So I invented my own maintenance diet. I wrote 'brown bread' on the shopping list, I stopped putting sugar in my tea and had artificial sweetener with everything. I stopped eating chips, and… I pretty much carried on as normal. Problem is, 'normal' involved an abnormal amount of food.

I missed the routine and order of my old busy pop star life so these diets, nightmare that they were, gave me something to concentrate on and adhere to. I liked that about them. In between these regimes, however, El and I were still going out and enjoying food together. So it was feast or famine. And when the enforced famine was over, the feasting began. The joy when you order something and people clock your meat's got skin on it, you've taken a piece of bread, there's no word of salad. 'What about the diet, Gaz?'

'Sod that! Now then, what are we having?'

I'm overweight and on a diet but my main hobby is eating out. Long before Take That had a hit, when I first signed up with Nigel, he took me for dinner to an upmarket Chinese restaurant in Worsley, outside Manchester. This was good food, more steamed sea bass with ginger, none of your greasy pork balls and glossy, gluey neon orange sauce. This was like a religious moment. Light came down from heaven and shone on my plate. The angels sang. Mind, blown. I was hooked on restaurants after that. I wanted to eat out every night. I loved the food, the buzz and the theatre of it all. I remember thinking, 'All I want is to earn enough money to do this every night.' That's how much I loved eating out.

* * *

It took a while before I stopped feeling like a passenger with El and my writing sessions. But soon we weren't doing badly; we started a company and called it True North. The laughs are back. We're flying transatlantic once a month; in New York, we're loving the power breakfasts at a restaurant called Michael's in Midtown and getting bumped up to first class by grateful divas, but these trappings of success were nothing compared to the fact that we were writing songs, making records, we were working in great studios with our favourite mix engineers, the sorts of things that only obsessive music geeks like us two would find interesting. It felt good to be around industry greats like the engineer Mick Guzauski.

We were working well together and people noticed. We were invited to a writing camp with a load of great international hit writers in Woodstock, upstate New York. It was a great week. The first night we got there, El and I go out drinking. He says, 'What's the craic here, what's the aim?'

'The aim,' I say, 'is to get a production deal with Sony. That guarantees us ten records a year.'

Now they don't give out too many of them. People like Walter Afanasieff, Celine Dion's producer, have one but your run-of-the-mill producer/songwriters? Nah. The head of Sony America is running the camp, he's English. We all got on brilliantly. That was the Monday night. By Thursday night we got that production deal. El sold his house and moved near me in Cheshire. Together we built a reputation. We took on a 17-year-old tea boy, Ryan Carline, who barely spoke for six months. Our first employee.

Where Eliot and I had an equal talent at that time, to the point where we became near enough the same person, was eating. So much of our work together was based around meals. Food is uniquely tricky to give up. If you've got a problem with booze you can thrive by never drinking again. If you give up heroin you won't be faced with a big pile of it for your breakfast every day. But food's there, in your face, all the time. You can't give up food, you'll die. But getting the dose right was difficult.

Any big eating episodes in between the diets could cause me major anxiety. Swapping sugar for Canderel wasn't quite cutting it. When a big meal out loomed, I'd reassure myself with the fact I could always make myself sick. Yes, I had turned a page in my head, I'm dieting but I'm still very uncomfortable in my own skin.

I didn't go out that much but now and again I'd have gone to something. One particular evening, I remember, I went to the ASCAP awards at one of those big Park Lane hotels. I'd lost a little bit of weight at this point but not much. I specifically pushed myself to go because I was trying to make this business with Eliot. At an event like that you've got pretty much everyone who's gonna give you work in one room. I didn't want to go, but I thought, 'I need to earn a living.'

For some reason Eliot wasn't with me. He's like my security. Els is a larger-than-life character and he'd take the attention off me. He is six foot six inches and great for hiding behind. Our Ian was the hardest lad in school, so I was protected from a lot of the casual bullying that went on in schools in the eighties. Now, it was El I used like a big brother.

Walking through the reception, people came up and went, 'Oh, wow!' to my face because they hadn't recognised me. They'd be talking to me with shifty eyes looking here and there because they were too embarrassed to look at me. 'Oh my God, that's Gary Barlow over there; he's put on a bit of weight...' I knew what they were doing. It happened quite often. Most people wouldn't mention it, it just hovered in the air above their heads like a visible thought bubble. Then someone would mention it. I hated being told. They'd go, 'Oh, you've put some weight on, haven't you?' Or, 'I'm sorry to say it, but I just wanted to say that I've noticed you put on a lot of weight.'

I'm sure it says in *Debrett*'s not to comment on a person's weight. I wonder if they saw the thought bubble above my head going, 'Piss off. Do you think I haven't noticed?'

It's why fat people have a stock of jokes, to distract people. Weight is an expression of vulnerability, isn't it? In this culture of size acceptance, of the whole 'Big is beautiful', there's a lie at the heart of that. I'm not saying people shouldn't be vulnerable. Vulnerability in itself is something I celebrate. I write about it all the time. The vulnerable side of me is lovely and it's in every one of my songs. But I hate being vulnerable on the outside. Vulnerability is only nice when you can't see it. All the weight says is, 'I've lost control.' And me, I'm always in control.

If I hadn't been me, no one would have noticed, and I'd have just been another person in the crowd. Unfortunately, once you've had a bit of fame, you're fair game. People have opinions, and when you've put yourself in front of an audience, you're putting your head above the crowd. It's like that old story when someone says, 'What's the best and worst thing about being you?' Well, the best thing is, when you walk in a room of two hundred people, everyone looks at you. And the worst? When you walk into a room of two hundred people everyone looks at you. People are going to have an opinion, whether they write it down, tweet it or just think it; it's out of your control, that stuff.

It hit me hard, that event. After all that El had done to coax me back out into the world, I could still be sent scurrying back like a frightened rabbit to my house with no doorbell. I went back home, shut the gates and didn't leave for three months. Even there, I couldn't escape. I'd put the radio on, and bam, there's Robbie being interviewed by Sara Cox in a Radio 1 studio. He tells a joke about me and everyone's laughing their heads off. What's the chances of that? Just putting the radio on and hearing the laughter, it was like Jimmy Tarbuck had told this joke – the cymbal's gone pud-ush – and everyone's rolling on the floor, crying with laughter. 'Right,' I thought, 'I'm not listening to that show again.'

When was it going to end?

3

... BUT EXERCISE IS NOT

'Give good feeling to me'

I wore swimming shorts 'cause I didn't have any others and I wore a white T-shirt. The trainers were mouldy with bald soles; the ones I used to slip on to walk down to see Mum and Dad in the gatehouse. It wasn't gym kit that's for sure. I ran from the house down the drive and into the forest. Dad was mowing on the mini-tractor and he gave me a surprised wave as I puffed by. He always seemed to be on that mower.

After the first painful minutes I hit a stride and for twenty minutes I disappeared. I took music with me on an early iPod, so heavy it was like two bricks strapped to my side. I was starting to love music again. I can remember the artist who pushed me down the drive that day: it was Basement Jaxx. I should thank them really, as they were the push that spelled the end of the depression and moved me out of slobbish mode. The running caused an amazing mental shift.

After the run I went to the kitchen to make my breakfast: the sweeteners, the skimmed milk and the cereals come out, and for the first time in ages I don't feel hesitant or uncomfortable about eating. I've been for a run, I've earned it.

Exercise kicked me into a new era of myself, one where I realised I could change my mood with a run. It's amazing; before you exercise you groan and think, 'What a day I've got today... I've got to see that bastard, oh and that tosser as well,' and then halfway through your run you go, 'Yay! I can't wait to see him today. What a guy, ah I love him.'

What just happened? Wow! Exercise gave me access to this brilliant drug in my body, the hormones called endorphins. I hated the thought of the running, but I loved having done it. As I ran it really made me see straight. It made me figure a few things out and the first thing that went was being sick.

The other sticking point was El. Our primary bonding activity outside of work is eating. I had to persuade El that he should go on a diet with me. El was no emaciated wretch either. He just didn't have people regularly telling him so in banner headlines.

I joined the local gym. It wasn't that good to start with. I went and met the top guy, who was gym manager and top trainer. His name was Jeff .

'So,' Jeff says, 'what's your aim? What's your goal? What weight do you want to get down to?'

'Oh, I want to lose a stone, please.'

'Right. Brilliant. Well put this key in the machine and you get ten minutes on the bike and then go over to the rowing machine and do ten minutes.'

The guy had some nutritional advice, too. 'What you need is to fuel up!' 'Lucozade is your best friend!'

Lucozade! What! I thought it was for sick kids. 'No, Lucozade is for replenishing,' he says.

'What, even after I've been on the bike for ten minutes?' I say.

I'm confused now because this is different from what the diet books say, but I do it anyway. I'd go on these machines. I loved having a programme. Another routine to follow. I went crazy on it. After six weeks of the same routine, it is interminably boring. But this is my safe place. This is where I feel secure. Systems, routines, schedules, personal bests to beat. And all revealed on the screen in the end-of-workout pie chart. It's a big leap from the dreaded cross-country at school.

Then this new guy arrived at the gym. He was also a personal trainer. I could see people talking to him. I was sticking my key in the machine and doing my ten-minute run, drinking my Lucozade, bored. The next day I went back and he was training someone. He was a bit older than me and in great shape; he was fast, lean, with an animal

quickness; he had the edge on poor Jeff who, dare I say it, looked a bit
podgy. He needed a bunch of keys, not just one.

So I dumped Jeff and signed up with Max. Now he *really* got me
into the training. I could feel that he really wanted to help me. He was
an inspirational guy, he made me feel great, and he didn't just stand
beside me on the running machine talking about Lucozade.

Dawn saw me loving it and wanted to shape up after having Emily,
so she went to Max too. Then El came on board. He was great, this guy
was, and he got me really running. Not with my key on the treadmill,
but outside. I've spent my whole life in the Cheshire countryside, but
for the first time I really started to notice its beauty. Max and I started
running all over the county. Sometimes we'd drive to a trail, leave the
car and just start running. Best of all was when it rained; it made me
feel so free, the rain. That same rain that in the 'Back For Good' video
I moaned about all day because it was cold and surprisingly wet; now
it was like a celebration of nature. I felt so happy and immersed in
these treks. We were totally alone, running these same hills that Paula
Radcliffe trained on for her marathons. Sometimes we'd get halfway
round a ten-mile run and Max would veer off towards a tree where
he'd stashed water for us both. What a guy!

After a year of training with Max, he got me a watch that
measured my distance and speed. Within six months, I was doing half-
marathons. The weight was falling off.

Max never talked about diets. If I started talking about diets he'd
just mumble something and change the conversation to the wonder of
the contents of his lunchbox. He'd have his brown bread, cheese and
pickle sandwiches at lunchtime. He didn't eat a lot, but what he did eat
was just sort of plain, home-made, everyday food, really. Max brought
some happiness and sanity to the whole weight-loss misery. He used to
hold up his banana as he unpeeled it and say, 'Look at that. God's gift.
Comes in its own neatly wrapped parcel!'

Your body knows when something's right. The exercise had a
simplicity to it and it was a relief to find the books were not the only

answer. My relationship with the books was complex. I hated them, yet I hung on every word like a religious fanatic. What was that? 'And' or 'but'? I took in every comma; every tiny detail might hold the crucial key to losing the next pound. Word by word, my life depended on these stupid books. I was that desperate. I had added a few more diets to the steadily growing list: the Dukan, South Beach, some bollocks to do with my blood group.

* * *

I had Howard to thank for my running playlists. He'd started coming over to mine a bit and because he was DJ-ing a lot he'd play me some really good stuff. H didn't live far from me. His daughter Grace was born in 1999 just before our Dan in 2000. When we both had our kids I saw less of him. When we came up to breathe after two kids I didn't really want to see anyone or look back at that point, but I love Howard, of course I wanted to see him. Howard would come round with old video footage of us in Taiwan hanging round in TV dressing rooms, taking the piss out of each other. We'd watch it and laugh. Howard loved these old vids because they reminded him of good times whereas they reminded me of lost times. Not that I said anything; this footage watching a life I felt so far away from then was bittersweet. If you asked any of the band about the nineties, he's the only one that said, 'Oh, I loved it. Every minute of it.'

I never talked with him about feeling shit about life in general. All I wanted was for everything to look under control. Howard's never looked anything less than a Greek god. No, I wasn't going to mention any battles with the scales to him. Those people who put on a couple of pounds at Christmas and lose it by February, by just eating less and exercising more, are probably reading this book and going, 'When's he going to shut up about the bloody diets and jogging? I wanna know about Robbie.' The fact is, at this point in my life, food and weight are both the symptom and the cause of unhappiness.

I'm a Liverpool fan; genetically, I'm probably more Scouse than Manc. So when I became mates with John Arne Riise, there was a little kid part of me that was dead excited. You know I'm going to be there when he says, 'Gary. Do you want to walk the pitch at Anfield?' As we line up for a photo with a few other players, I heard the midfielder Danny Murphy mutter some aside about my size. Well, that hurt. Later El, John and I are driving back east to Cheshire. John's got that strangely deadpan Norwegian way about him.

'Hey, Gha-rhi,' he says, 'did you hear Mur-pheee say he hardly recognised you because you're fat?'

'Oh, yes, John, I did but thank you for mentioning it.' That hurt too. El winced. John didn't have a clue.

This time, though, I didn't lock myself away. With the running I'm starting to come back to life, and I'm stronger. Whatever I got, footballers get it worse; I felt sorry for myself back then but those guys really go through it. They never stop getting abuse, even from their own fans. The fans were always sweet to us. I mean in the nineties it was a complete pain in the arse, not being able to go anywhere without security and a quick getaway planned. By now, though, those fans have dwindled to a hard core who might turn up outside Delamere on my birthday. I remember once coming back from a trip to New York with El when I was still a big lad and this girl waiting for me there. When she screamed, 'Gary!' I just waved and said, 'All right, love, I'm amazed you even recognise me.'

I wasn't even in the minor leagues compared to the fat people in Vegas, though. If you're fascinated by the way people eat, just go and sit in a buffet at the Wynn in Las Vegas. El and I got stranded there on the way to LA; we found ourselves in the middle of the Strip with a night to spare. Neither of us are gamblers, it's got to be a show. There was an advert for Cirque du Soleil's 'O' at the Bellagio. We dropped a couple of hundred bucks on good seats and sat down to enjoy the show.

★ ★ ★

I hadn't sat in a theatre audience for years. Settled in my seat I found it quite emotional sitting with people staring in one direction, sharing the magic. I remembered the feeling of being up there. For the first time in ages I felt a longing. By 2004 I hadn't been on stage for nearly five years and it had been some time longer than that since I'd really enjoyed it. Even back in the later Take That days we used to just wander on, like it was just another night, like we were driving a bus or working in a bank, and all these people going crazy in the audience was just another day at the office.

The feeling in Vegas was the same then as it was when I was eleven (Remember the talent show at Connah's Quay – I didn't win, but was offered a gig?). That feeling of looking out, watching people watching you – it's more than thrilling, it's a need. For the first time in so long, I felt that familiar urge again, the desire to get up there and make people happy by entertaining them. I'm lucky enough to have been given a few talents and writing is only one of them. I'm a performer. You can only turn away from who you are for so long. You can't run away from your DNA.

Desire is one thing and without question I felt it that night. It was so frustrating. I was watching the performers knowing everything going through their heads. Even when you're going through the paces, it's the ultimate expression of your talent – whether you're a gymnast or a singer or a diver – to be able to do it for an audience. What's the point of talent if you can't share it?

Why was I thinking like this? There was never a point, not a single moment, when I thought, 'Right, I want to get the band back together.' I never considered it. There was no band. And certainly no one was asking for me back on a stage, anywhere, any time soon. I hated the sound of my own voice. I avoided singing on demos. Didn't even sing in the shower. Singing symbolised the nineties pop star and all the criticism and failure that came with it. Being a pop star had resulted in such a brutal kicking, it was like aversion therapy. There in my seat at the Bellagio, the idea of being a singer again was nice, but not at that cost. No thank you.

* * *

By the end of 2004, I'd lost four stone and gained two back on my own-brand dodgy maintenance diet. High fat one week, no fat the next, constant denial combined with the odd massive blowout. There was never a book about maintenance. I wonder if the diet industry never really wanted me to succeed. What a conundrum.

When I started training with Max, I took a break from all the crazy regimes: all the rules, weighing food and all the miserable, always hungry habits of the dieter. I just started eating a bit more like Max. After we did the Wilmslow Half, also known as the Sting in the Tail for its last half-mile up a killer hill, Max ordered me to go straight to the pub to eat a steak and kidney pie. 'You've achieved something there. Now go and celebrate with your favourite meal.'

To this day, pies and pastry are the only things I miss from the old days. That bit, where the pie crust meets the meat's juice, that's a glimpse of heaven there. Brilliant. I met Dawn at the Goshawk down the road from ours, and we had a proper guilt-free feed for the first time in ages. I can still see the two little golden brown pastry leaves decorating the crust. Thanks, Max.

Ridiculous isn't it, that eating a pie should be such a memorable event in a life that's been pretty extraordinary. Since Fat Day in 2003, I had become obsessed by food, obsessed in an unhealthy way. It was my tormentor. It had got me into a state that I hated. Food was my enemy. With exercise and Max's sanity it just became less important for a bit. For the first time in years I was sleeping well.

The other thing about exercise is that if I'm on one of my diets, which I usually am, and someone offers me a handful of chocolate buttons, then that's it; if you eat them, your whole day is lost. The guilt! The despair! Once you put exercise in the mix you can combat it. If you eat that handful of your kids' chocolate buttons, you can exercise them off. Some tedious, pious person told me once that endlessly compensating for the food you eat with extra exercise is another form of bulimia. Did I care? They clearly had no idea that until exercise came along I was compensating for eating too much by throwing up till my eyeballs popped out. If exercise is bulimia then bring it on.

As I ran and my brain unfolded, one thought came back to me again and again, to the point where it bothered me almost constantly. I didn't like Delamere Manor any more. We had to leave.

Dawn and I moved into Delamere Manor in 1997 and Our Ian did it up. Back then, there was only the studio fit to live in. Dawn and I put a mattress on the floor and lived there for six months. It was heaven; happiest times we ever had in that house were in that studio.

But now I didn't want to be there any more. I loved the fact that it brought my family together because they all had houses on the estate. It felt like a nice thing to do at that point. Mum and Dad lived at the bottom of the drive in the old gatehouse, and Our Ian was also on the estate. My mum had two hundred chickens in her garden, laying eggs which she sold with an honesty box at the side of the road. ('You'll never have any problems selling those Take That eggs', Nigel used to say to her.) The kids just ran around feral and free with their cousins and had a great life there. All lovely apart from the fact that the place had become my prison.

When I bought it in the mid-nineties I loved it. I loved that it had gates and a drive to keep everyone away. At that point, it represented me: a big star with a massive ego and an army of fans who set up a permanent Girl Guide campfire, waved their arms in the air and sang 'Back For Good' outside the house every day. It was the answer to everything.

By this stage, frankly, I hated it. I actually have nightmares to this day about waking up back in a place like that.

* * *

In January 2005, Dawn took me out for my birthday to this local hotspot with a Michelin star. We sat in Cheshire's latest place to be all alone. Around us were thirty empty tables and somewhere in the shadows one other couple. We sat there listening to our cutlery on the plates waiting for the next course to come. I took a deep breath and said what'd been on my mind for months.

'Babe, I can't do this any more.'

Dawn looked at me shocked, horrified. 'Do what?'

'We've got to move. We've got to go to London. I want to get back; I want to get back to music, a career, life, people...'

She started crying. Oh Christ, what a disaster.

'Bloody hell, Gary, I thought you wanted a divorce. London! Thank God, I've wanted to move for years.'

'Babe, you could have told me?'

Dawn's from Yorkshire. She's like her tea so strong you can stand a spoon in it. She's cheerfully taciturn. We don't feel the need to endlessly talk because we understand each other very well. But the lack of communication had been off the chart since two kids arrived; it was too much. We both felt like we were fading away in the country, while assuming that the other one wanted to be there, hived away miles from the nearest shop.

Dawn had lived in London since she was 15 when she went to dance school. She was living in Islington and in and out of Pineapple Dance Studios while I was still sweating over my GCSEs.

It wasn't Dawn I wanted to divorce, it was me. I hated who I was and that house was a big part of it. I'd always kept a place in London but I considered myself a Northerner and I still do. The wilderness years plus the brilliant and banal, inescapable reality of parenthood made me a very different guy from the one who left the band in 1996. I had to leave Delamere. It was far too big. I mean, even with our family now, it'd be far too big. We'd only need half the house.

Leaving the North was going to be an upheaval. The kids were happy there, and they lived with their cousins who were like siblings to them. El's son and Dan were as thick as thieves. God. Eliot.

My parents would deal with it but I dreaded telling El we were going. He'd moved his whole family over to Cheshire to work with me. He'd picked me up off the floor. Our company is called True North and I'm buying a house in the Royal Borough of Kensington and Chelsea.

El's more northern than me. The North is a thing that always tickles us; we love playing the comedy Northerner with each other, to the point where I don't even know if it's me or not. You have to be a Northerner, really, to understand it. But the North is just funny. It's funny. If an American came to London I'd go, 'Come on, son. We're going up North. I want you to see what England's really about because it's not London, that's for sure. London's for postcards. You need to get north of Birmingham to really understand what England is.'

It's harsh, up North is. The people are harsh to one another. They take the piss out of each other. You can't have too much of an ego being from up North because the level of banter is brutal. No one's getting away with anything. But there's usually a warmth in this sharp banter. Warmth is a key part of that humour. If someone insults you, that's a sign of affection where I come from.

I asked El over and he turned up in an incredible mood, which I was about to piss all over with my news. I stood next to Dawn in the kitchen, presenting a united front. 'El, we've got something to tell you. We've been thinking a lot about this and we wanted to tell you that we are moving to London.'

He just stood there expressionless, then he beamed and said, 'That's cool, so am I!'

* * *

A few weeks after Dawn and I decide to leave Cheshire, I felt brave enough to sit down and watch the Brits. I turn it on and what's the first award? It's those *Little Britain* guys coming on, and I'm like, 'Oh, no, no. Please, no.' And guess who's won? Yeah, that's why they're dressed like me and Howard. And then he mentions me in his speech. I snapped the TV off. It's not going away this. It's ten years now since

I left the band. I'm still a laughing stock. It's never going to end. Just as I thought it was safe to go outside…

We made the move very quickly, which is a sign of how keen we both were to get out. We bought a house near Kensington High Street. Our Ian stayed living on the estate. Mum and Dad left the gatehouse. I hope all the chickens that laid the Take That eggs didn't find the move too tough. There was a positive for Mum and Dad. They'd lost their son to That London but Dad got to move back to his home town, Frodsham – home of the Barlows.

We got ready to move into a white stucco semi in Kensington. A semi sounds far more humble than a manor house, and in size it was humble compared to Delamere. But with it being Kensington, it cost about the same. Welcome to London.

One of the greatest pleasures of moving was selling all the antiques in the house and chucking out nearly two years' worth of diet books. In fact, I might have even burned them.

In this busy period of hammering more nails in the coffin of the old me, I got a text from Nigel. I'd hear from him every few months; we had a fractious, on/off friendship. He said he'd been approached by the label who were putting out a *Greatest Hits* album on the tenth anniversary of Take That splitting up; 'a repack' as it's known in the business. They were entitled to do that, whether we liked it or not. Old Nige wanted to discuss digging out an unpublished Take That song to go on the album. He wondered how much we wanted to be involved in promoting it. We texted back and forth a bit. I knew he was in contact with the others.

It's a sign of how insignificant it was to me that I didn't tell Dawn for a while. When I did she was wary. She was so protective of me and after years of Barlow bashing and living with a recluse, she really didn't want me walking back into the lion's den. 'Hmm. What does he want?' she said.

Eliot and I were making a name for ourselves; our industry rep was good. We were doing all right, working hard and having a laugh while we were at it. Just like Nigel had written a script for our lives in the nineties, now I had a whole new script for who I was in my head. I used to actually say, when I refused requests for interviews, 'No comment. I used to be famous.'

What went unsaid between Dawn and me, something both of us knew, was that I was stuck in a rut. I might as well hear Nigel out. Something was missing from this new script I'd written for myself. The texts flew back and forth for a couple of weeks more and then I rang him.

'I think we should get the band back in the same room,' he said. 'Can you come to my house?'

4

FOUR SPARKLY SHIRTS

''Cause the scars run so deep'

I could feel Nigel's eyes on me. Before I even got out of the car. Before I even saw him. It was clear, the moment I turned up his drive, that he had got us all together to get a feel for where we were at individually and as a group. He was sounding us out. Is it worth getting them together? Is everyone up to it? Who isn't? Whose face doesn't fit any more? He wanted to see what he was working with, which made me feel terrible. I may have lost a couple of stone since Fat Day, but I was still a pretty chunky fella. I know Nigel. I can read his mind. He was thinking, 'We're gonna have to sort him out. He's going on a diet.' All this before I even got out of the car. The Manager was back.

There were a couple of assistants at the door and they led us into the house. It was all very professional. We were shown into this room, where we joined the others perched on armchairs and sofas. For the first time since we'd split up, we all came face-to-face with each other. Mark had won *Celebrity Big Brother* and had a bit of solo success. El and I had produced a track on his album, *Four Minute Warning*. Howard was DJ-ing, Jay had done some acting and a lot of travelling. At that time I was probably working more than any of them, El and I were going great guns, but that didn't make a bit of difference. I felt awful. The lads all looked in great shape, exactly as they did on the day we split up in 1996. No one looked any different, except me. I got the pat on the back and a coded 'You look well'.

For some reason I'd thought it would be a good idea to have a brutally short haircut and in an effort to make myself look thinner, I'd shaved myself a weird little goatee because I'd heard it made the face look thinner. I don't know what the plan was with that because the overall effect made me look even fatter than I was.

Jason said, 'Right, let's have a look at everyone.' They all stood up. I stayed sitting down.

There's a lot good about Nigel. Like, you'd never know he's a wealthy guy. He didn't wear his money on his sleeve. As we all got sort of educated and got into things and started buying gold watches (which we never wore), Nigel never did. In that respect he was right. I was due to pack up my whopping country house in a matter of weeks and I had to acknowledge that Nige had got it right. I wish he'd told me this in 1995 when I bought my massive pop star's pad in Cheshire. Driving up to his house you wouldn't have known he had made all this money. It was just a new-build house out by the airport; nice but no different from loads of houses in Manchester. I always liked that about him; nothing ever changed him. He still lives there now.

They've been together for years, him and his partner Danny, who is a genuinely lovely guy, and they really don't give a toss. I went to the toilet at their house and when I flushed, the handle came off in my hand.

Nigel's controlling side overrides everything else. It sends shivers up and down my spine. Being around him I felt a loss of control, a subservience. With Jay, Mark and Howard all standing there, and me with my strange hair situation, I felt like I was in the audition for the band in 1989. With everyone there, the clock had turned back...

When we'd all gone to the audition for Take That, I remember how impressive Rob, Jay, Mark and Howard were. When they started to move, my heart had sunk. Perhaps I wouldn't make it. My only hope of success was this other lad at the audition. His face just did not fit. He looked like he'd driven one of the other lads to the audition. I'll never forget when Nigel turned to me and said, 'He's got to go, 'im,' pointing in the lad's direction. Then he turned to this lad and he said, right in front of me, 'You're not gonna make it, son, you may as well go.'

This lad's face, oh he was destroyed; this normal lad who was really hoping he'd get in this group. When Nigel did his hardman business, ouch, it was brutal. This was the man who was going to help me make it. Seeing his power in play was thrilling. He dismissed that lad in front of me for a reason. He wanted to show me that he was the boss. I know him now. I now get what he was doing back then.

I'm in this new world with this impressive guy who clearly knows his stuff. He's got a gold disc. I get this uncomfortable feeling in my gut of being way, way out of my comfort zone. And that's exciting. I needed to up my game, especially with these other guys. Compared to them I'm like the kid who's a few years out of date, not just style-wise, everything; they were acting their age, whereas I was turning up with all my songs in a briefcase.

At that point in 1989, despite the briefcase, despite the crap dancing, I was the only one writing music and making a living out of singing. Nigel took a huge interest in me. He started coming to all of my gigs in these seriously old-fashioned working men's clubs. There was always one seat spare in the audience with a sign above it, 'Turn's Wife'. Nigel sat proudly underneath it. For a metropolitan guy in his thirties, he was strangely impressed by my act. He loved coming to see me. And I loved having him there. My route to the charts was finally in the audience. There may as well have been no one else in the room.

Night after night he told me, 'You've got to get out of these clubs.' Nigel always saw the band built around me. He even described the others as 'a vehicle' for my talent and they knew it. Nigel was already working his magic on me to make me feel special and set apart from the others. Like Napoleon, Nigel was master of divide and conquer; that was old Nige's game.

Doesn't matter how many years separate me and Nigel, if I was to go for dinner with him when I'm 80, it'd always take me back to when he was the manager. The Manager. He still feels higher than me. Nigel is never off, and he's never not watching. He's always looking for the angle.

Back in Nigel's living room in spring 2005, I felt separate from the others again. This time it wasn't my talent that set me apart, it was my size.

The awkwardness didn't last long. Someone cracks a joke and you're back to being in a band again. Then Nigel said, 'We've got this tenth anniversary coming up. Whether we like it or not, the label have the right to release this *Greatest Hits*. We can get as involved with the promotion and do as much or as little as we want.'

We all agreed that we'd talk to the label and listen to their ideas.

I knew what Nigel wanted. He needed me to engage with it fully. If we were going into the record label he needed his old Take That partner with him. The problem-solver. The guy who goes, 'I know how to do this. I'll write something new. I'll tweak this or that. Let's put the end at the start. Let's do a medley.' That's how it used to work. I'm a good problem-solver; I love it. It's what I was good at back then. We're in Japan, we're due on stage in five minutes, the speakers have gone down. 'Right, we'll get them all to be quiet, and we'll sing it a cappella till the speakers are fixed.'

In the band my department was Problems and Worrying. Launching a *Greatest Hits* with a band that haven't been together in nearly a decade would require a lot of both.

There's another thing, says Nigel. Syco Productions want to make a documentary: a history of the band, a 'where are they now' type thing. I'd get asked to do these sorts of nineties nostalgia shows every now and again and I always, without hesitation, said no. The last time I was on TV was in 1999. A starring role in *Heartbeat*. Nuff said.

*   *   *

My reluctance to be on telly was nothing to do with music, being in a band, or a fear of publicity. It was about one thing: being fat. On the bright side, the TV show was, if nothing else, a new spur to get fit, a proper goal. The producers told me the day they were going to come and film and I worked towards that date with a new focus.

I lost about half a stone in three weeks. I think I am about 15 stone in the doc. I've still got my weird little 'slimming' beard on, which made me look fatter.

The next move was to get us into the label to talk about this repack. I wish I could say I felt nothing; I certainly pretended it stirred nothing in me. But the truth is, it was lovely being back in a label. Music coming from every doorway. There were twenty other people sitting in that boardroom with us. Visuals, campaign ideas, marketing shots. And we were at the heart of it. Everyone was so enthusiastic.

I've always loved the business of music but my faith in it had been shaken. It was hard to shrug off my pessimism. I wondered how much money they were putting into this album because they were clearly not gonna make anything back. Howard and I left that meeting thinking we knew something they didn't. No one cared. Mark and Jay didn't even bother turning up.

The documentary came at a time when car-crash reality telly, painful TV, is what people were loving. That was the pinnacle of Simon Cowell being vile on *The X Factor* and saying things like, 'I can't believe the size of your mouth. It's so big.' And the audience would be laughing along with him. 'Look! It is! Look at her massive mouth. Massive!' Everyone's rolling in the aisles at some poor woman with a big mouth. This was reality TV's prime gladiatorial era.

All the way through the making of the documentary, it was clear we were being played. I remember the cringing realisation that we'd been set up as they shot this finale that pivoted around whether Rob would turn up to meet the rest of us in a hotel. It made me feel queasy, the whole set-up. I remember asking Dawn, 'Do you reckon he'll turn up?'

'It'll be better telly if he doesn't,' she replied.

The closing shots of the documentary are us four sitting like lemons on chintzy sofas in an English country house hotel, watching Rob deliver his messages to us all by video from Los Angeles or somewhere. There were some nice words for the lads while his contempt for me was barely concealed behind a reluctant compliment about my songwriting.

I rang Dawn. 'Well, you were right. Rob didn't turn up. What a mess. We've been royally stitched up here.'

Dawn said, 'Is all this gonna go on the telly then?'

'Oh yeah, you bet. Our faces, sitting in that hotel. It's the money shot.'

While they edited the documentary together, I had a bad feeling. What was the price for me personally? I didn't need to be putting myself out there to be humiliated again. Sure enough, they show us an offline edit really late so we can't change anything; that old chestnut. We all watch it through our fingers, cringing. We're pawns, we've been played. We agree, they've got a story. It's not *the* story.

The album and the doc would come out within a day of each other in October 2005. The doc was a promotional opportunity for the repack, and of course I saw the logic in that. But oh God, where's it gonna go? You've got to remember, I'm still switching the telly on to watch the Brits and seeing megastar Rob having a laugh at my expense with a fat comedian dressed as me. It's not looking good.

* * *

Suddenly, out of nowhere, a new player enters the game and with him the first real sign of a pulse in this whole thing.

Mark calls me and says he's got this proposal he needs to discuss. We arrange to meet Howard at 190 Queen's Gate, a bar not far from my place in Kensington. Mark pulls out one side of A4 from a guy called Simon Moran who had been promoting his solo tours. He'd done all the big nineties Manchester bands like the Happy Mondays and the Stone Roses. He's got a hunch, he's a gambler. This guy put Oasis on in front of a quarter of a million people at Knebworth. He's convinced we should do a comeback tour.

'He thinks we can play arenas,' says Mark.

'What's wrong with these people? They don't get it, do they?' I say sharply.

The proposal was for eight arena dates including London, Manchester and Cardiff, but Simon was sure that would be the start of it, and he had many more on hold. Next to the list of cities was a number; it had a few noughts attached.

That woke us up a bit.

The big questions hanging in the air are 'Is this guy for real?' and 'Should we turn back time?' We spend a lot of time taking the piss. 'How many people do we know?' 'Have we got enough mates to fill Wembley Arena?' But as the evening progressed, the pitch in our voices grew less cynical and more excited. We had always wanted to do that one last tour. Perhaps we should head out there one more time? After a couple of drinks the offer's looking better. 'Well, we might not have enough mates to fill Wembley, but maybe Jay does.' And we're suddenly going, 'Ring Jay, ring Jay. We've got to tell Jay.'

By some miracle, we get hold of Jay and he's only twenty minutes away. We caught him in a good mood; yes, he'd come by.

He strolls in, arms out wide, and with a massive smile he says, 'Where's me boys?!'

We're all here. These are my brothers. I really haven't needed them in the last ten years but by God in this moment I need them. This is a huge decision. For the first time since we split up, it is just us four. At all these other meetings there was always some bod or other there: managers, label people, someone with a view or an agenda. Just being alone together, the energy ramped up another notch.

We showed Jay this pitch and ordered another round. Red wine for Jay, white for Mark, Howard's on the G'n'Ts, which is always a good sign because he never drinks. I'm on Jack Daniel's and Coke – *Diet* Coke, it goes without saying.

In that moment I dared to dream. I think we all did. I looked at Howard. I knew he was thinking the same. Imagine getting the old Cuban heels on and the sparkly shirts, getting back out there and doing it all again. The thrill hit me with an electric jolt. I thought, 'I'll be able to show the kids what I do.' You know, for one night they'd be able to see their dad doing what he used to do best. The thought was quickly crushed by another. 'Would I still be able to do it?'

This Simon Moran had written a bit of a seduction. He listed all the gigs and said something about 'your amazing shows in the nineties'. We always prided ourselves on our shows; it was the right thing to say.

We ended up back at mine. More drinks. We'd been through the downsides. We started talking about how the show would look 'if' we did it. As we talked about the upsides, the ideas started forming. Once creativity starts, it answers its own questions. It gave me goosebumps. We'd gone through the night, talking, laughing, taking the piss and imagining the show in our minds. After 6am, Mark said, 'Look, we'd better clear off. Is it yes then?'

Time to call the manager. 'Right, Nige, we've got this offer...' He was full of questions: 'Simon Moran? Never heard of him. Let's go and see him.'

The thing that fascinated me about Simon was that he was talking like Nigel talked the first time round. When our third single bombed Nigel kept pushing and pushing. He talked like we were already global megastars while we were still doing school assemblies and provincial gay clubs. Simon had that same conviction before he'd sold one ticket.

Turns out Simon had come up to me years ago backstage at a gig at the Bridgewater Hall to ask if we'd ever get back together. The guy's straight up, transparent, soft-spoken, humble. 'There'd have been no Knebworth without Simon,' according to Noel Gallagher, 'and he's the most honest man you'll meet.'

But the cynicism keeps creeping back. Nigel says he'll go and see Live Nation, which is the massive global equivalent of Simon's SJM Concerts. He rang me with their answer, the one we both expected. 'Live Nation aren't interested. They're saying, "Without Robbie Williams, I can't see it."'

At this stage, I'm more into bad news than good and all the hype and enthusiasm of that night at mine is waning. 'Nigel. They're right. It's not gonna work; this Moran guy's got it wrong.'

But this Moran guy isn't taking no for an answer. He's constantly calling Nigel, 'You've got to do this. You've got to get the band to believe in this.' On and on, day after day, he rings. When he hears about the album and the documentary, he calls even more.

This is how it was going to run. Album released, album sells well, documentary comes out, interest ramps up, album sells a bit more; following Friday, tour tickets go on sale. It was a well-oiled machine... There were a lot of professionals involved now, and these people knew what to do. Best-laid plans and all that. Would people buy it, though?

* * *

The repack was called *Never Forget* and was released on 14 November 2005. It went to number two in the album charts, behind Madonna. Three days later *Take That: For the Record* would air on primetime ITV. We were all dreading it. We agreed to go to a little premiere at a cinema in Notting Hill. We'd get the black suits on and be there for it.

We sat in the bar of the Berkeley Hotel in Knightsbridge beforehand and toyed with the idea of not turning up. Four Mercs pulled up to ferry us there but we all piled into one. Three times we told the driver, 'Take us back to the hotel.' We were scared to death of failure.

The film went down a storm; within two minutes everyone was in stitches at old footage of us on Lorraine Kelly. Within ten minutes it was clear that people were lapping it up and we all relaxed. We stayed the whole night. We had all the journalists from the old days coming over, lots of friends and family to cheer us on. It was a buzz and I loved it. We even went to the after-party, which Nigel had always told us a band must never do. Simon was there, discreetly showing us a printout of all the extra venues he had booked.

The show went out on ITV and people fell in love with the whole story of it.

Now we had to wait a week after the documentary until the press conference at the Berkeley Hotel when we'd announce the tour, the Ultimate Tour.

This gave us a little time to think about Nigel. It was one thing him managing a TV show and a repackaged greatest hits. Quite another him being around for the next six months. I didn't want to be someone else's bitch. This time round we would not work for the manager, the manager would work for us. There was too much history with Nigel. As the manager of Take That first time round he'd made us stars, yes, but he'd also used dirty tactics in my view: unfair treatment, favouritism and a feeling of constantly being manipulated. I'd worked hard to remove all this from my life. None of us wanted to go back there. We were not boys any more. Nigel and his ways could not come between us four as men.

We were all at the Berkeley in a holding room before the Ultimate Tour press conference. I bumped into Simon in the corridor; he looked worried. 'Look, I can't get hold of Nigel,' he says. 'He's not picked up my calls for a couple of days.'

'Can you come to our room a minute, Simon, we've got something to tell you.'

Us four sat there. 'You deal directly with us from now on. 'There's no more Nigel. Now it's just the boys.'

5

JUST ONE MORE

'Come on, come on, come on,
come on take that and party'

We announced this tour two weeks before and we barely got through that press conference. It scared the life out of us. Just getting to the press conference from our rooms was a feat. Just looking at the press was a feat, let alone talking to them. It was like a massive blag. Here we are telling the world about this great tour, this fifteen-date extravaganza. Once again, we know something they don't. We haven't got a single idea how we're going to do this. We aren't the Fab Four, we're four thirtysomething blokes and all we know is next year by some crazy turn of fate we're going to embark on the biggest tour we have ever done. Is this really happening? Do reunions ever really work?

It doesn't feel like it here in this room at the Royal Garden Hotel. We're all staring over Hyde Park in shock. It's our first official meeting about the tour with Kim Gavin. Kim was the invisible Take That member who had made our shows so much fun back in the day. He had been creative director of all our tours since the start. Without him, I'm not sure we'd have been the band we were. If we were coming back, then without question Kim was too. Obviously we've got to do it because the tour's not just sold out, we've added fifteen more shows with six stadiums at the end. Stadiums? We've never done a stadium. Perhaps we'd better ask Rob what it's like?

Howard and Jason brought Apache to the table way back in the early days; it's a famous breakbeat from the eighties that every breakdancer knows. That's their heritage, that is, and it demands movement. An hour later, this was the first idea on the table, and the energy in the room had completely changed. We dared to believe we were a band again. We'd only ever used it on our first arena tour in

71

1993. Kim wanted to use a version of Apache, and we agreed. Apache 2006 appeared halfway through the show. We all worked together with Kim on the direction but when it came to the words for this part of the set, us four sat down alone to write it. A white-coated mad scientist character comes on, answering the booming demands of 'The Manager'. It showed us being popped off the end of a production line like Barbie dolls. Then we slowly come alive to Apache's beats as The Manager's ominous voice boomed around the venue.

'Rule one. The boys in a boy band must love, honour and obey their Manager, and must have no other Manager than me. Rule two. They must sacrifice their privacy. Rule three. The boys must not have girlfriends. Rule four. Some of the boys in the boy band will have to take one year or two off their real ages. Rule five. The boys must always be ambiguous about their sexuality, never confirming their sexual orientation will encourage the homosexual sector of the market. Rule six. They must always be prepared to smile.' Mark turned and smiled at the audience and they went absolutely berserk.

'Rule seven. They must always be gracious and humble like the boys next door. Rule eight. The boys must be prepared to wear make-up. Rule nine. They must never become too close to one another. They must never become real friends in case one of them breaks down and has to be discarded [audience roars with knowing laughter]. Rule ten. The most important rule of all. The boys in the band must all be very, very, pretty...' The audience went completely insane.

Jason wrote the words and Howard and I set it to the music. It was a massive in-joke, for us, for the fans, for the press – everyone got it. It was cathartic. Nigel was not a good thing for us. We didn't want to regress. He couldn't possibly continue. Jason told him in the end. He lived up in Manchester at the time and he's good at things like that. He grew up in a big family, and he had an emotional intelligence none of the rest of us had. Jay was the first to spot the mind games and the divide and conquer stuff the first time round. He's always been the best at that stuff. Not afraid of the truth is Jay. I felt terrible about the whole thing and I wrote Nigel a long letter not long after. There was no alternative.

The Ultimate Tour had sold and sold. It was unbelievable. The first eleven dates sold out in half an hour. Simon put more dates up, and they sold out. He put out more dates, stadiums this time. Two Wembley dates specifically sold out in thirty minutes. More stadiums went up. In the end we did 32 dates in the UK and Ireland, six of them in stadiums. They couldn't build the new Wembley Stadium fast enough for us. It wasn't built in time for us to perform there. Instead we did two nights at Milton Keynes Bowl. Nothing could change how totally shocked we were. The whole thing was totally unbelievable.

There was no way we could do this tour without a manager, so after a few months of me working perfectly happily with Simon Moran, we asked Jonathan Wild to step in. Jonathan is Mark's manager, and his mate since primary school days in Oldham – he'd come to our first ever Take That gig in Huddersfield. He's one of us. It made sense for him to pick up the ball. It was only for one tour after all.

*　*　*

When we started working on ideas with Kim, we made it clear: it's us now. With Nigel gone, we'd shape the band on our own terms. When we talked to Kim about the show we were adamant that the dancers should not be too young and the boy dancers not too good-looking.

Not long after this discussion he suggested Dawn join us and I can't tell you how ecstatic I was – that extra bit of support gave me confidence. Considering I had barely sung in a decade, I needed Dawn on that tour. We were friends, us lot, but still far from being a band at that point and having Dawn around was key to me having the balls to get back up there. As much as she loves dancing, this was about getting back the man she married. I didn't want to be picked on again or have a critical light shone on me. My attitude at this time was, 'If you don't do too well you can carry on being unnoticed and no one will ever hurt you.' Going back on stage and being in the charts was going to propel me back into the firing line.

Take That are devils for an in-joke; we almost speak a different language. There was one phrase that followed us throughout those rehearsals and on, constantly, to this day. 'Yeah, but where is he?'

We'd finish a song in rehearsal, and Kim would go, 'Yup, that's great.'

One of us would come back, 'Yeah, but where is he?'

We'd be in a bar, toasting our success, and in unison we'd say, 'Yeah, but where is he?'

A good review came in: 'Yeah, but where is he?'

This was our shorthand. It was a way to keep Rob in the room. Mark found it a bit annoying, but we all wished he was sharing this with us.

Dawn and I would catch each other's eye in rehearsals and snigger. It was faintly ridiculous. She felt too old – I just felt lucky. But it was only for this one tour – so, hey, sod it, let's go for it. This was like when we first met on tour in 1995. I remember falling in love with her in those rehearsals, catching the odd look and my stomach leaping into my mouth. Back then that magic teenage new love feeling was amplified by the fact we had to keep it a secret. 'What would Nigel say?'

On the Ultimate Tour, Kim kept us apart on stage and made Howard her partner on stage. Dawn used to say, 'Poor Howard, stuck with the old lady while the rest of you get fresh girlies.'

Joking aside, the prospect of these shows was about as serious a goal as you can get.

If people are going to buy a ticket, drop the money on a babysitter and a few stadium lagers then I needed to get in shape. I owed it to the audience. I'll be more confident. I'll be a better artist. No one loves goals more than me, they propel me forward.

The weight started to come off again. I didn't make the connection then but the power of positive thinking is crucial in all of this. Those wilderness years had been a struggle. Now I'm working incredibly hard but life feels effortless.

Stepping out that first night on tour, I was calm, almost too calm. I had to be.

This first night in Newcastle, though, was obviously a massive deal for us. I'd shunned all this for so long but now we were back here. I remember that night vividly. I put my ears in, which always detaches you from your surroundings, and go on stage. Over the next two hours I'm looking at these crowds of people while my life flashes before my eyes. I'm back in that tiny room with the giant telly, that massive house with nothing to do, a broken man-child trying to make sense of the world. I see it all. I see myself laying down the towel to kneel down and be sick. I see myself clomping off stage in silence after bombing at Clive Davis' Grammy show, dragging the corpse of my dreams of an American career behind me. I see it all. Being the laughing stock of the Brits. Hundreds of negative column inches. The Spice Girls movie, and all the other c**** who kicked me when I was down.

This night is like an exorcism.

And the future? Where are we going next, what do we do? Do we give up after this? Do we go on? Look at the journey I've gone on to get back up here. Look at everybody and the history we've got together, not just the boys. Everyone. Look at the audience who've grown up with us and the weight of life and the hours lived of every person in that stadium.

It was so immense, it was incomprehensible and humbling. And it went in a second. I'd never experienced anything like that before and I never have since. There were very few moments in that first show when I was actually present.

If someone was to ask me about my greatest moments with Take That I would include that show. I'd look around and there they are, Jason from Wythenshawe and Mark from Oldham, the northern boys that I met outside La Cage waiting to go into Nigel's audition. Behind them slightly out of focus are 10,000 people going crazy. Look the other way and I see Howard from Droylsden singing his heart out and punching the air. Behind him, another 5,000 people. The support we felt from the audience that night was unbelievable. They wanted us there, and my God they let us know it. The sound that greeted us was no longer the screams of teenage girls; this was the roar of an army.

We knew it would be good: we had the songs, we had nostalgia on our side, but the one thing we never banked on was the love.

We went on timid, apologetic almost. We came off feeling like kings. Yes! The boys. We're back.

That's being in a band, that is. That's the magic of being in a band. It's equally as much about these crappy private gigs where no one's standing up or even really looking at you; they're drinking their champagne and talking about their art collections. But knowing your fellow band members are going through the same absurd experience, dancing away like performing monkeys in front of these world-weary people who have seen it all, that's being in a band, too. And it's great. It's all great. It can't compare to anything I can think of.

Let's compare this time, this first night, to when you first go on at an arena, which for us was in 1993. The lights are flashing and all you're thinking is, 'Look at me. Aren't I amazing?' Fast-forward to this time around: yes, I felt amazing, but I also felt lucky and grateful.

When we came off stage we hugged each other. We'd played a gig and felt like a band again. Mark's a very self-contained man. He never gets in people's space. But every now and again he gives these hugs; they're gentle, almost celestial. I hadn't had one since the nineties. He went round the room doling them out. Those hugs are always markers of a moment. It means we've done well. 'Yeah, but where is he.'

It was so brilliant being with Dawn, and it made everything that was good about that tour even better. It was the best. When we got to the hotel rooms we'd set up our family photos and had our own teabags for a proper northern brew. We loved having breakfast in bed. We loved the drink in the bar after the show. We were like Terry and June on tour. Dawn said it made her happy seeing me happy again. That whole tour was a bubble of bliss and excitement for us. The kids came to see us a lot. Emily was too young to get it, really, but Dan was five and beside himself, jumping up and down at the side of the stage and singing along; oh, he loved it. Our tours are so colourful, so they're great for kids. He'd sit down in the pit with James, our long-time friend and security guy. I'd look down and see him looking up; huge, unbelieving eyes that said, 'Is that really Daddy?'

Em and Dan would come on the tour bus with us, sitting at the front, looking out of the window and waving at all the fans.

When they weren't at the gigs, Mum and Dad took care of them up in Cheshire; that's home for them so we knew they were happy there. We couldn't have done it without Mum and Dad. It's only now I realise how lucky we were to have them right there for us.

Both of us missed the kids when we were away from them, Dawn especially. Despite the magic, I think she regretted doing the tour once we had started as she really wanted to be at home with them. But we also had a great time. We laughed a lot. We generally do.

Back doing the onstage workout, I regressed a bit, relaxed. Before long I was eating big bowls of Golden Grahams after the gig every night on the tour bus. Worry not, skimmed milk not full-fat. Some nights we went mental, and I'd join Howard for a cheese toastie at 2am. By the time we hit the stadiums towards the end, we were playing in front of 70,000 people. I started to feel untouchable. It's not gonna happen now, the fat, I think.

By the end of thirty shows, the clothes were getting unbearably tight. None of the tour clothes would fit. It was unbelievable. It annoyed me so much because I thought, I am sweating my bollocks off every night but still I feel big. I stand on the scales and, whumph, my spirits go through the floor. Does fat not know who I am again?

I realised then, no matter what happens, this isn't going away. I've not got to think about this for the next four weeks on my next diet. This is forever. You're always gonna have an issue with this. I had to choose. Diet misery or fat for good? (There's a song title in there somewhere.)

★ ★ ★

While life was looking up for us, in another galaxy far, far away, Rob wasn't too well. He'd go to rehab the following year and Russell Brand would take the piss out of him for it at the Brits. They do love to kick a man when he's down. It's only a year since those *Little Britain* guys were on stage at the Brits taking the piss out of Howard and me. Neither of us have quite got round to laughing about it yet, but we will. We're Northerners. What bothers me more than the actual sketch is the thought of them all sitting around at a meeting discussing the script, planning it, thinking about how funny it'll be.

When we came back as Take That, I could see the audience had changed. With the Twin Towers in 2001 we'd come back to a different world. The year before the comeback, on 7 July 2005, I had been on a train that collided with one blown up by terrorists at Edgware Road in London. It was something that haunted me for years. There was the immediate horror, the cries of pain of the injured and dying. And then there was the trauma, the constant waking nightmares about my wife and children dying. I was just one person. So many of us were dealing with this new savage world.

What better place to escape from all that than at a Take That concert? Coming back in a harsher world, we found our old audience and a whole new one in search of escape who'd found a new antidote. I saw far more male faces in the crowd, and some of them were even straight. Imagine that!

We'd scared all the blokes off in the nineties with our bloody red PVC hot pants. Sexuality was a big part of Nigel's vision for the band, in a very homoerotic, adult way that Nigel was convinced was our trademark. The dancers' clothes were never sexy enough. Nigel loved all the Madonna *Sex* era stuff with her hitchhiking naked for Herb Ritts. That's Madonna; it's not us. And it's particularly not me; it had no connection to the music I was writing. I was sitting in the corner writing 'Back For Good' thinking, these two worlds ain't meeting. In the last couple of years of Take That, Nigel was hustling me to write R. Kelly-style bump and grind and all I wanted was to write these power ballads like 'Nobody Else' and 'Holding Back The Tears'.

In 1995, when we got signed in America by Clive Davis at Arista, the first thing he said was, 'I don't want this band on TV in America. The way they look doesn't match the record.' He's hearing 'Back for Good' going, 'This is a hit. I want this.' Then sees us at Earl's Court and is horrified by us in our devil horns gyrating around to 'Relight My Fire' and Howard with his arse hanging out. He's going, 'Where's "Back For Good"? Where are the guys sitting on stools strumming guitars? Who are all these red devils in hot pants flying in from the ceiling?' It's part of the reason why the band split up, that whole sex thing. When Nigel told me what Clive had said, I agreed. Tour by tour I felt less and less comfortable trussed up in all this kinky tackle. Davis was saying what I was thinking. With Robbie gone, I felt like we'd reached the end of the road.

I never feel sexy, not in that way Howard can pull off with his six pack and all that; it's natural to him. He's an extremely sexy guy. I've never felt like that. I always went for the darkest, the most covered-up version of what I could get away with. Those costumes of Nigel's were torture. I dreaded the moment when costumes came for the tour; what fate lay ahead for me and my dignity. I'd be looking at a three-foot-tall crown and a cape for our opening outfit, thinking to myself, 'Oh shit. I'm gonna have to seriously edit my guest list for this tour now.'

Yet for all my self-consciousness, I felt those costumes kinda made it. They were part of the magic and they kept people coming back. They did scar me for life, though. When we came back we got a new stylist, Luke Day. He's always going to battle to get me out there in anything wacky.

We came back and stripped out the sexuality but ramped up the showmanship. We love that about the Take That shows – the high camp; we're proud of it. We picked over every detail in that show, just the four of us, long before it was handed over to the 'professionals'. We all loved the flamboyance. It wasn't just because it looked fabulous, it was something to hide behind on this first outing.

It didn't take long to discover that Take That had evolved in an extremely exciting way.

Mark brought his eye; he saw everything in universal stories; theatre's great subjects: love, birth, death, loss. Jason bared his soul: everything we did he saw in terms of the struggle of men with their identity in the modern world. This was undoubtedly formed while living the insanity of being in a boy band. He was well read in philosophy and psychology. Everything went so deep with him. He was always attached to some well-thumbed paperback and bringing its message to our chats.

Round a table, we were all fizzing with tour ideas, which we approached in our different ways. Mark and Jason conceptualised everything and would argue into the early hours, pushing each other into ever nuttier realms. Jason, so against the mainstream, so repelled by commerciality. Mark wanting any message to be carried by an eye-popping show.

Howard had his fair share of ideas but most crucially played the role of arbiter. He's naturally got fantastic taste in music, he's got great style, he's a dancer so he always knows a truthful expression. He'd swiftly dispatch any bogus posturing or try-hard ideas. No one understands the Take That brand like he does; he mentally puts himself in the audience and they always come first for him. The final word belongs to Howard.

I'll be honest; what had initially felt like four losers being dragged back for a bit of nostalgia and novelty now looked like a future. We'd all gone away and lived, and we came back with opinions this time. This was no boy band, these were great minds working in harmony. I felt the possibilities were endless.

6

BLOOD, SWEAT AND PATIENCE

'I know we'll try, try through
the laughter and the tears'

We came off tour and went straight into making an album of new music. We'd all changed. Who were we now musically in 2006? The only way to find out was to get in the studio. We made a promise to each other. We'd give it a try and if we got to deadline day and didn't like what we'd written, we wouldn't release it and pack in the whole thing. Jason was the one pushing hardest for this. He always liked the car door open, ready to jump.

The boys all said, 'We all want to write this time.'

In what I had thought was my misfortune, I had learned everything we needed to know about writing collaboratively through my work with Eliot over the last five years. I was able to put my hand up and go, 'I know how to do that. All we've got to do is be in the room together…'

I admit, I was curious and nervous about how I was going to deal with this. If the band had all wanted to be in a room in the nineties, I'd have been far too controlling and wanted to have it all my own way. I was a different person then. I never said, 'Hey, everybody stay out of the studio because this is my domain.' It was more that everyone just left it to me and, aside from a couple of rare occasions ('The song' Sunday to Saturday), I never invited any of the boys to work with me. I wanted it to be all mine.

This time all four of us would be credited as writers, and we'd share the royalties equally. It was the right thing to do.

I went to the label and they offered us a recording contract. The deal looked decidedly average. I needed a second opinion.

'David, can I come and see you?'

We'd first met Dave Joseph in 1993. He was the junior press officer at BMG. He'd always stayed in touch with me as he climbed the ranks to become CEO at Polydor. He asked me to be a judge on the prehistoric TV talent format *Pop Stars: The Rivals*. Talent shows? Yuck. That'll never work. (And with me then at 17 stone, I'd take up three chairs.) He's a cool guy, really quietly spoken. Some people when you meet them, in a second, you think 'music business'. You don't with him.

'Yeah, yeah, come down this afternoon.' The Universal offices were not far from our flat in Kensington. I went down. He greeted me in this lovely way, saying, 'Congratulations on all the music. Brilliant, really brilliant.'

'I've got something I need to discuss with you. We're going to do new music and I've got a contract here from Sony. Will you tell me what you think of it?'

He didn't even pick up the contract I'd put in front of him but fixed me in the eye. 'Are you really going to do a new album, the four of you?'

'Yeah. We're going for it,' I said. 'We've got an opportunity, it's now or never.'

'I don't need to see that contract. Have you got five minutes now? Can you come and meet my boss?' He made a phone call and we walked upstairs past two receptionists and straight into Lucian Grainge's top-floor office with its views across west London. Lucian is God at Universal. He's the complete opposite to David. His whole being screams music industry. Mind-blowing confidence. He's in a suit, but he's off the page and unpredictable and wild. Quite often these guys are basically accountants or lawyers. Lucian's reputation was always as a music guy. I liked that.

I sat down, and his first words were, 'Who are you? What is Take That? I don't get it.' It's a test.

I know the answer.

'It's simple. We're a vocal group that sings enormous hit records.'

'I love it!'

A car is immediately sent to pick up our lawyer.

★ ★ ★

Take That have a three-album deal with Polydor. Now all we need is to find those enormous hits I've promised. We all see it as a new start. New label. New energy.

Our new A&R man is a fabulous human being who also happens to have the same name as my dad. As soon as the handshakes are over, I ring Colin Barlow. 'Signed. Deal's done. What next?'

'Great. Let's listen to some music,' he says.

We sit in Colin's office all afternoon working through his suggestions of people we can work with. An A&R's job is to support you on your music-making journey. This Sheryl Crow record comes on and I love the sound of it. 'That's John Shanks. We'll get you some flights to LA. Go and work with him for a week.'

At this stage, we're midway through the arena tour. We go to LA to meet this Shanks guy in the break before we start on the stadium dates. We land on Sunday night, go to bed at the Mondrian, have a sleepless night and turn up to work the next day ready for bed. We're in John Shanks' room at Henson Recording Studios, which is where Carole King wrote *Tapestry* and where all Joni Mitchell's albums were recorded.

John comes into the studio: he's all biker boots, faded Ramones T, trucker cap and Ray-Bans. I can't say I warm to the guy, but I like his edge. It's just what we need. Not sure that feeling is reciprocated. He clearly isn't excited to be working with us; we are just some English guys in his studio.

'Take That, eh'; he goes to his laptop and types us into the search engine. Wouldn't you know it, up pops the 'It Only Takes A Minute' video. Vests, quiffs, breakdancing, oiled muscles. We sit cringing while he provides a running commentary. 'Wow. Well. Look at these guys. Are you guys straight?'

It is the worst possible start for a group trying to be taken seriously and evolve musically. He gets straight down to business, strumming away on his vintage Gibson acoustic. This guy is a serious player. Reaching for credibility, I run to the piano to show him I can do something more than lip-synching in a boxing ring. We don't get much done that day and go back to the hotel underwhelmed. Where are we going to find these hits I've promised Lucian? I've had these experiences before while trying to write a hit for the great Clive Davis. America can make any British person feel very small. The cars, the buildings, the portions, the voices, the egos. Everything's big there. I would not be beaten this time.

The next day is a whole different story. We all come back in a new frame of mind, not least John. He is working with Rod Stewart on an album of rock classics and has mentioned his session with Take That. Good old Rod has sung our praises. John looks at us through fresh eyes.

By lunchtime we've written 'Patience'.

We're warming to John; for an American he has a respectably dry sense of humour. We are ordering sushi every lunchtime – my favourite, so healthy! By the end of the week we're sad to say goodbye.

Four days later the demos arrive via email. I listen through: sitting proud among four other songs is our comeback single. If he's ever asked about 'Patience', Colin always says, 'I knew how good it was by the look on Gary's face. He looked so excited.'

Colin puts the CD on and by the end of the first chorus – '...*have a little patience*' – I know.

'Well,' he says, 'that's it. I'm going to play it to the company this afternoon.'

'Playing it to the company' is an extremely important part of record-making. It's when everyone gets onside with the task of pushing your work out into the world. He plays it without an intro. No names. The company likes it. 'It's a hit but we don't know who it is. Is it Take That?'

* * *

One of the great things about delivering your hit single first is that the label then leave you to get on with it. We had the freedom to make our album.

John arrived from LA, recovering from pneumonia.

The most significant thing about *Beautiful World* wasn't the writing of it. It was the recording. John normally worked with bands – you know, guitar, bass, keyboard, drums, vocal. We weren't a band in that respect – we would be called a 'vocal harmony group' in industry-speak. John plays everything. He'd do all the guitars, Jeff Rothschild, his engineer, would be the drummer, I'd play piano and keys. In the past we had multiple producers on each album. This album was being made by one guy, one sound, one message. This time, when record-making began, it was fast, intuitive and exciting.

The last album we'd made in the nineties we'd done on borrowed time, scheduled to be in the studio for thirty minutes to put our harmonies down, literally recordings dropped into a schedule of promo and haircuts. To the people in charge of us, music was the least important thing.

This album, ten years on, could not have been more different. We had become a studio band. This is how great music gets made.

One big discovery for me in this period was my voice. I'd barely sung for years. The tour was one thing; being in the studio with John was a whole other. He pushed my voice into new ranges and sounds. He was obsessed by my falsetto, which had been unexplored in the past. You can hear it a bit on 'Back for Good', but this time round it had become a trademark. He was gentler with the other lads, but he practically locked me in the vocal booth.

'Again … higher.'

'More emotion.'

'Meh. Pitchy.'

On and on until he said, 'Great take! Now do it again.'

I'd sing until I was hoarse. I'm sweating in that vocal booth. And loving every minute of it.

John is a real seen-it-all, done-it-all guy who has worked with loads of great people. He's a bit older than us and one of those songwriter/producers that likes to be the boss. He wasn't bowing to anyone, he wasn't scared of his own opinion, and he'd take people on if he thought they were wrong. We'd steered clear of characters like this to a near neurotic degree since getting back together. Memories of Nigel.

It started to dawn on us. John Shanks was like Robbie and Nigel rolled into one. He's an incredibly talented guy, sharp, sensitive – *very* sensitive – but very direct with other people.

Processing this authoritarian figure we had in John was psychologically interesting for us all. Having a figure like this back in our lives meant only one thing. It brought us closer together. It wasn't long before we started calling him 'The Producer' in the same way we called Nigel, 'The Manager'.

One thing's for sure: he was central to Take That getting our act together second time around. The therapy side of the process was inevitable. We recorded the album at RAK Studios near Regent's Park. In between sessions we'd go upstairs to the canteen and talk a lot and pick at the scars from the first time round. This was great. Progress! Dealing with this just bonded us even more.

We're still a bunch of northern teenagers at heart when we get going. Like it was with El, we revel in our northernness. It's a constant pleasure. Being northern outwardly involves a lot of huffing and puffing but what you need to understand is that, for a Northerner, moaning is an extremely enjoyable pastime.

The vast majority of Northerners hate the word London – it's a place we can't ever be seen to be enjoying but actually we're fascinated by it. On the way out of the city it's always good to say, 'Can't wait to get home' and away from 'That London'. If something's too cool we like to do it down by saying, 'It's all a bit London.' There's no finer sight than a Northerner sitting in a restaurant like the Wolseley. See the sheer joy on their faces at being somewhere exciting and posh and then watch the lip-curling moment when the bill arrives.

Northerners do like to travel. They just enjoy getting home more. Especially if you've been to somewhere gorgeous and hot and on your arrival home it's freezing and raining. That's the cue to sit back and pronounce, 'Ahh, that's better.' A cold wind is a pleasurable experience for a Northerner. We label it 'brash'. Winds like these are usually found in Blackpool, the north of England's premier beach destination. I love Blacky.

More than anything, Northerners love being northern. We have endless jokes at our own expense that make it all right to do pretty much anything. Get fat, get pissed till you fall over, wear no sun cream, never tip anyone, get in a fight, steal a car… The answer is always, 'Fuck that! I'm a Northerner.'

You hear stories about all the great bands and their big fallings out, and I can't imagine it. I can't imagine what it's like to be in a band where no one likes one another. Take That's a happy band. We don't fall out… no one has arguments. We solve problems with humour or we just say, 'Fuck that, we're Northerners. It'll be 'reet.'

Saying all that, my sense of humour isn't quite back to full health yet.

Dawn sat me down one night and said, 'You've got to watch this, it's the best thing I've ever seen.' She's recorded a comedy called *Star Stories: The Take That Story*. For the next hour I sit in stony silence beside Dawn who was wetting herself.

I showed it to the lads and they thought it was even more hilarious. Howard is played by Chewbacca. I'm this controlling egomaniac swot. Sounds about right. Robbie is a sweet young innocent. That doesn't sound right. They loved it, and the quotes went on for years.

Me? I thought it was the most painful thing I'd ever watched in my life. It was like someone sticking a spear in my side repeatedly. Why? Because it was spot on, they got it just right. It was more accurate than most of the documentaries about us, even the ones made and approved by us.

Difficult as it was to watch, it was also quite useful. There's a bit in *Star Stories* where the actor playing 'Robbie' is begging the actor playing 'Gary' to let him have a go at writing, and 'Gary' turns to his Ivor Novello statuette and says, 'I don't know, let's ask Ivor. Ivor says no.'

Now when there's some debate over a point of music, I'll say, 'Let's ask Ivor, shall we?'

'Patience' was number one for a month. If you'd have written our comeback as a script, you'd read it and go, 'Nice story but it can't possibly be true.'

Your only dream when you write a song is for people to hear it. Certain songs resonate with people more than others. They connect on a different level and when those songs come out it's almost like a date stamp in your life. A big song can take your whole life in a different direction.

After 'Back For Good' came out in 1995, I think people realised I could write a song. People are going, 'That Gary Barlow's a good songwriter.'

'Patience' is another one. 'Patience' is why we're here. People were surprised by it; they couldn't believe it was us. 'Patience' brought us right back.

After the release of 'Patience' through the Beautiful World Tour, we were riding one huge bloody wave. We were all struck by a too familiar feeling of the machine taking over. The way we worked in the nineties was constant. Whatever the question, the answer was yes. Second time round, we were the band that said no to everything.

'We want you to go to Poland next week.'

'Guess what. We don't want to go. And we aren't going.'

Part of these 'nos' came from experience. One lesson I'd learned from the nineties is that we did anything and everything. All the good stuff; all the shit stuff, too.

There was no need. Another reason for the 'nos' is that we could just say no. We were men, we could say no thanks. No. It felt good. You should try it some time. We definitely hadn't said no enough. Now it was our favourite word. No, thanks. No one died. Record sales were great. Just, no.

No matter how sweet all this success was, it didn't make me feel any better about the way I looked. Plus, being on diets really wound

A member of the pathological staff at Bootle General Hospital, Miss Marjorie Cowan, daughter of Mrs. Cowan, of 31 Wilberforce Road, Walton, married Mr. Colin Barlow, son of Mr. and Mrs. Barlow, of 8 Clifton Crescent, Frodsham, at Walton Parish Church, on Saturday. Given away by her uncle the bride wore a classic gown of white satin with a shoulder-length veil and rose head-dress. She was attended by the bridegroom's sister, Miss Sandra Barlow, and the best man was Mr. Kenneth Nield.
(Photo by J. Baron Williams, Great Crosby.

Mum and Dad's wedding day,
21st January 1967.

There was only one part for me
'Joseph'. Although that white suit on
the pharaoh looked pretty damn sweet!

Love reading this report. It's slightly unfair to laugh at the comments as at this
point of school I was working six nights a week as a paid musician.

NAME Gary Barlow		TUTOR GROUP 4B	
SUBJECT	SET	ATTAINMENT	EFFORT
Music		71%	A

Gary has worked well throughout the year and deserves this good examination work. I have been pleased to see him preparing tapes for the purpose of the practical assessments and have enjoyed his performances. It is also encouraging and pleasing to see him producing composition work of a high standard. However he must improve the presentation of his compositions if he is to do himself justice in the final assessments. At present they are rather untidily presented and not well documented. It would be a shame if he were to lose V.J. Mason. marks because of this. I would SUBJECT TEACHER like to see Gary involved in some music making at school.

All photos in this section © Gary Barlow

Such a thrill to see yourself advertised in the local paper.

This was my first job at the bar in Connah's Quay Labour Club. Can you imagine my face when I saw they had put my name above the stage?!

This was taken at my friend Mike Croft's house in Heysham. He had a few synths and a reel to reel recorder. His daughter used to sing too – it was always fun going to his and making music.

Black & white – yes – Duran Duran were still big at the time. Classic '80s Burtons attire. I thought I was the bee's knees.

The news headlines always tickle me. I'm pretty sure I wrote these myself!

I won a record tokens song contest for 'Best Song', called 'Now We're Gone'. Posing is Bill Buckley and me stood outside Abbey Road. What a day making a record in the penthouse studio and then watching it being cut onto vinyl.

Winning songwriter of the year at the Ivor Novello Awards was incredible. To top it off, my idol presented the award. We sat and gossiped over lunch before this. Elton is the best company.

This shot of Elton and me was taken at Alexandra Palace for the BRIT Awards. He was presenting with Ru Paul. It was a great night – we performed the Beatles medley and in our cast was a certain Dawn Andrews!

Meeting Princess Diana was brilliant. This was actually the second meeting, as she had invited us to the Palace for a chat before we committed to the charity concert. Great memories. We all got a Christmas card from her that year too!

Enter our very own Jean Claude Van Barlow. Constant touring was keeping me in very good shape in 1995. Can we rewind please?

Mum and me at my 26th birthday dinner. I think Dennis Taylor was big at the time hence the over-sized goggles!

Dawn and me in Venice. We took some pictures but we really shouldn't have bothered, as we had a tabloid photographer who followed us for the whole weekend and shared it with all their readers!

Our wedding day. Very simple. Only close family there. Dad was my best man. Don't tell anyone but Dawn was three months pregnant with Dan. Don't know how that happened from kisses on the cheek!

Now there's a guy who loves a dessert!

Dan and me at the piano. These were tough times. Sleeping a lot. Spending most of the day in pyjamas and track suits. It was hard to see a way back from this point.

Dan and Emily's christening. My dad insisted on the kids being christened. He used to say 'they won't do well at anything until they are christened'. He was very quietly religious. He also used to put Bibles in some of the drawers in our house without us knowing.

me up; I didn't sleep well fretting about what I'd eaten or not eaten. It's hard to sleep when your body is too full or too empty. It's hard to diet when you're tired. This vicious circle meant that sometimes, sick of all the anxiety, I'd say, 'Sod this, I've had enough, I'm going back to eating normally.'

This is how the yo-yoing would go. When we toured I would be off the diets because I thought if I'm sitting near Howard I won't put weight on because he never does. I'll eat the same as him: nice fat hotel club sandwich with the crisps on the plate at two in the morning. It'll be fine. Lo and behold, I'd come off tour a stone heavier. Then I would do a diet, something quite drastic and completely joyless, usually involving fat-free eating and rabid all-day hunger.

At busy times I started falling back on a regime that I christened the one step forward, two steps back diet. It's very effective. You feel great one minute and shit the next. In a nutshell, it consisted of:

1. Breakfast, no thanks, I don't eat breakfast, I'll have black coffee.

2. The next meal I had was the epitome of what I thought diets were: piece of steamed fish and steamed broccoli. Tastes of nothing. Diets meant tasteless food. I'd eat that for lunch in this pious, thin person way because that night I was going out. I felt like I'd got it all under control. I'd be reassuringly starving and have honking bad breath because of it. I didn't drink much water, so I'd refresh myself and fight off hunger with coffee and Diet Coke.

3. In the evening, on the one-step, two-step diet, you eat and drink 'normally'. 'Normally' means double the calories you would've eaten on a normal day.

The problem with weight loss is it seems to always entail eating bland food, which is unsustainable long term because it's dreary. Even when I try to eat normally, I can't shake the paranoia. I wasn't able to tightly manage my diet like I had when I was less busy.

The label wanted to take us out to celebrate the success of the album. We went to the great River Café in Hammersmith. Everyone's chatting away and the wine's being uncorked with a lot of ceremony. Suddenly the waiter's there with an enquiring, 'Sir?'

Panic. What should I eat? Haven't even looked at the menu. Pasta. Can't eat pasta. Lamb. Too much fat. Steak, what if it comes with chips? What's everyone else ordered? Pasta. Oh, okay, okay, yes, pasta please.

It arrives.

There's no way you should be eating pasta.

I'll just have a couple of forkfuls and leave the rest. Self-control, self-control. Oh my God, this is delicious. One more. I'll use a spoon. Pass the shovel. What's yours like? Can I try some?

For a moment, you're in heaven. Greatest Italian restaurant in London.

Pasta.

Then the guilt sets in. Food was an enemy that made me feel bad about myself, made me big, made me angry, made me so many things that I didn't want to be. That puts you in an anxious eating disorder state, doesn't it? I can't tell you how petrified I was of finding myself back in 2003, beached on the mattress. 'Fat Day' was a ghoul that haunted every meal.

* * *

I wore Dior for *An Audience With...* Back then, I took a 36-inch waist. I'm not obese any more, maybe about fourteen and a half stone. *An Audience With...* was a massive moment for us; it was my idea, as I always used to watch these things as a kid. There's no better way to get new music out to your audience than putting it on the telly. So I spoke to ITV ... when you look back at it, it was bloody ambitious. It was a live version of that show, which they'd never done before. They offered us a host, Jonathan Ross or Dermot O'Leary, but we were full of confidence by now. *Beautiful World* was a great album.

We said, 'No, we're going to host it ourselves.'

It worked a treat. After that the album went through the roof. We had an after-show party at a Japanese place called Sumosan on Dover Street; we went to that, too, despite Nigel's instruction back in the day that we should never go to after-parties. I remember feeling special. John flew in for it. David Joseph of Polydor and Colin were there. Even God – aka Lucian Grainge – came down from his top-floor office to see us, and brought Mrs Grainge with him. We had been blessed.

There were a few old faces in the audience who'd had bitchy laughs at our expense over the years and kicked us while we were down. Did I find it hard going, 'Hello, how are you doing?' while thinking, 'Fuck you.' No, if anything, it made me lay on the showbusiness hugs even more. I loved it. Whatever awkwardness I might have felt I knew they felt it ten times worse. 'Darling! How lovely to see you!'

Our confidence was coming back. I was already making plans for the next album. At the writing stage of *Beautiful World* we had leaned on co-writers for most of the tracks. This time I wanted us to write the whole album ourselves.

7

FOUR GO
MAD AT SARM

'Silence please 'cause I've got something to say'

I took an Aston Martin for a test drive. The sales guy comes to the house and says, 'Here you go, take it. Enjoy.' I took this purring beast out on the open road. As we were pulling up, the guy said, 'I've been doing this job for twenty years and that's the slowest test drive I've ever experienced.'

Still, I bought the car. Couldn't drive it. I kept bumping into other cars. It was embarrassing so I sold it. I think it worked out about ten grand every time I took it out. I'm not a particularly good driver. I'm not interested in driving fast. Cars are wasted on me. I'd say to Dawn, 'I'm gonna buy a sports car.' Dawn would say, 'Okay, babe. See you in nine months,' and literally to the day I'd go, 'Sod this. I'm going to go buy a Mini,' and I'd be off puttering about in my Mini happily for years. Then I'd go and buy a Porsche. Again, I'd bounce off a few parked cars and a few months later go, 'This is a waste of money, I'm going to buy a little Audi.'

Point is, I don't have many vices. I love pies. I love pâté. But I don't eat them any more. As I keep telling you, I'm on a diet. I only eat pâté on my birthday. And pies? Never.

Are pies and pâté a vice? I like a drink, and I can drink a lot if I feel like it, but I'm never a mess. I can go a month without and not miss it.

Weed? Yes. I used to love getting stoned, way more than drinking. Back in the late nineties, when my career was tailing off and Dawn was touring in Germany, I was on my own in my pop star palace, Delamere. I spent the entire time off my box on weed. I used a rolling machine, but the trouble was that by ten at night I was too pissed and stoned to work it, but for some reason a new skill would come to the fore and I could build these big joints using three Rizla kingsize papers. I'd smoke the first third and put it out and then I'd go to bed leaving the rest so I could wake and bake. Weed's great for filling the hours. I wasn't unhappy back then, but I was getting there. I'd never wake and bake these days. That's just escapism. It's a waste of time getting wasted.

But if you want to know my real vice, it's studio equipment…

* * *

I'll never be truly rich because of what I spend on my studios. When I order kit, it's rarely something new; it's got to be a very specific piece of vintage tech from 1979 Berlin or an old synth from the eighties. I'm an obsessional person by nature. If I took up golf (which I never will), I'd have all the clubs by the end of the week. Studio kit, oh, I love it. I can be on that stuff all day and all night.

When I first got some serious money I made a point of buying all the synths I dreamed of. The ones that I used to watch Vince Clarke, Gary Numan and OMD play on *Top of the Pops*. I bought them all and then I was broke again. I was only 20.

Someone told me, 'You should spend your next royalties cheque on buying a house.' So I bought a house. And filled it with more keyboards. Since then I've never stopped. I spent six grand on a Hartmann Neuron. They only made 150 of them before they went bust. It's crackers. It's proper weird and produces sound by granular synthesis, so you don't get notes, you get atmospherics – real *Doctor Who* sounds. Looks mega too. The other thing with synths is that it's love at first sight; you've not heard the thing yet but it looks great with all the lights, knobs and buttons. You're like an eight-year-old. 'Oooh, shiiiit, look at that! I'll have it!'

The Yamaha DX7 – that keyboard I sat on the wall waiting for – I've still got that. I kept it because it just felt so special. It's the second biggest selling synthesiser of all time. It's worthless because there's so many of them out there, but despite how much I played and gigged it, mine is pristine. The bug I've got goes beyond keyboards. There are things called cartridges that go in these old synths. I've collected them over the years. I must have sixty that I've found scouring Japanese websites, constantly dropping bits of text in and out of Google Translate so I can get a rough idea of what I'm buying. I've got thousands of pounds' worth of these cartridges stashed in a drawer.

There's a place called SchneidersLaden in Berlin. It's paradise. If I wasn't happily married, dropping a mention of this place would be the ultimate chat-up line for me. El, Rhino (that's what we call Ryan) and me go to all the music techhead trade fairs – NAMM in LA, to Cologne for the Musikmesse – where they announce all the new kit to the eager geeks. Just talking about it makes me feel weirdly, dare I say, aroused.

A good time, for me, is Abbey Road. That's a day out, that is. I love it. We've recorded every string section since 'Back For Good' there and it still feels magical. I go and spend an hour in Studio Two and take pictures of the microphone in the mic room. Proper trainspotter, me. Studio Two is The Beatles' room. I'll just sit there and listen to the room. The history knocks the wind out of me.

I love sleeve notes and I love the credits. Who wrote this? Who played on that? The characters involved in music are part of the wonder of record-making. Not just the well-known artists, I want to know who the session players were. Who was the engineer? What mics did The Beatles use?

The producers would work in white coats like scientists in a lab. I'm sometimes disappointed I didn't have my career in the sixties when the three-minute British pop song was something so iconic. That era is the greatest for British pop music and it defined us to the outside world in a way that's gone on for generations.

Then again, I love the fact that I can walk into any room, open my laptop and make a record. Early on, when I was a kid in the eighties, I knew music was going to be computerised. I could tell by watching what bands like Human League, OMD and Ultravox were doing.

Back then I'd get on a train all on my own for day trips down to London. Mum would pack me a ham bap from the Devonshire Bakery, some Ringos and a Penguin biscuit. I was quite a picky eater then, and only baps from the best bakery in Frodsham were good enough for me.

I'd go straight to Denmark Street where all the music shops still are – but only just: the flats are creeping in. You only had to hang around those music shops to realise what people were up to and where music was going. Music-making was becoming affordable. When I first got into music as a teenager, the pop stars at that time would have been using these $200,000 Synclaviers. That's what a big star used (of course now you can buy a Synclavier app for £200). Computers? They were a different story. I realised if I slogged away at the clubs for six months, I could have one of those. I got my first computer when I was 15: an Atari 520. It cost £1,000 and I bought it on my mum's Access card. It'd take me about six months to pay her back.

There was this program called Steinberg which let me plug my keyboards into the computer. I could play a melody and the computer would lock it and quantise it to dead on the beat. The first time I hit the quantise button, the sound of my own digitally perfected song blew me away; it was like I had *Top of the Pops* in my bedroom. It sounded like all the pop records that I loved. The world lit up. I was breathless.

This Steinberg program kept me entertained for about two years, and I was making song after song with this secret sound and barely left my bedroom. Ask Mum about the difference between me and Our Ian when we were teenagers and she'll say I was always in and Ian was always out. Not that unusual for a teenage boy to lock himself away in his bedroom, but at the end of those two years I had these tapes to show for it – the ones I gave to Nigel. The ones that decided my future.

* * *

Everywhere I have roots, you'll find my gear. When I fly to LA for a writing session or a family holiday, I ship a studio-load of equipment out. There's bits and pieces stashed in my mum's barn. At home, the kids are up in the attic, while the studio in the London house is opposite our bedroom. There's another full working studio up the road.

Not long after we moved to London after the Beautiful World Tour, we bought a house near Oxford. Goes without saying, I built another studio there. London is great but I've come from Frodsham and I want my kids to have a bit of what I had – freedom, space, green. Not 122 acres of space, more like half an acre – a normal garden, not 'grounds'. Our house in Oxford's big but it's not ridiculous like Delamere was. We use every room there. We've got massive sofas and light fires every night, the whole place smells of wood smoke, the dogs get up on the sofas. It's a freezing old seventeenth-century house and we love it there. It has a pub within walking distance, which is extremely important. I'm a lot wiser now about what luxury is. It's not a fancy sofa that matches the curtains and the rugs; it's a home, with all the things you love that probably don't match. Heaven.

I've still got all those original cassettes I made in my bedroom with my name and all the song titles neatly written on them. One day I'll stick them up online.

Thank God I taught myself chords and had unpicked all the sonics and scales. My spelling and grammar might be erratic, but I can speak and write the language of music fluently. Those pre-computer years meant I understood the technicalities of music. I'd done my homework. When the computer arrived it was like taking skills I had and putting them on a throne. The opportunities became endless.

Those years in my bedroom between 11 and 18 were the building blocks of who I would become. How you spend your teenage years is more important than people like to recognise. Things you learn as a child become completely effortless as an adult. What a gift that is. Thank God I didn't become successful overnight and then have to learn about music at the same time as doing *Smash Hits* interviews. I used my time wisely, though I didn't realise that at the time. Learning an instrument is hard; it takes tons of time and you have a lot of that as a kid and none as an adult.

In many ways I could blame my complete ignorance about how to eat on any number of different things: rubbish education, rubbish industrial food, the sensible eating traditions of my mum's generation going down the toilet in the convenience age, working-class chip eating, middle-class fine dining; hey, I could even blame it on my genes – my dad's a big lad. Take your pick. I could come up with all sorts of clever reasons that aren't my fault.

But none of them are as true as this one.

As a kid, as soon as I sat at that keyboard and got some attention off the back of it, that was my obsession and it is well and truly ingrained in my life forever. Every waking minute for years I spent immersed in the ecosystem of music – if I wasn't writing I was playing, practising, performing. When I was asleep, I dreamed about it.

To be good at music you have to dedicate your life to doing it – and I did just that – I literally never stopped until I got dropped in 1999. It was way beyond a passion. Music was all I ever thought about. Anything other than music seemed a waste of time. Not just food; friends, money, love, family, fun. They all took a major back seat and were neglected.

When you come out the other end, you're like 'Shit, I know nothing about life. I'm this emotionally stunted, 28-year-old teenager. All I know about is music – and airport lounges.'

* * *

Going into the next Take That album we hired Sarm Studios in Notting Hill, which is in an old church off Portobello Road. Bob Marley, the Rolling Stones, Queen… the list of pop legends who have recorded there is long. What it'll always be best known for is Band Aid. Sarm is another historic studio that's been turned into flats now.

Since we'd moved to London, and I was working less with El, I really needed an assistant and remembered Ryan ('Rhino') from the Cheshire days. We put Ryan up in a flat over the road from the studio for three months. I wanted him with Take That full time for *The Circus*. I asked him to come and work for me.

I could not have guessed his talents when he started with us as an excruciatingly shy 17-year-old kid. He barely spoke for two years. One day the main computer broke and the entire system went down. El and I were effing and blinding while Ryan quietly had the screwdriver out and was taking the side off the hard drive. He only went and fixed the bugger.

Not too long after discovering he was an IT wizard, I was trying – and failing – to play a complex piano part. Ryan makes a suggestion, very quietly. 'I think you need to do it like this,' he says, stretching his fingers across the keys. Clearly he'd also spent his teens doing the right thing. Yup, he's an amazing piano player, too. This was no ordinary tea boy, not least because he was famously bad at making coffee. He only mastered this extremely important skill when we got a coffee machine with lots of knobs and buttons. Then he was in his element.

He's family, Rhino. He lived in Chester back in the early days and until he passed his driving test I picked him up every day from Cuddington station like a devoted dad.

It was just us four at Sarm, with Rhino engineering. Unlike Take That albums in the past, the tour ideas came first. Right from the start of Take That our intention has always been to give our audience the best night of their lives. We started to picture *The Circus* not just as an album, but a full 360-degree experience in sound and vision; a magical mystery tour with a classic Beatles, British harmony group sound. The whole thing slotted together naturally.

With this ambition in mind, I tailored my equipment to suit the brief. I shipped in my original Mellotron from the studio in Oxford – that's the kit that gave The Beatles' 'Strawberry Fields' its distinct sound. I pulled out my original Neumann U47, the same one used on *Sgt. Pepper*. I went on eBay to buy an old Wurlitzer piano, another nod to Sir Paul – this time from my favourite Wings album, *Band on the Run*. We had all the ammo. Now we needed the songs.

The next three months we were extremely focused. Thankfully we're the band that says no; none of us had anything else to do except crack this difficult second album. Initially it was slow. There were no co-writers on a day rate, checking their watches and clocking in and out. It was just us. Some days we'd amble in around midday, sit and chat, drink coffee, eat, laugh a bit and then go home around nine. What must Ryan have made of us?

We must have got down to work at some point but the early days of making this album were extremely relaxed. We were just enjoying each other's company. It became clear, though, that these casual conversations were crystallising around some common ideas.

We wrote some titles – always a good place to start – 'The Circus', 'Greatest Day', 'Hold Up A Light'. Music and live show working hand in hand.

Writing like this lifted a weight off my shoulders. Those writing sessions at Sarm were the precise opposite from the songwriter I had been in the nineties, jealously protecting my role as the sole writer, locked away working alone. It was fantastic to share.

I am starting to look back on the wilderness years less with horror now and more with gratitude. Because the way I'd put myself back together was, without question, a better version of me. Had I been confronted with everyone wanting to be in a room writing in 1995, I'd have had a total meltdown. This time, all I can say is that recording with the boys at Sarm was a golden time. *The Circus* is the most collaborative we've ever been as a band.

The writing of *Beautiful World* was us finding our feet. By the end of *Beautiful World* we had found our confidence and wrote our song, just us, 'Rule the World'. Its success told us what we needed and were able to do next.

We were in a place most artists only reach once in their careers. Our new music is highly anticipated. It can be hard, even for established artists, to escape the label's prescriptive demands. 'We want to put three new tracks out. It's got to be the sort of thing that'll make a

Spotify playlist called Easy Sunday Morning. And iTunes will want a special version. Then for Radio 2 we've got to make sure it's upbeat for Chris Evans. Make sure you can sing the chorus after one listen.'

It was no better in the nineties. Back then the label and management were completely obsessed with *Going Live*, the Saturday morning BBC kids' show presented by Phillip Schofield and a puppet called Gordon the Gopher. 'Gary, make sure it's got a good beat for *Going Live*. Don't forget about *Going Live*, will you?' Imagine their faces when I walked in with 'A Million Love Songs'.

Everyone would stick their oar in: your manager, the label, everyone knew how your music should sound, but no one could write it. It's a horrible feeling being crowded by The Brief. The Brief piles into the room and all the creativity flies out of the window.

The times are rare when all the noise and expectations stop, and recording together at Sarm was one of them.

Eventually it was brilliantly chaotic in the studio. We're in this split-level room with a spiral staircase with access to the roof so Mark and Howard can smoke. Often there'd be three songs being written at once. Jay's on the laptop, doing lyrics. Howard would be hitting the pads on the drum machine, Mark's on guitar.

On one of these chaotic sessions where everyone's bashing away, the chords appeared for 'Greatest Day'.

Being a songwriter is definitely a process. You don't just sit down one day, pull up your sleeves and go, 'Righty ho, time to write that big hit song.' God, wouldn't that be great, to be an actual hit factory. You have to fight your way through a lot of ideas and a lot of songs until you find that one that gives you goosebumps.

After two months, Colin said he wanted to come down. He came down one night in April, excited to hear this difficult second album. We played him 'Greatest Day', 'Hold Up A Light' and 'Said It All'.

'That's all I need to hear,' he said, and left us to it.

We told him then about our plans: 'Listen Col, we're calling it *The Circus*, and this isn't just about the music, it's a tour as well.

Tightrope walkers, contortionists, clowns, the whole shebang.' Just telling him was getting us excited. It was the most creative we'd ever been together.

The Circus was a title Mark suggested. Imagine the opportunities a title like that would give you.

Mark really blossomed on that record. It's funny; back in the nineties, there wasn't really anyone who was in charge of the tours. I'd choose the setlist because of all the time in the clubs. But when it came to the creative ideas, we all did it. You'd never look back to the nineties and go, 'Oh, wasn't Mark a great creative!' When we did *Beautiful World* he was really involved, but so were the rest of us.

He just took off on *The Circus*. He was fizzing with ideas. He came in one day with a load of pictures torn out of books and magazines. 'Look at this blue sky here. Wouldn't it be great if we had a picture of a guy on a tightrope against a really strong blue sky; what a great shot.' Album cover. Tick. We'd be writing lyrics and he'd say, 'I like that chorus now because I can see sunshine.' (Note to the lighting engineer.)

Don't get me wrong, we all saw our ideas come to life in *The Circus*, but Mark was the ringmaster. I think, with 'Shine' being such a big hit, Mark had grown in confidence since *Beautiful World*. I've had knocks but you know what? So has Mark. We share stories about being dropped by record labels. He's been through it. He's got some thick skin from somewhere. I think 'Shine' gave him extra armour plating. Pretty much since that record, he just went through the roof. *The Circus* was testament to his vision.

* * *

First, a Rock-It Cargo container arrives with John Shanks' name on it. Twenty guitars, 15 amps, numerous vintage guitar pedals. This guy was here to stay. Then in comes the artist, John Shanks. The uniform: ray-bans, vintage Ramones T-shirt, cap on backwards – the ego has landed. He greets the room, 'Anyone wanna make a hit record?'

We were already feeling on top of the world and now The Producer had arrived. A producer's job is to make your music come to life in the most magnificent way, to make it sound the best it could ever be. We knew he was good, but this record. Oh my God. John produced the fuck out of *The Circus*. He gave it his trademark Wall of Sound. We couldn't wait for people to hear it.

One by one, in they come to Sarm for a listen: heads of label, radio producers, TV bookers, sponsors… They all love it. I might have even had a pizza. Yes, I was that happy.

In the UK and Ireland, *The Circus* went straight to number one and stayed there throughout Christmas 2008. The tour sold out 600,000 tickets in five hours, which was the fastest selling tour ever in Britain.

After all the uncertainty since this cautious return to the stage, we were finally finding our feet again. Once you have a few hits and a few gigs under your belt, the old attitude does return. The 'who gives a damn' came back. It's good that, it's really powerful stuff. It's not about arrogance, it's confidence. You stop caring what other people think. You lose a fear of criticism and what other people think can't crowd creativity any more. You start to celebrate vulnerability. It's hard to come by that stuff. You can only feel like that when you're winning.

It was around this time that the old Gary paid me a visit. A touch of the nineties ego wormed its way back. 'Greatest Day' was out, it was number one, and we were doing some promo on Chris Moyles' Radio 1 show. Rob is on a big downer by now and people were really rubbing it in that we were back. And me? I was enjoying watching the wheel of fortune come full circle.

8

THREE GORGEOUS KIDS, TWO MAD DIETS

'Just the other day somebody said to me,
"Hey, maybe you are oh so slightly OCD"'

Dan was only 20 months old when Em was born so it was chaos for years. It was like a zoo, the house was a mess, there were Honey Nut Loops all over the floor, sick everywhere. When you come out the other side of that, you wash the shit off your hands for the last time and say, 'Christ. Never again.'

Dawn had danced on *Beautiful World* and again we'd absolutely loved being with each other. But she'd nearly killed herself trying to be a mum at the same time. Every other day she'd go home after the show so she could take the kids to school then travel back to wherever the show was that night. Dan and Em were four and six and she hated leaving them. I can remember how happy they were whenever we came home. I know she missed them. So did I. She told me she wasn't going to join me on The Circus Tour.

'Don't worry girl,' I said, 'I'll replace you with a nice 26-year-old.'

'You'll be lucky,' she said.

In fact, she retired from dancing altogether. She came home one day from a shoot for a Shirley Bassey video and said, 'The leg warmers are going back in the drawer for the last time.'

We felt safe then. I was flying, the band was in a good place. Life was good. Dawn and I had reached a point where we were getting far too much sleep. We weren't arguing enough. We looked at each other. 'Is this it? No more cuddly babies?' To which the obvious answer was, 'Let's have another one!'

Pregnant with our third child and retired from dancing, Dawn had some fun; oh yes, she really went for it. She put five stone on and was having a fabulous time. I used to say, 'Get my order through first before she starts on hers,'; she was eating everything, twice. She enjoyed being pregnant with our little Daisy, she was always cuddling her bump and I get a bit cross-eyed thinking about it; I fancied her more than ever. She was loving it. When I think of her then, I think of her looking absolutely gorgeous eating muffins and Hula Hoops. Putting on weight didn't bother her. She's tall and naturally athletic and had always eaten well as a dancer. We don't share an unhealthy obsession with food. I was alone in that.

I was due to shoot the video for 'Up All Night' on a housing estate down in Croydon. Dawn had gone into hospital the night before. She'd thought she was going into labour, but then Daisy changed her mind and decided to stay put a bit longer. We went back home while Daisy left us on tenterhooks.

'Should I go and do this video, then?'

Dawn said, 'Yeah, go and do it, just keep your phone on.'

The set was built to look like the Silver Jubilee; you know, big tables full of food and a band playing at the end of the street. Us lot always talked about the 1977 Silver Jubilee. We all remembered the bunting, the mums and dads and everyone in the street round at yours. So that's how we made the video look. Got there, got in make-up, got it all done, literally sitting on the set at the piano, and Dawn rings. 'I'm going in. I can't cross my legs, I'm going in.'

I thought, 'Shit. Right.'

Can you believe, I did an interview with *This Morning* before I left? Priorities! The presenter, Alison, gave me some nappies. I whizzed off, nappies in hand.

Daisy made her entrance bang on time. More precisely, half-time in a Manchester United vs Arsenal League match. I was watching outside with the obstetrician who was meant to be delivering our third-born. Us two useless sods sitting watching the football while, next door, Dawn was in labour. At half-time the midwife came through to say, 'She's ready.'

Perfect.

I went into the delivery room where I had all the cameras lined up. Digital had really taken off, and I had more cameras lined up than Dixons on the high street. I put the video on: battery light's flashing; put the fancy stills camera on: battery light's flashing. Phone, phone. I patted down every pocket in a panic and only just in time did I find some technology in a functioning state ready to capture Daisy's first moments in the world.

* * *

Three kids; three completely different births. Dan held Dawn in labour for 24 hours, eventually delivered with forceps and a lot of blood and gore. A birth straight from the *Hammer House of Horror*. All we needed was Peter Cushing to complete the cast. We always tell him he's a bloody nuisance, that even before he took his first breath, he was a royal pain.

Emily was right on time. Two polite hours of labour. Dads with little girls can mean only one thing. Tears. It was only sixteen years ago, but the midwife felt comfortable telling me, 'Pull your bloody self together, man.' Dawn nodding in agreement over her shoulder. 'Give me a break, you've not done anything.'

The girls love hearing about their births. Dad always adds a few more details every time, usually to make himself look better... 'Yeah, and then Daddy came in and helped Mummy with the most important thing.'

After the tears, we celebrated with a nice cup of tea. I popped down to the hospital shop and got us each a bar of Dairy Milk.

Dawn delivered Daisy like a pro, shaving an hour off her previous record. No tears this time. We were far too experienced for that nonsense.

The next day I picked the kids up from school and we went straight to meet Daisy at the hospital. I can still see them now taking turns to hold her in their smart blue school uniforms. We always say, Daisy is the most kissed baby ever.

Meanwhile, back on the shoot it was left to the director to pick someone to be my body double while I'm at the hospital. When I watched the playback a few days later, I couldn't help but note he was a big fella. I felt myself smarting.

'Why did you pick him? There must have been a queue of people wanting to be me.'

'Oh, he was the only one...'

'Rubbish!'

The truth is he was the only one large enough to play Gary. Dan the cameraman is a cracking bloke but looks 'well'; he's not thin.

'I bet you had a giggle picking him out, didn't you?'

'No, no. Honestly, he was the only one.'

Everything in my life is perfect. Except for one thing. In all the happiness and harmony at Sarm, these were long days which meant no time for exercise. The result of this was that I was even more hopelessly neurotic about what I ate. I couldn't compensate with exercise so I restricted myself to very safe, basic, bland food. The obligatory chicken with broccoli and loads and loads of caffeine to fill the void.

I'd sit chewing joylessly while Mark and Howard wolfed down a pizza or a sausage sarnie. Heartbreaking.

I had Jason there and he was always so healthy; he'd sussed early on that he could fix problems by eating well. And when I say early on, I mean *really* early on. We were once stopped at Manchester Airport back in the early days because the security guys thought his little sack of healthy seeds were drugs. For Jay it wasn't because he was trying to lose weight; he was healthy for health's sake. Even back in the early days, we used to take the piss out of him. 'Hey, Jay what's in your lunchbox?'

Jay was diving off at lunch and coming back with all these crazy salads, big spicy bean stews, street food in all the colours of the rainbow. I wasn't interested; it all looked a bit foreign.

I was doing some online stuff at the time and trying to live fat free. A lot of those diets were fat free, and in the end you get the hang of it. Which is mostly that when you take fat out of your diet, you go crazy. Everything tastes disgusting, slightly chemical, if it tastes of anything at all. You're hungry all day and edgy. All the deliciousness in food comes from fat. Fat is delicious. Fat-free diets made me feel a bit twatty. I always think of diets in terms of a day, and it's an odd one on a fat-free diet. There's no satisfaction. A spaced-out feeling – like your body is running on dust and worry. You don't feel strong, you're shaky and light-headed. It's no life.

On and off, I'd visited dieticians and nutritionists, listened to personal trainers' advice and picked up tips from other people. Some had good tips, some were just the pits. The trouble is, I couldn't always distinguish between them. The worst ones always seemed to appear when I was most desperate.

Sometimes these gigs would come along that sent me into crackers diet overdrive. You have to remember, I never felt that I looked good, let alone my best self. A shoot, an album cover, a tour, a TV show... That's when I'd get cracking on the nuttiest, most out there regimes. Any dieter will understand desperation. That's why the papers can sell themselves on the latest pre-holiday or New Year regime.

Then our manager Jonathan told us Marks & Spencer wanted us to do their megabucks Christmas ad campaign. *Circus* the album's just out, and we're on the telly. Right. That's a cracking goal. This time I'd train like a commando and eat like a supermodel. I'd fight not to feel uncomfortable on the shoot: like I'm a bit awkward, a bit embarrassed, a bit *big*.

The M&S ad campaign probably didn't mean much to the others, but for me, who'd spent years hiding from cameras, it whipped up a lot of complicated feelings. I wanted to look good. Who wouldn't? I was being paid to look good. I needed to step it up a notch. My current caveman regime of sacks of fruit wasn't cutting it. I was a bit desperate. I wanted to feel good about this ad that'd be playing on a loop on everyone's telly over Christmas.

Dawn had always been dubious of my obsession with Canderel and sweeteners. But as what I could eat narrowed down more and more, fake sweetness felt like my only pleasure. 'Artificial sweeteners aren't good for you, babe,' she'd say. I ignored her. She's naturally a lean, strong and healthy woman, my wife. She gave up coffee when she was pregnant with Dan; now the only caffeine she has is in her thick, orange, Yorkshire-strength brew. The Diet Coke went after she got home from a retreat where she'd learned about some of the effects of artificial sweeteners on her body. She told me this and I hmmed and nodded while clicking a few more white tablets into my tenth coffee of the day. Didn't listen, didn't apply to me. Because I was on a diet. Yet despite busting a gut on stage all night and eating near to no fat, I still weighed nearly two stone more than I wanted to. The man I wanted to be didn't look back at me when I looked in the mirror.

⋆ ⋆ ⋆

I found Scott at the gym. He trained at Virgin Active in Kensington and had got to know the trainers there. I was saying to my trainer, 'Listen, I need to put a spurt on, you know? I've got this ad campaign coming up and I want to lose more weight, fast.' The trainer said, 'Well you could try this Scott guy.' He hooked us up.

I went to see this Scott and he said, 'Go low on the meals, but go high on these bars… When your dinner arrives, cut it in half and give the rest away, then enjoy one of these bars.'

They were real space food, these bars, called something like Q2, and in the small print, it said, 'for the treatment of obesity'. As with a lot of these diet foods, when I first had them, I was like 'Jesus Christ'; they were sweet, insanely so. They were made of sweetener and probably some kind of protein substance. It was basically a bar full of aspartame or saccharine, some lab-built, zero-calorie, mega-sweet chemical. If I did 'go high on the bars', by the end of the day I'd have barely eaten anything. The schizo side to all this, as I keep saying, is that I love food and eating out, but that pleasure was lost a bit because after eating these bars, food didn't taste that great. It tasted sort of weak: there was that much artificial sweetener.

I lost quite a lot of weight eating these things as I'd effectively cut food out. He said he wanted me to exercise, too. So I've got to work out like a bitch while surviving only on artificial sweetener. It's spirit-sapping stuff.

I was losing weight and eating more and more bars. Dawn is not an aggro person; she is a gentle, steady person. And she knows me better than anyone on the planet. She knows there's no point moaning at me as I don't hear it. But she's getting quite upset about these bars. The guy also had these choccy pot puddings that were incredible, even sweeter than the bars if that's possible, and she really took against those. They made sticky toffee pudding taste savoury. I'd go days just eating them.

'I'm telling you now, Gary, read the side of that. I cannot pronounce anything that's in there, Gary. The use-by date is 2030.'

They came from Neptune, I think. An alien wrapped them in silver foil and dropped them to earth, to LA first, goes without saying. They were not from this planet. The problem is, I'm getting sucked into this Scott. He gave me a little bit of therapy when I started with him and I liked it. He was asking me about what my relationship with food had been and I told him about the towel in the studio bathroom and the numbing quantities of Golden Grahams. I hadn't spoken to a therapist before. I'd never done anything like that in my life. It was emotional. It was incredible how much shame I felt. I felt embarrassed that I'd fallen apart after losing my record deal to such an extent. I'm meant to be the rock, not Dawn. She was the one who needed the help. She had two small kids and didn't need a giant baby eating himself to death. I still feel the embarrassment now, writing this; the shame that I couldn't step up.

The psychology side of it had woken me up; it was just nice to speak to a stranger and get some of it out. Because, a lot of what happened in those years, I hadn't really shared with Dawn. The point being, I've invested in this Scott with the space bars *and* I'm dropping weight.

Dawn lets me do what I want, she is not a nag. If I bugger off and write music for two months in LA, she doesn't grumble. For the last few years, as I've been lost at family mealtimes because I'm always doing Daddy's Special Food, she's not complained. But these bars drove her nuts. Eventually she started to get through to me.

I had to be honest with myself: for all the weight loss I felt weird. I think I must've been acting weirder. 'Enough. You're the worst you've ever been. The worst. The bars have to stop. It's me or the bars from Mars.'

I started to see through the guy. He was struggling with his weight as well. I could see it in his legs: they were watery, blubbery legs. They weren't the legs of a god. That should have rung some alarm bells earlier on, shouldn't it? He was an American guy and there was something odd about him. I wouldn't have been surprised if he was very religious. He used to get me to take my top off a lot. When Dawn first mentioned the word gay, a few things started to drop into place. It wasn't quite right. If I'm honest, I felt a bit abused by the end. I'm fine with it now. I think it's hilarious. But it shows the lengths you go to when you're desperate.

Dawn didn't think my diets could get any worse. She thought Scott's Canderel bars were as bad as it got. She was wrong.

I'd met the producer and director Matt Vaughn in 2007 when we wrote 'Rule The World' for his film *Stardust*, and I'd go on working with him for years. We did the soundtrack for *Eddie the Eagle* and the main credit song for the first *Kingsman* film. I connected straight off with Matthew. I respected him. We're the same age, and he's an ambitious guy. And he's a problem solver, too. We'd have our modern man chats. We'd sit for hours talking about work/life balance – or our lack of it – and the best places to take the family on holiday. It was during one of these conversations that he mentioned he was trying to lose weight; it was a given at this stage that I was, too.

'There's this guy,' says Matt, 'who gets actors camera-fit...'

Goes without saying, I've got his number in my phone before you can say 'Daniel Craig'. I booked in straight away.

This Derek wasn't a dietician. He didn't have any clear qualifications at all from what I could see. He looked like the stuntman in *The Fall*

Guy. He was this shaven-headed ex-army type: ripped, serious, no jokes, zero banter.

'Right. How much coffee do you drink?'

'Oh, I drink decaf. I was drinking far too much coffee, see, having trouble slee...'

'Fuck that. We're gonna get you straight back on coffee.'

'Cigarettes? Do you smoke?'

'I used to.'

'Time to start again, bud. If you want to lose weight quickly you need to ramp up your metabolism. Two days a week you eat only green apples.'

He wasn't polite considering I was paying him a fair bit. He wasn't taking the therapy route like Mr Canderel. There was no, 'Right, I'm going to suggest a plan here now for you Gary, is that okay?' His vibe was, 'Fuckin' do it and if you don't I'm gonna beat you up.' (He didn't actually say that but that's how I felt.)

I left. 'Mate, wicked, thanks. I'm on it. On it.'

I went home after my first appointment and started telling Dawn all about Derek. She listened patiently, leaning against the counter in the kitchen, laughing a bit because it was kind of ridiculous, until I got to the smoking bit when she crossed her arms, crossed her legs and looked me in the eye. 'If you start smoking again I will divorce you.'

I never rang Derek again. In hindsight, I can see he had some good ideas in among the lunatic ones. Like, he was the first person to introduce me to fasting. Fasting, as I'd discover much later on in life, is actually pretty healthy, but not Derek's way. He wanted me to do two days a week only eating apples. I did try it and got to about half past one. I couldn't do it. You could eat apples and you could have a coffee every two hours. I mean, how bonkers is that! It'd taken me so long to wean myself off coffee. I didn't want to go on it again. But he was adamant. Coffee would drive up my metabolism. Black coffee. And a few sweeteners, obviously. I didn't take up smoking again, but I did get back on the caffeine. He also talked a lot about going to bed early and being in bed by ten o'clock at night.

Thing is, it's hard to sleep when you're on ten coffees a day. It's hard to sleep when you're hungry, too. I started taking sleeping pills. Sometimes I'd have a sleeping pill for my dinner if I'd already used up all my calories for the day.

Dawn was worried about me; I'd go so far as to say she was frightened. All she saw were these diets getting sillier and sillier. At this point I'd done a lot of different diets, and created many different rules around my eating that meant I rarely sat down with my wife and kids to eat. It wasn't just a couple of weeks, it'd been years now. And wouldn't you know it? I was still disappointed with how I looked in the M&S shoot. All this effort seemed to reap me meagre rewards.

9

TWO ELEPHANTS

'And in their houses there will be pictures,
like the ones of you and me'

The Circus was just a magic moment in time. This is a band that couldn't get any bigger. Everyone has their fifteen minutes of true, *true* fame and we knew we were at our peak. We were good. We were on it. We'd got it back. Let's go for it. Every detail of that show was obsessed over. We left nothing to chance. We were celebrating all this, loving it. You take none of it for granted when you come back like this. This time you remember to say thank you to everyone.

I could write a book about The Circus show. It was incredibly complex and used up every inch of experience we'd gathered up to this point. Back in our little bubble at Sarm, we started by imagining the audience's first impressions. They're excited. The trick with any show is to tease them. What do they wanna see? Us. Out we go into the middle of the stadium down the walkway and onto the centre stage surrounded by people. Everyone can see us, everyone feels close. We give them five uplifting songs, using only white light. Remember we're still in daylight. Then something needs to happen. Why don't we climb on an elephant and ride back to the main stage while singing a song?

Nearly an hour of the show had passed and only now were the audience getting a glimpse of the main stage. What a great time to introduce them to the other thirty cast members and the Take That band. The stage was now full of colour, movement and acrobatics. What a great time to call on nature to play her part. The sun goes down. We enter dusk, the golden hour; for the first time the coloured lights blaze up. When they least expect it, the stage empties, leaving just us, a four-piece, playing drums, bass, guitar and keyboards. Just four lads from the North West who'd been thrown together and were playing like a rock band on a stage. And guess what. That stupid boy band from the nineties? They're in stadiums now and killing it every night.

It's time for a few laughs. Let's dress up as clowns, apply our own make-up, then hit them with some in-jokes, the big hits and the dance routines from the nineties. The audience are starting to wonder: will they dare drop their trousers and have Take That written across their eight buttocks. Probably not. Too big for that now. Then we all come out on unicycles. No one will expect that. Then a run of hits to bring us home. What do you reckon?

These were all great plans for a stadium show, if a bit over-ambitious. Maybe we should think a bit smaller. Or maybe it just might work…

That show had everything, including the 30-foot elephant and half the Blackpool Circus on the stage. It was precisely choreographed mayhem. We had 48 branded lorries that rolled into town like the Coca-Cola Christmas trucks. We splashed out on every detail. The jackets alone that we wore on the elephant cost £20,000. I don't know where it came from but the one thing we've always invested in is our live shows. We wanted it to be the best it could possibly be. Our audience deserved it. And we want them to come back. And they did.

The Circus became the biggest selling tour in British history.

*　*　*

There was always something going on round that period, even though we were saying no to everything. I liked being too busy to think about my next meal. It made everything easier. Don't forget, in all this magic, nothing had changed about living with diets. Worrying about food is a near permanent anxious noise in my head.

It was a shame I didn't eat with the family. It wasn't only that I wanted to eat mashed potato, sausages and frozen peas or chicken and bacon pie (though I did want to eat that stuff, a lot). It was that I was embarrassed that I was having to eat different food. I didn't want to eat the shit I was eating in front of anyone. So I'd either eat later than them, or, far more likely, I couldn't wait and I had to have it early because I was so hungry. The lunch I'd have would have been thin on nutrients, low in fat, and completely unsatisfying. Then I'd realise I'd used up all my calories and it was only half past three. I like a puzzle, but this one was unfathomable.

Meanwhile, in the other room, Dawn's casually dropping the five stone she put on with Daisy. She's in there chatting to the kids about their day as they shovel down their spaghetti hoops, on toast, with butter, and some grated cheese. And I'm sitting in the other room eating cardboard. Bloody hell. I mean, I know no one's died, it's not a tragedy, but the whole thing's a shambles.

Not long after Daisy was born I went off to climb Kilimanjaro for Comic Relief. I'd done a film piece for them the previous year and wanted to do more. I'm always blown away by how easily someone like me can make a difference. How annoying must it be for all those decent folk who dedicate their lives to helping others and then some pop tart turns up and makes them three million quid in a week.

I took a few mates in the business out for dinner – Moyles, Ronan Keating, Alesha Dixon and Fearne Cotton – and floated the idea for us to climb the highest mountain in Africa. They were all into it. Once word got out we were fighting people off, to be honest. Everyone wanted to do it. Someone told me, 'Be so careful with the personalities, as one bad egg will ruin the whole trip. You don't need to be a bunch of famous people for that to happen.' But it was sound advice and I said 'no' to a lot of people.

I spoke to Richard Curtis about it and he said, 'I've got this guy you should all meet. He's the best Kili guide in the world. He'll tell you all about it. He'll look after you all.'

His name was Jeremy Gane and this old boy had climbed Kili about sixty times. He's the sort of guy you want to be with if anything bad happens. We meet up and he says these magic words: 'Eat what you want 'cause you're all going to come back a stone lighter. By the end of the week you won't want to eat chocolate ever again.'

Any doubts about the project I had at that stage vanished. My brain tuned out all the difficult bits he was explaining.

'Dairy Milk,' you say. '"As many as you want", was it? Now that's a challenge I can rise to.' I'd love to say it was entirely noble causes and doing good that made me decide to climb Kilimanjaro but the 5,000 calories a day also played their part.

They watched us as we hiked up to make sure we ate enough. It was like going back ten years to a time when I never had to think about what I was eating. The first day we were up there, we weren't even very high, it wasn't steep, and I was already crying, 'Oh I need chocolate! Freddo! Freddo! Bring me a Freddo bar.'

Ronan Keating and I were absolutely caning the chocolate. We were in heaven. But I tell you what, after a week my chocolate interest was flagging. It's ten o'clock in the morning. Freddo time! Oh no, I can't face another one. 'Come on, eat up everyone. Kit-Kats!' It was just sugar, sugar, sugar constantly in your system. 'Gary! Have you eaten your Fruit and Nut? Time for another Mint Club, lad!'

All food aside it was a magnificent challenge made even harder by the fact that I injured my back two weeks before we left. There was even a meeting where I had to beg the Comic Relief doctor to let me go. I think I offered him a couple of The Circus Tour tickets to persuade him.

The real memory of the trip is out of focus. I was on opiate painkillers throughout the eight days. I smiled a lot at nothing and kept up the rear, assisted by my old friend Ronan, who never left my side. The guy literally had my back.

We arrived home heroes, all of us. We made a tonne of money for a great cause, had a laugh, and your old friend Gary had lost a stone.

* * *

We knew Jason wasn't going to stick around forever, but when we started thinking about our next album, he was already on his way out of the back door. I know people would give their left arm to do what we do. But at times I felt like Jay'd give his right arm not to. In that respect he's like Dawn: hates the publicity.

There was only one thing that would keep Jason for one more record: Robbie. Jason would stick around if the old Take That were together again. And wasn't that where all this was headed since the comeback? Rob.

'Yeah, but where is he?'

Rob still felt so far out of reach.

Around the time of The Circus, we were in LA doing a photoshoot. We invited Rob to the Beverly Wilshire. He came up to our room. He was wearing a cracking pair of black and gold trainers – he's always got a pair of boxfresh on. He sat there for ten minutes, then left. It was uncomfortable and fleeting.

The following day I got an email from him: 'I can't just meet up because there's an elephant in the room. When you're ready to talk come up to my house.'

Despite being in Africa, I hadn't seen any elephants in Tanzania. I was about to confront an elephant in Beverly Hills instead.

Robbie's emails are always written in block capitals. It's like he's shouting. It'd be a proper battering, I knew that; all the demons would be brought to life. Rob had a lot to get off his chest.

I showed it to the boys and we all agreed we should go up. I emailed him, 'We can come up tomorrow.'

We arrive at his place. A bottle of water appears on the coffee table for each of us and we get down to business.

Whenever we had seen him before, the elephant was always there. Living with that kind of feud isn't right. We've all done well; why carry that burden when you don't need to? The Chat was like an exorcism.

This is how I understand it, but there's always two sides to any story, isn't there? This is mine. The others may see it differently.

Robbie found me threatening. I was a strong personality, I came into the band, confident and with a honed skill. I was writing all the music. I had all those years, week in, week out, doing the working men's clubs. I had a strong hold on what the group was. I was also old beyond my years and acted like I was Nigel's partner in Take That; in terms of decision-making and business, I pretty much was. Nigel loved me and back then I loved him, too. I think that whole thing was a nightmare for all of them, but Rob especially didn't like it. He felt like Nigel had bullied him for years, and that I didn't listen to him. He was right about that.

As time went on, and people said, 'I want a piece of the action now,' if it didn't happen, then of course people weren't happy. All of them felt the same way towards me at times, and this was only made worse by The Manager's divide and conquer methods.

Rob felt that for the last year of Take That, he was crying out to every one of us. 'Help me. I'm not happy. I don't want to be here. You're all doing things that I don't like.'

In the end he left, and we handled that badly. We let him leave the fold and walk out of that rehearsal room and no one looked after him. Robbie was barely 21 and when he walked it was into the arms of Paula Yates and Liam Gallagher. People see that as a period of him redefining who he was, of establishing some kind of rock 'n' roll identity. Maybe, but there's no doubt that it could have destroyed him. He was angry at all of us but most of all he was angry with me. I look back now and I feel bad. What happened between me and Rob always bothered me.

We never talked about our feelings. I'd been in a band with Rob through half the nineties, we lived closer than brothers and yet we'd barely ever spoken. We never went below the surface back then. It was all building site banter, nineties Take That. We talked endlessly about birds. It was our world. Just girls and, now and again, music.

Once he'd survived that and it didn't destroy him, then he wanted to destroy me. And that lasted a long time. He said that I was always the subject he could fill an empty interview with. It was the easy gag he could reach for to get a laugh. It wouldn't have bothered me if I hadn't lost so much in terms of career and gained so much in terms of stones and pounds. As it was, when Rob slagged me off in public, I felt a victim.

Over the years that feeling of 'poor me' has turned to 'I was a right idiot'.

The Chat ends with me passing judgement on myself: 'What a dick!'

Then Rob goes, 'No, *I* was a bigger dick.'

Me: 'No, I'm sorry Rob, I was a waaaay bigger dick.'

And on and on until it got to the point that we were sick of saying dick and started laughing instead.

'Yeah, but where is he?'

He's here.

It was an emotional moment that turned into a funny one. Usually works out that way when you put five Northerners who love each other in a room.

Throughout it all, even though he wasn't there, or even really speaking to us, Rob was often in the room for Circus. We'd be thinking about pulling off stadium shows and interested in what he might have to say. The guy played Knebworth for three nights; he should have some ideas.

The refrain continued on and off, 'Yeah, but where is he?'

* * *

We all felt unbelievably good about *The Circus* album. It didn't surprise me when a guy from Universal's International Division came to congratulate us. 'We love this music, and you've done amazingly well here in the UK.' I smiled in agreement. 'But...' – eh? I wasn't expecting a but – 'we've found it harder in the rest of the world.'

I knew he was wrong. We're kings of the charts, and we make the rules. I dismissed it. But, as always, these things whirr away at the back of your mind. What this guy was saying, intentionally or not, was, 'You need to update your sound.'

And he was right.

I was talking to my friend David Massey, who at the time was running Mercury Records in New York. 'I love that new Killers record. I can't stop playing it and it's all over the radio. Do you know the producer?'

Take That had come back the second time round to find that guitars are our friends. And not nice sparkly acoustic guitars; we're talking the big gnarly electric ones. What the Killers had done in that brilliant album was integrated their roots as a rock band into electronic music. The result was a big, beautiful radio hit. I fancied a bit of that. And so would our friends at International.

'Their producer's Stuart Price, and he's just up the road from you in Notting Hill.' I rang him and invited him round to the house. He turned up two days later. Daisy was only five days old and lay beside me in a Moses basket.

'Listen, we're going to do a record. We're going to start writing at the end of this year and I'd love you to produce it.'

I invited him to come and see The Circus show. Our next record was a long way off. Isn't the music business cold? *The Circus* has only been on the shelf six weeks and I've already got another young blonde on my arm.

Stuart Price is a producer with a super-impressive résumé who started out as a credible underground DJ. He crossed over and lost none of his cool. Quite rare that. For someone who'd had so much success he was incredibly softly spoken and humble. And he clearly loved music, which is another thing you can't take for granted in this business. We chatted about this album and he seemed interested.

Stuart Price was the sort of producer Robbie Williams would love and Rob was on my mind.

We went on a family holiday to LA, to a rented place in Pacific Palisades. I'd touched base with Rob before going out there on holiday, and said, 'I'm going to be here, if you fancy coming over.' I'd invited him in an abstract sense, no specifics on when. I wasn't angry with Rob any more. I don't think he was angry with me either. We're still prickly around each other, though – circling each other like a couple of tomcats. 'Yeah, yeah, I might come,' he says.

I knew Jay would stay if Rob came back. He and Rob are great mates by now. Fact: if we weren't five, we were three, no two ways about it. I had to get Rob back.

Most importantly, I wanted peace for Rob and me personally. Our falling out was something I thought about every day and with real regret. It was time to put away the Rob and Gary war stories.

Not far off our first day in LA, the doorbell goes. It's Rob. He had driven all the way from Beverly Hills down to the beach where we were staying: Rob, Ayda and two little, white, fluffy doormat things, Pomeranians. Crap dogs. The kids are all over that and love Rob already. Ayda went off with Dawn, talking in the kitchen.

Rob's a fractious character, nervous. He's not comfortable in social environments. You can't sit and have a cup of tea with him. He's always agitated, always moving. He makes you feel uncomfortable, you know? The one thing I know is that music stops that in him; it makes him still. Thinking on my feet, I said, 'Do you want to hear what I've been working on today?' That broke the ice. Just a little bit.

'Oh. I like that! It should be one of ours, this song. Yeah,' he says. 'It should be about how it's a shame that all these years have gone by and we've missed each other.'

They'd only been there about seven minutes, they'd driven all the way over from Beverly Hills and now they turned round and went back again. It's a long way to the beach. Yet in that little time we came up with the chorus and a story for 'Shame'. As he went off again with the little dogs, 'I'll email the song to you,' I said. 'By the time you get home, you'll have it.'

'Yeah, great, and why don't you come over one night, bring all this equipment, and come and write at mine?'

I emailed the track to him and in a couple of hours he'd sent me back all the words. Straight back, I said, 'I love this. Shall I bring my gear up and we can get it down tomorrow night?'

The next night I went up. I set down the laptop, two speakers and a mic on his massive coffee table. Rob's old place in LA was in a gated community. The neighbours are all famous: Paris Hilton to the left, Slash to the right, Tom Jones down the road. He was one of the first collectors of Banksys – they're everywhere and they're huge, bigger than any I've seen. Every time I knelt down or moved, a dog squealed.

There must have been twelve of them in total, all shapes and sizes and yapping around this lovely house.

There are so many layers of excitement to this, it's making me nervous. Primarily it's great seeing an old friend. There's a good sensation, and it's a wound that's starting to heal. I'm writing together with my old bandmate, *for the first time*. That's mad. I'm telling myself, 'Don't dare to dream; don't dare to dream… I can already picture the five of us on stage. If people knew that we were even here together; we know it's a big deal. Add to this that there's a new guy in the room: Robbie Williams superstar. I've never met him before.

When I think about my behaviour in the 1990s, a lot of it wasn't nice; most of what I was in the nineties was unbearable. I thought I was above everyone else and my ego drove everything. I was like Nigel, trying to play everyone off, and saving the best songs for myself. My bandmates had to put up with me, poor buggers.

Of the five of us, the one who is most sensitive is Robbie. It fills me with shame remembering the day in the nineties when Rob called me with a song idea and sang something down the phone. I couldn't even tell you if it was good or not because I rubbished it immediately as I didn't want him to become the songwriter in the band. My input was so protected. Howard had to go and do a co-write with somebody, because I was guarding my position so much. This is how bad it was. When Howard wrote 'If This Is Love', he had to go outside the band unit to make a demo. It would have been so easy for me to go, 'Hey come round to my studio, we'll do it together, it'll be fun.'

I never had the chance to say, 'I'm sorry, I was a twat.' There's something else, though. And it's something that I feel uncomfortable about. This song 'Shame' we're writing is clearly a duet between Robbie and me. I'm in a band. How's this going to work out? There's an undercurrent of guilt. I'm being unfaithful to the boys.

Rob walks in with two bottles of water in his hand. If I'm thinking all this, what the hell's he thinking? Like good Northerners we didn't talk about it. We just sat down and wrote a song.

He's like an animal, Rob; he's alert to shifts in energy. When he came back in the room I don't know if he knew consciously but he made it better straight away. 'Oh I can't believe it. It's great having you here. Can't believe you're here in my house. You, here with your keyboard. Ah, it's great news, Gaz.'

We gave each other big hugs and nothing was said about the past.

'Shame', the song we wrote in those LA days, is a funny one. I can't make my mind up whether I love it or not. People say it sounds like The Beatles' song 'Blackbird' and my response to that is, if only. But it served a great purpose: it broke the ice for us. 'Shame' is about us, it's about two men discussing their regrets about a complicated friendship.

It was a joy seeing Rob with new eyes, as a writer; his writing was superb and he loved showing me his skills, loved it when I reacted to something he'd written. In the five years of Take That we never wrote together. I was really impressed by the way he went about it, and his ideas were always great. Rob was a big, inspiring, creative presence in the room. God, I thought, Mark would love this.

The last time I was with Robbie was in 1995 in Stockport army barracks. Whether he left Take That or we kicked him out is still an ongoing debate between us all to this day. Whatever happened, it left us in a right mess five weeks before we toured the UK, the Far East, Australia and the States. I'd bumped into him here and there but never for long and never with any meaningful interaction. Here I am now, thirteen years later, in the middle of Beverly Hills, in the middle of Robbie Williams' living room. We worked on one more song that night.

'We've got two crackers here,' I said.

'My producer's in town. I'm going to play these songs for him tomorrow,' he said. His producer's Trevor Horn, one of my heroes. He's produced loads of artists I love: Grace Jones, the Pet Shop Boys, Frankie Goes to Hollywood.

Now, above all else, I'm thinking, 'We do this duet, Trevor Horn's going to produce me.'

By now it's early September and the kids are due back at school. I said, 'Listen, Rob, we're leaving town next week. Can I put something in your mind? You should do something with us. Come back. We should do a record together.'

I'd opened the door. 'We've got to see this through. This is great.'

It felt like a pretty weighty moment, I thought. Boom, I'll leave him with that to dwell on. I wasn't expecting an answer. 'Ah, Gaz, it's such a long way back from here,' he says. 'I feel like I'm too far away from it all now.' He was nice about us. 'You guys are killing it right now.'

'I'm just putting it out there,' I said. 'We land in New York in a couple of weeks. We're there for Mark's stag do, and we've booked a studio. Electric Lady. We're going to do a bit of writing.'

'Oh, no, no, not New York. Oh, no. I can't stand New York. Too many people. I hate people.'

'All right, I hear you, but in case you change your mind, we're staying at Soho House.'

10

DAD

'Breathe deep, who knows
how long this will last.'

Dad was around a lot on The Circus Tour. He'd recently retired and was enjoying his life. He loved the shows. All our mums and dads enjoyed Take That more second time round. The audience were grown-ups, the screams less piercing.

I came off after our last night in Manchester at Old Trafford Cricket Ground. I had just two nights off before the last push and four nights at Wembley. Home town, day off tomorrow, I was looking forward to a drink.

Dad had been standing in the pit right in front of the stage. He had Emily down there on his shoulders. Simon Moran had spotted him down there and invited him up to his box. I don't know if he ever got used to all the hospitality. Apparently the sherry trifle was very good, and the whisky.

When I found him after the show he looked merry. 'Dad?'

'You're gonna have to drive son, I've had one too many,' he chuckled.

'You what? I can't have a drink? I've got to drive myself home? You're kidding me.'

He smiled and possibly hiccupped. He wasn't merry – he was absolutely leathered.

'Sorry, son.'

So the great pop star drove himself home from his stadium gig and once we pulled up outside my parents' place, Dad went tumbling and wheeling back down the drive, giggling like a schoolgirl.

There was only Em, no older than seven, there, and me. She had to help me cart her grandad back up the drive. Em looked shocked, a little bit scared. Did he start singing? I think he might have done.

137

'Is Grandad all right, Daddy?'

I was made up to see him having a good time, enjoying it all. That's what it's there for. My dad had worked his whole life like you can't imagine. First he was a farmworker, that's what he wanted to do, but the money was better in the local fertiliser factory, so he moved there when we were children. I don't think he enjoyed it as much. When he officially retired at 65, he went back to work as a farmworker. Even at home, Dad was never far from a tractor or a mower.

He was tractor mad, Dad. You could usually find him mowing or towing something. Even in the early days, when I'd get back to my first big house in Knutsford at 5am after a gig, I'd often be woken after an hour or two by my dad getting a head start on the mowing at dawn. I asked him to take a look round Delamere Manor before we bought it. I wanted to know what he thought. He did the whole tour of the estate, the acres and acres of grass to be managed, and at the end he asks the agent, 'One question. Where do you put the grass cuttings?' The agent got back in the golf buggy you needed to get round the huge estate and drove Dad off to show him.

Dad was this great big guy. Action Grandad. He would scoop up the four of his grandchildren, our two and their cousins, in his massive shovel-like worker's hands and bounce them on his knee. Up they'd go a foot in the air, their heads wobbling all over the place, as they screamed with pleasure.

Dawn and I wrapped our precious kids in cotton wool. Then the day comes when you ask, 'Dad, can you just look after the kids for half an hour?' We're hardly out of the door and there's the sound of a tractor rumbling past and all the kids hanging off the back of it and screaming with laughter.

Action Grandad would have them hammering posts in with a mallet, all the things I'd be scared to death of doing round kids: massive bonfires, lawnmowers, the dummy dipped in whisky, chocolate for breakfast, chocolate for lunch. I bet he did the lot.

He was calm and quiet, my dad. A gentle man and a gentleman. In the twenty years I lived at home, the shouting only ever came from one direction. Mum's. He lived outside, always doing something, tending to some animal or other. Sporadically, he'd quietly appear at the back door, with his horsewhip in one hand and a bucket of freshly laid eggs in the other. 'Now, now.'

'Dad, guess what. I've got Donny Osmond in the studio.'

'Is 'e be God?'

And he was off, back to the rake and the manure.

He didn't talk much, a bit like Howard, but when he did, you listened. One day when I was about 35, I grumbled to him, 'The kids aren't sleeping; we're up all night.'

'Don't worry, son, the first forty years are the worst.'

In the last couple of years he'd started enjoying a drink a bit more. He'd always worked so hard, it was like he was letting himself have a bit more fun at last. It was harmless. I walked in the door one day dragging a film crew from iTunes behind me. I was always walking in with some film crew or journalist or other; I always had some angle I was milking.

'Hiya, Dad.'

'Oh all right, son,' he said, as if it was dead natural to be sitting in your dressing gown sipping whisky at four in the afternoon. He got up so early in the morning. I think he'd just got in and out of his overalls, had a bath and now he was quietly unwinding. We stood there, me, them and my dad, in his dressing gown and holding a tumbler of Glenmorangie.

He never felt awkward. 'Afternoon,' he said, nodding at the film crew standing there with all their equipment.

My mum's a hard worker. However much money I made, she never gave up her job at the school, but Dad took it to another level. He worked from early in the morning until late at night and never complained. It was normal for him and he's passed it on to Our Ian and me. The Barlows are grafters.

For such an incredibly grounded and humble guy, he was tickled by the perks and the treats of the high life.

I can't pretend this life is not all I've known as an adult. Take That were successful so quickly in the early nineties that we jumped from being a tour bus band to a chauffeurs and private jets band in the space of one tour.

Dad carried on with his pigeons, his hard manual labour and his lager and lime, but he mixed that up with a joyful enjoyment of the luxuries my work brought us. He liked a fine old single malt. He liked a nice bowl of trifle in a private box at a gig. But his favourite thing was to take a private jet to Padstow in Cornwall for a birthday lunch at Rick Stein's fish restaurant. We'd eat and have a potter round the pretty old harbour town, like normal tourists. Then, like abnormal tourists, we'd buy a box of 20 pasties from Chough's down on the quayside and load them on to the Learjet at Newquay airport.

I am protected by three things: optimism, hard work and family. Mum and Dad gave me all that. They gave me a great start in life.

I was having lunch with Simon Moran at Le Caprice in the October after The Circus. We'd always catch up after a tour, talk about what had worked, what hadn't. We were both basking in quite a glow after that one. When I left the restaurant I checked my phone. Seven missed calls from my brother. He never rings more than once, Our Ian. Something was wrong.

In the end I got through to my mum. Her voice was shaking. 'Your dad's died,' she said.

That was it.

I went home, told Dawn. She said, 'Just go. Now.'

I got in the car and drove straight to the North. I went into coping mode: making calls, making plans in my head, being practical. Then halfway up the M1 I had to pull over. I sat in a service station car park and cried.

* * *

There'd been no warning letters and no grave chats with doctors. One minute he was here, the next, he was gone. Heart attack. Three hours later, we met up at Chester Hospital. Our Ian, Mum and me. Dad was still in the hospital bed, covered by a sheet. Mum said, 'Do you want to go and sit in there?' I wandered in but it just felt wrong. I could tell Mum wanted to stay but I couldn't. I suggested we all leave. We went back to Mum and Dad's empty house and started to deal with the logistics of death.

Death really is rubbish. It's absolutely devastating. But while you're on the floor, don't forget you've got to organise an event. Enter stage left, strangers in your home. People you've never met telling you how sorry they are and asking whether you want brass handles on the casket. Death's got a price tag. And the ultimate sales tactic. Guilt.

All this is the last thing you need. You just want to tell the world to piss off so you can give your mum a hug. But no, you've got to go to the crematorium to hear more meaningless condolences and discuss the order of service cards, hymns, poems, music. Enter stage right, more strangers, the religious ones this time.

This is the joy of death. It was a ten-day extravaganza between my father's death and the funeral.

Our new friends at the funeral directors' asked, 'Would you like to spend some time with your father before the cremation?'

Having not spent any time in the room at Chester Hospital and feeling like I had cheated my mum out of a few more moments with her husband of 43 years, I said let's go.

The lid of the coffin was leaning against the wall and on it a little silver plaque said, 'At rest.'

Very apt for a guy who had worked every waking hour of his life.

I stared at Dad and felt disappointed by what you take with you when you die. Think of all the crap you go through in your life, all the worries, goals, fights and stuff, the piles and piles of stuff. There lay Colin Barlow. He had a shirt, a pair of trousers, shoes and a couple of his AAA passes from Take That tours. Not a lot for 71 years on earth.

But then it hit me. This isn't it. It's me and Our Ian, our kids. That's what Dad leaves. That's what you leave when you die. All the good stuff I've done is because of Dad.

After the funeral was over, I stayed up with my mum for another week. It was getting kind of nice being there with Mum. We were talking about Dad a lot and we were making dinner together. We were just keeping each other amused in a really shit time. It was lovely; she cooked for her little boy every night. Mum's old repertoire from childhood: spag bol, roast chicken, and sausage and eggs. And a few new ones from Nigel Slater. We had The Food Channel on all day.

Sometimes we didn't talk. She just cooked.

I remember we were listening to Radio 2 and Terry Wogan had sent his condolences on air, a little thing but Mum and I were tickled by it. I loved being there, it felt good – too good – I was getting used to our little routine. It was such a mountain, the funeral; we just hibernated. Mum loves a routine, and so do I. Breakfast at eight, lunch at one, dinner at five, cheese and bicos at ten. As the week went on, I worried more and more about leaving her alone.

Life was moving along as normal despite our world being shattered. Dawn and the kids were missing me. I needed to go home to my own family. We hugged, I left and could only begin to imagine how she felt as the door shut behind me.

I had just buried my own father. But when I got back to London I'm Dan's dad again. I felt a whole new rush of feelings when I saw my son. Fear of that day coming for Dan, when I die. You've had this protective loving canopy of your parents all your life. You feel safe because they're still alive and then it's, 'Oh, shit! We're going to be next.'

The passing of time is always more vivid when kids are born or people die.

Dan was at the funeral, but my head was all over the place, and what with the organisation and the weird spaciness of grief, I was somewhere else that day. When I got back to London I just couldn't leave Dan alone. He'd come in from school wearing his school uniform, his little tie, cap and blazer. He hadn't seen me for over two weeks. He was climbing all over me like a baby chimp. I couldn't let go. To the point where I was slightly scaring him: 'Let me go, Daddy.'

I loosened my grip – a bit – and we sat and looked at pictures of my dad. We enjoyed it. Kids find it fascinating when they see pictures of older people at their age. Holding Dan, I held a piece of Dad.

Of all the letters and emails I got, the one from Jason meant the most. He always took time out to talk to Dad, and his sadness was sincere and it was beautifully written.

Not long after Dad died, I went round and Mum was having her dinner on her knee. I'd never ever seen her have her dinner on her knee. It shocked me. Dad was gone, and this solitary meal said everything about what Mum, and all of us, had lost.

11

PROGRESS AND PROGRESS

'At last, we meet on no man's land'

I had landed back in London from that LA trip with mixed feelings. I've met with Rob, we've written, had a laugh. That's enough progress for now. I was desperate to tell the others all about it, but I didn't want to get their hopes up.

'Okay everyone. I saw Rob, we wrote some songs, spent a bit of time together. I asked him the million-dollar question about coming back. Not much of a response to report, sorry. He's having a tough time working through some stuff. It's the last thing he needs right now. But I planted a seed and I invited him to join us in New York next week.'

Mark and I flew first, with Rhino. We wanted to get a couple of days' head start before Howard and Jason arrived. We landed and got a car from the airport, and went straight to the Meatpacking District.

Stepping out of the lift at Soho House, I see two laden trolleys of Louis Vuitton cases. I turned to Mark and said, 'Blimey. Someone's got some bags here.'

From behind one of these towers of bags appears Robbie. I can't believe it, he's turned up.

Mark gives Rob a hug; he won't let him go. It's lovely to see great big Rob and little Mark together, the band's nippers. I think Mark had put up with us three for these last few years. I suspect he was always missing Rob. They were as thick as thieves back in the day.

I say, 'Rob, the studio is only down the road. Rhino's setting up. Fancy it?'

We write 'The Flood' that day. I have an instrumental, no melody, no lyrics. Rhino sets up two mics above us all and we riff. An hour later we play it back and right in the middle is this fabulous hook.

We dive back in, find the verse, write the bridge. Rob opens up his laptop and as the screen turns on there is this blanket of stickies all covered with lyric ideas, mined from Rob's paranoia and genius.

Another half-hour passes. We've got some lyrics. Rob wants to go in the vocal booth – we all do and we're scrapping over who'll be in next. These are the best moments when you're a writer. You're circling your prey, you're high on it. More humming, more tapping away at lyrics, more grins and high fives. It's done.

It feels like a battle song, one we could sing with one arm in the air, feeling like kings. It's a song that could only have been written in that first nervous burst of creativity of us all back together again. It's like a relay. Whatever we do only makes it better. Mark tweaks the melody, Rob trims a lyric, and as this is going on I can't help but see us on stage at Wembley Stadium singing this song.

It's about our survival, despite everyone's best efforts to write us off. We'd all not only come out the other side, we carried on going, too. Every one of us has our stories about being at the Brits and seeing an Oasis member look sideways at someone from Blur and snigger, or hearing an Arctic Monkey call us 'bollocks'. Doesn't matter how many albums you sell, pop is always the underdog. Don't forget the continuing theme: we're always trying to prove we're good because everyone thinks we're crap.

* * *

The party gets better. Howard and Jay arrive and another wave of creativity begins.

Howard and I, when we're out in a club, we do what we've always done, since the first time round. He'll tap my arm and say, 'Oh, I like this. Yeah.' And the two of us will have a magic little moment of grooving to some ace beat. It's a little thing we've always done, 'Hey, this bit.' And off we go. Heads nodding and grinning.

Howard's interesting to write with because he thinks like a dancer and a DJ. There's a track that happens in New York when we're meant to be on Mark's stag. Howard and I get up and while we're still at Soho House having breakfast he says, 'Gaz, I wanna come down early today 'cause there's five of us now. It's hard for me to get my ideas in and so if I come down with you now we can start it together and then I've got my ideas in before everyone else arrives.'

We run to the studio, just a few blocks away down in the West Village. And he's got this Afrika Bambaataa breakbeat. I put this break in the computer and we loop it. He plays bass sound. I listen: 'Brilliant, brilliant.' Immediately I can hear the chords. 'Yes, I've got a bridge that will go with that.'

These are my favourite times with Howard; it's just me and him. No pressure. He's very musical Howard, yet for someone who is so creative, he finds it hard to raise his voice above the crowd. But what he brings is essential. He brings rhythm and grooves: the stuff you can dance to. Watching him at times like this fills me with love.

In fifteen minutes we've got an arrangement for the guys to write to.

Bang! There's a thunderclap as the door goes. Robbie's arrived. It's like it's never one door with him, it's two. Both doors slam against the wall as he comes in. Even if it's one it feels like two.

Mark and Jay are behind him, so I go, 'Listen everyone, we've been at it, here, so we'll just give you a little sneak preview.' We put it on the ego speakers and turn it up to 11. It starts with strings, it starts really slowly, and then the unexpected beat kicks in.

Rob immediately gets up and starts singing. Then Mark adds to the melody. Rob fills the bridge. It's melody battle. And they're all good. As they're shouting words out, Jay will be there scribbling them down. We're starting on the lyrics. Another ten minutes and we've got a verse, bridge and chorus.

Almost twenty years to the day, and Take That, all five of them, are writing their first song together. No one knows we are all here together. The biggest secret in the world just got bigger and better. This writing is like a complete organism; this is stars aligning, real universe will provide stuff. We're all as high as kites. It's so exciting.

We work up the rest of the track while the others are doing lyrics next door. Within twenty minutes we've put vocals on it. Whole thing takes an hour. From one Afrika Bambaataa breakbeat to Wait, a Take That song like you've never heard before.

* * *

Somehow Rob landed in the room next to mine at Soho House. We did not shirk on our responsibilities of being on a stag. We went out every night. Rob was teetotal and we were gong to bars drinking. We never expected him to come and Rob always said very happily he didn't want to but God did he absolutely love hearing about our plans. 'Where are you going tonight?' 'Where are you going after?' 'And after that?'

Crashing in at three, leathered, I'd find Rob's door ajar. 'Gaaaaz?'

I'd then have to go in and relay the entire evening's events, course by course, bar by bar, drink by drink. And he loved every minute of it.

Night after night, for a whole week. It was exhausting. 'Gaaaaz!'

After NY, Rob came to us in London later in the year. The writing was good but the whole set-up was complicated from the off. When you take four people and put them in a room, they all take a little time to shuffle into place and find their position and role to make the band work harmoniously.

Someone is the leader, someone is like the official opposition, someone will be the one to support the leader, someone will be the diplomat. Someone will bring cool and soulfulness, someone will bring a system. Someone will push the creative limits. Someone will be there to provide harmonies and quietly make a call on something when no one else can agree.

He's one of the funniest people I know, Howard, although when it comes to band decisions, he doesn't speak up often, but when he does you listen. So in a situation of an album where you're just second, third, fourth-guessing a crucial decision, ask Howard – it's usually right what he says.

I look at us all, including Rob, from when we first met and to now and what we've all become. I watch how we've all dealt with what's happened over the last twenty-odd years and I believe that some of us are acting out our lives a bit. But I think that, out of all of us, the one who has stayed the most true to who he is, is Howard. Howard, for me, is the most real of us all. It doesn't matter if he's going to upset the whole room, he's himself, always.

I'm always checking myself. Is this me? Or am I being who people want me to be? I have to check myself all the time because basically I don't stand for a lot. There was one thing that Nigel always drummed into me on this subject. Always consider what you say in public. Whatever you say you can make other people believe in it. When someone – anyone – is in the public eye, rightly or just as likely wrongly, their public utterances carry more weight. So unless it means a lot to you, keep your mouth shut. (That lesson rings even truer today in the age of social media.)

I do have views, of course, but for the most part I keep them to myself. I don't want to impose them on anyone. I'm a guy who sings and writes songs, entertains the odd crowd. And when I'm not doing that I like to be with my kids and my wife. I'm not an intellectual. I'm not a politician. I'm definitely not some kind of moral compass.

When you become famous at 19 for being in a boy band, the privilege of deciding who you are is taken away from you. All you ever try to do is live up to someone else's idea of you. You lose the freedom to just be you, forever. There's always an idea of who you should be and what people expect from you. If you're driving the car, eating in a restaurant, tweeting or just walking down the street, people are looking at you to be that famous guy. And in 2018 it's worse than it's ever been. It feels like the pop stars we know now live their lives according to Twitter polls and Instagram likes. This isn't complaining,

I'm telling you how it feels. I know, in the social media age, you all feel or have felt a bit of it.

In a more normal life, a person finds out who they are gradually, by looking backwards and slowly working it out. I think all I'm saying here is: stop looking up to the famous guy. They're already flawed: they wanna be famous.

Part of the confusion in a pop star existence, especially at 47, is how do I feel being me? Unfortunately I have no answers for you. Monday, I might not give a shit what anyone thinks; Tuesday, what everyone thinks is so important to me that I feel suffocated by it. Being famous is a total head fuck. Somehow Howard deals with it.

* * *

There are five different takes on *Progress*, and this is only mine. For me, there was a problem. Since we got back together, we were writing partners. Now this new fella has come in and he wants to be the one sitting by my piano as I am programming a song.

Robbie's bigger and louder than pretty much everyone, isn't he? His voice is bigger in sessions and his presence is louder in life. He's Robbie Williams. He's got a massive voice, he writes good songs and he brings chaos and star quality that is as exciting as it is unsettling.

All this made for an amazing five-piece but a less settled four-piece. We've all got to shuffle into new positions. And some people feel more left out, some people feel like they've got a partner, some people feel like they're out in the cold. Everyone's shuffling around again trying to find their place and they need to do it quickly because this person's not *just* someone else, he's big.

His manager had warned us, 'Look, he's hot one week and cold the next; you need to be ready for sudden changes.' Sure enough, just before that Christmas, we get an email. 'I'm feeling differently about this now. Maybe it's for another year.'

I think there's a million things going round in Rob's head at any one time; he changes one day to the next.

'I'm the best at SS,' he said to me.

'What's that?'

'Sweeping statements. I'll throw them out and then the next day I go back to doing the complete opposite.'

His Christmas gift to us is he's not doing the album. Bloody hell. I knew we had good music. Hits!

Why did we jump into this? We barely knew the guy. We haven't worked with him for fifteen years. We've only ever heard stories of how unpredictable he is, and those are from his own people, let alone industry gossip. At this point our brother Rob was a complete stranger again.

I was frightened. This was a nightmare, and way beyond anything I could control. My mood hit the floor. I paced up and down the London house like a demented cat. I didn't dare tell Dawn. She would have only been proved right by this. I couldn't hear her say the words, 'I told you so.'

I felt sick with it.

Might be a good time for a pie. And not just any pie. There's a restaurant called Sally Clarke's less than a hundred yards from the very house I was pacing. On Friday she does a special pie: chicken and mushroom with puff pastry; no, it's flaky pastry. I know because I paced straight over to Clarke's and came back smothered in pie crumbs. Oh my God. This is what Rob had done to me the first time. He's done it again.

Mark had a better solution. 'He's in London this week. I'm going to go and see him.'

Fortunately, even though we hadn't finished recording the album, Stuart Price had worked up a couple of the songs. One of them was 'The Flood' and the other was 'Underground Machine', which sounded mega.

Mark went round to see Rob. 'Listen,' he said to him, 'we all understand. We always said, "No pressure." But we've got something good as a start here. We'll come back to it another time perhaps... Oh, but before I go and leave you be,' he pulls out these two big guns, 'I'll just play you this...'

Within seconds of hearing Stuart's fat intro to 'Underground Machine', Rob's up dancing around the room, 'This is amazing.'

Five days after he buggered off, he's back. I let out a sigh of relief, and went back to my sushi. Panic over.

* * *

In early 2010 we decided to spend two weeks finishing writing *Progress* before we fully jumped into the recording. *Progress* is about us. It couldn't have been about anything else. Before we sent the complete album to Stuart, we all needed to discover the thread, the idea that pulled the whole album together. Rob had come to us in New York; it was time to write in LA, on his turf.

We went at the end of January, just after my birthday. I'm an LA old-timer now; it's my second home after Britain. LA's sunshine and healthy living culture give you a bright and breezy feeling about life that London can only muster on the occasional sunny day. People eat sushi all day there. So I'd be feeling incredibly smug as I drank bucketloads of fresh orange juice and started the day with an egg white omelette with spinach. I'm so pleased with myself I order an extra piece of toast, butter on the side obviously.

We set up in a studio called The Village, which is by the I-405 on the edge of Santa Monica. Rob had invited us all to stay at his house. He loved people staying over, and having his mates around.

We said, 'We don't want to impose.'

'Come on, we'll have quizzes.'

We insist we're staying at the Beverly Wilshire, 'But we'll definitely be up for that quiz.'

It was fascinating really, the whole performance, because he nominated his dad, Pete – top man – to be quizmaster for the night. Pete had slaved over Google all day. His question 20 was a trick one, which I've borrowed for my own quizzes ever since. (Yeah yeah, no one's too cool for a quiz.)

I love a quiz for the same reason as Rob; it's about getting everyone together, all his mates, having a laugh, relaxing them without needing booze or being on their phones and all the other bloody distractions of life. Couldn't we all do with a bit of that?

There were thirty people all piled into his sitting room, falling off sofas, sitting on cushions and crammed together. It was a good night that only got better when, halfway through, sushi for thirty arrived. Healthy food in American portions. My favourite.

I know a few people who can fill a stadium – artists, comedians. None of them could've hosted a night like that without being the centre of attention, and a pain in the arse, frankly. Watching from my seat it was lovely to see Rob, the perfect host, enjoying his mates, just happy that we were happy.

We wrote a few songs in LA, including 'Happy Now', 'Kidz' and 'Eight Letters'. The day we wrote 'Eight Letters' we found the soul of the album. That whole album, lyrically, is our story. It's us. Most people, when they think of *Progress*, they think of 'The Flood'. But for us, the song of the record was 'Eight Letters'.

'We became the parade on the streets that we once cleaned / Expendable soldiers smiling at anything / Raised on a feeling our lives would have meaning eventually.'

We were from the North West of England. Put in a manufactured boy band. Told not to think. Not to complain. Because you can always see another very, very pretty boy waiting to replace you.

We spent about six months writing *Progress* and then, after that LA trip, we handed the album over to Stuart. Stuart Price wasn't collaborative like John. He works more like a DJ doing a remix. It was, 'right, give me the files' and he'd go off into a darkened room and you wouldn't hear from him again for a week. Stuart left us to it; then we left him to do what he did. I was excited to see how he would produce that album.

At some point the whole John Shanks thing had to come up. He's more than a producer to us, he's The Producer, and he's a great friend. We needed to tell John face to face he wasn't producing the album. Letting John go was a big thing for us. We all met him down by the pool at the Beverly Wilshire one morning. The whole thing felt more like a break-up than a business meeting; it was very uncomfortable. I asked John if he wanted to stay and have a drink. John shook his head. Just said, 'Good luck and party on' and he was gone.

We're friends today. We're forever indebted to that guy. John Shanks is the man who put Take That musically together again. He is an awesome producer and everything he touches turns to platinum; outrageously talented. I still work with him to this day.

I felt bad about John. He'd seen us through our transition from boy band to man band. I kept texting him and calling him, 'Hey mate!' He'd text me back in true dramatic John style, 'You broke my heart, man.'

12

ON THE BOX
AND AT THE PALACE

'Ain't life so cruel when
you're just not good enough'

Perhaps it was time to introduce the outside world to the secret we'd all been keeping. I asked Rob to do Children in Need Rocks in November 2009 at the Albert Hall. We knew us introducing him straight after us on the bill would stir up a bit of gossip, especially on this newfangled Twitter job.

One of the good things about these big charity gigs is you can pull some really surprising bunnies out of the hat. I love that thing of breaking out of genre and bringing musicians together. One of the most exciting things I ever watched as a teenager was Live Aid. When musicians get together, pigeonholes and genres go out of the window. It's lovely that. I dropped it on Shirley Bassey in rehearsals at Maida Vale two days before. 'Dame Shirley, how about you and Dizzee Rascal doing a rap in "Diamonds Are Forever"?'

You've got to know what you're doing when dealing with music's royalty. Not sure I did. But, thank God, Dame Shirley's granddaughter was there and she did. 'Oh my god! Dizzee Rascal?!?' I had Dizzee waiting in the wings. What a sweetheart. On he came and blew her away. We had a moment. Showbiz hugs all round.

I'm sitting in my dressing room halfway through the show and this guy knocks on the door. He's incredibly polite, this guy, 'Good evening, Mr Barlow. I work with Buckingham Palace. I'm interested in talking to you about how you pulled this together.'

He said he would be in touch. Normally, that sort of thing would hover in the back of your mind, wouldn't it? Buckingham Palace. Be in touch. I'm knee-deep in the complexities of *Progress*. I miss my dad. My heart is heavier than a stone. It's not long after Robbie says he doesn't want to do *Progress*. The furthest thing from my mind is Buckingham Palace.

A few months later my PA reminded me I have this lunch at Buckingham Palace to discuss the 'Diamond Jubilee event'.

'Wha'?'

My life in 2010 is starting to get insanely busy. I'm taking on loads. We're the group that never says yes, but I'm the man who can't say no.

This lunch at the Palace comes round. We've got a milestone album coming out; it's all-consuming. Mixes, re-recording, choosing directors for videos. This isn't an album, it's a military operation. Wherever I was I can't remember, life was nuts, and the car was late collecting me. I wanted to go home and get changed but the traffic would've been against me so I had to make a call: incredibly late and well-dressed or only slightly late, badly dressed and possibly a bit smelly?

I'm passed efficiently and politely from one member of the Household Cavalry to a footman to a butler to a private secretary, all immaculate in their tailored coats and shoes so shiny you can see your face in them. All too polite to let on if I am a bit whiffy.

After a ten-minute walk down Buckingham Palace's deep red carpets, we arrive at the Centre Room, which is this sunshine-coloured room full of silk and gold and priceless Chinese porcelain. It's lavish; even the lining on the curtains is gold. It was like our old house in Cheshire, basically – but not quite as nice.

There are about twenty people here in this dining room. No member of 'The Firm' but a fair number of showbiz aristocrats and Whitehall functionaries. There's one spot left at the table. Mr Gary Barlow is last to arrive. We ate our lunch, no one drank the wine that was served in crystal glasses. The china is beautiful and has tiny food on it: quails' eggs, lettuce, a smear of pâté, you can imagine it. Gone in three mouthfuls. I noticed that everyone had presentations in front of them. Some were glossy prospectuses, others were pimped out documents inside a plastic cover; whatever they were, everyone had one except me.

'Should I have one of these?' I said to the bloke next to me.

'Oh no,' he said. 'These are *our* proposals for the Queen's Jubilee event.'

* * *

It's like one of those dreams where you go to school without pants on or you wake up on the day of an exam having done no revision. Except I'm awake, standing before a dining room of important people at Buckingham Palace. We finish eating and the woman from the Queen's office, this nice Kiwi girl called Sam, says, 'Right, we're going to hear everyone's suggestions now. Let's start with Gary.'

What! I've got no one's homework to copy. I got up and winged it. I winged it for about twenty minutes in fact. Because while I was making it up I found that I was imagining it in vivid detail. I could see it in my mind's eye. I was dialling in on how I felt in 1977 for the Silver Jubilee with everyone sitting on those trestle tables, all the mums and dads serving the food; I wanted to get that feeling back of a simple, good time.

'We live in a time of constant bad news, so let's shut the noise for the day and have some fun.'

'It will be a celebration of all things British. A cross-section of music, young to old, it will include British eccentricity and greatness.' It felt right, what I was saying; even though I was making it up, it felt good. 'Of course, we will have Paul McCartney, I know him, Elton John, I know him, Stevie Wonder, I don't know him, but we'll get him. All the great songwriters. It will be a gig for free. In the middle of historic London. Everyone waving flags...'

I went over towards the windows and pointed out to the bloody great fountain outside the Palace on the Mall. I couldn't remember what it was called, didn't know in fact. 'And the stage will be...' I looked out over that famous forecourt and imagined a stage there, then the fountain caught my eye, and I got quite excited, 'the stage will be there. Right there.'

'You mean the Victoria Memorial?' Sam said. 'Let's not get carried away.'

I sat down. A lot of what I said wasn't much but there were definitely some inspired bits. I surprised myself with how passionate I felt about that gig. It'd be the last big Jubilee many of us would see in our lifetimes.

I finished my stint and the baton went off round the greats at the table. Some spoke for one minute, some for five, none for twenty. And it landed back at Sam at the head of the table.

'No one has suggested a song,' she said, sounding disappointed, 'and it would be amazing to have one of those, wouldn't it, Gary?'

Make no mistake, I really wanted to do that concert. At this juncture I'm saying 'no' to nothing. This song, however, is the worst idea in the world for a songwriter like me. No one's made one of these records work since Midge and Bob. 'Wonderful idea, Sam. And we should have artists from all around the Commonwealth sing on it.'

'Yes. The Commonwealth!' The assembled greats murmured their approval. 'The Commonwealth...' 'The Commonwealth. Yes.'

Oh dear. How am I going to get myself out of this one?

I kept my Buckingham Palace lunch menu card embossed with the royal coat of arms and gave it to Emily when I got home.

'Have you been to see the Queen, Daddy?'

'Not quite, Em...'

The kids started their dinner and my phone started ringing as LA woke up. Business as usual, back to work.

The next day Edward, the guy I'd met at the Albert Hall, called. 'Gary, we want you to do it.'

Instead of punching the air, I punched the wall. This was going to be a nightmare. That night Emily asked if I'd got the job organising the Queen's birthday party and I said, 'Yes, I'd better start working on my bowing, hadn't I?'

I turned to Dawn and told her how I really felt. 'It's not going to be fun, this gig. Because not only have I got to deal with Buckingham

Palace, who will be a nightmare of formalities and protocol, I've got to deal with BBC1 as well, and I know that will be a nightmare.'

All I can see ahead is a bloody big mountain of red tape. I'd love to be excited but I'm not. I've got a tour, an album, a new baby, I'm doing another Children in Need next year, and… And now this. I'm anticipating seventy people copied into emails. I'm dreading it.

These anxieties played on my mind so much that I called a meeting the following week with Jay Hunt, who was the head of BBC1 at the time. I walked into her office at the BBC TV Centre with my own glossy prospectus under my arm this time. I opened the door and there was Guy Freeman, only the King of OB – outside broadcast. He's the safest pair of hands for al fresco telly out there and especially a Diamond Jubilee event being shown to the world. Maybe he'll even let me sing.

This was my one contact at the BBC. Sorted. He was brought in by an executive producer called Ben Weston who was in charge of all the BBC coverage across the Jubilee weekend.

Next up, the Palace. 'Listen, I'm excited about this gig, I really am, but I'm giving you an opportunity…' I'm doing a Jedi mind trick on them: 'I'd love to do it. I would. But I've got a bomb to drop. I want to deal with one person. That's it. I don't want to get into a spider's web of bureaucracy and endless dead ends of people going, "Oh I can't give you permission to do that – it's got to go to my boss." No offence if you don't want to do it that way, but it's the only way I can. Unless I can do it like this, I don't want to do it.'

God bless them. Both of them agreed.

Very early on, the idea of Grace Jones came up. Commonwealth, Jamaican, 'Slave To The Rhythm' is one of my top five favourite songs. I remember loving it when it came out. I loved the song, her image, Jean-Paul Goude's insane album cover, and the sound. Oh, the sound! I'd sit in my bedroom as a kid wearing my Yamaha studio headphones just studying the sound. I always dreamed of doing that, what Trevor Horn did to that record. I was a bit scared of her as she looks like she'd kill you and eat you afterwards; she's proper Amazonian. She scared me even more now, thirty-plus years later, because she's developed quite a significant rep for being unpredictable. It really depended day to day whether she'd turn up, behave herself and be any good. But we needed an edge, some risk; I didn't want it to be just a boring set-up of one act after another. From all the communication with her manager, the one thing she absolutely promised was that she'd behave.

Aside from the contractors, everyone did the show for free. I sent an email to Robbie who got back to me in two minutes with a yes. For the artists there's the little incentive of performing in front of the 500 million-strong audience watching around the world. It's going to be a nightmare to put together. But Christ, the dinner stories I'm gonna get out of this. Bloody mega.

Why did I say yes? Well, you don't say no to a gig like that. Also, I'm ambitious, a grafter, there's that fear of saying no. I will never get the chance to organise a Diamond Jubilee concert again. So many reasons to do it.

However, I'm really working at a new level of intensity now. You're looking at an unusually busy person choosing to be even busier. I couldn't start to count the hours I spent on that concert alone. I worked all the time.

There's something not quite right. It went further than that. My PA would say, 'Radio 2 want to meet to talk about something or other.'

'Book in a dinner!' I'd say.

Why? It could've been done in ten minutes on the phone. I don't want to spend the whole night doing it.

Oh yes, and I'm also working out twice a day.

I remember thinking, 'I've got to slow down here.' Even though I was in London and was coming home every night, I was seeing very little of the kids. I'd leave the house before they woke up and get home after they'd gone to bed. Mine and Dawn's date nights weren't happening.

Two-phone Gary has recently arrived. Yup, I'm typing an email on the Blackberry while talking on the iPhone. I'm constantly agitated. But I miss it when it's not there. On those busy days, the great positive is that you never think about food. In fact, you buzz off the hunger and the stress, which only makes you feel even busier. Coffee. That's all I need. If I felt hungry when I finally came down off my busy buzz at bedtime, I'd take a sleeping pill for dinner.

Living a life like this, of course I was going to crash. That was my time with the kids. All they see is Daddy on the phone, phones, or crashed out on the sofa. I never went outside to play football with them; I was knackered and docile.

The only time I'm not docile is when I'd lose my temper. I tried never to direct it at any of the family, but I'd lose it. Traffic jams. Especially in London. I hate traffic jams. Waste of my time. Damn! I'll never get this hour back. A queue in the airport would have me growling and sighing with fury. I was never angry at the kids, they've always been good kids. I wasn't a horrible, angry dad. And I let Dawn do all the disciplining anyway.

Once we got stuck in, organising the concert took about eighteen months. Every two weeks it was off to the Palace. We had fifteen A-list artists, ranging from proper old national treasures to the kids at the top of the charts that year. It was a fun mix: Stevie Wonder, McCartney, Annie Lennox, Rob, Elton, Tom Jones, Will.i.am, Grace Jones, Jessie J... The Queen was asked very early on what she wanted at the concert and she only asked for two things: Cliff Richard, and she said, 'Don't make it too long.' (I only told Cliff that recently, that she'd asked for him, and he had tears in his eyes.)

Oh, there's another thing. Have I not mentioned I'm in talks to take over from Simon Cowell for three years on *The X Factor*? At this stage it was just a conversation. No one knew. But what arose from this was a schedule so insanely packed that even if I'd dined on sleeping tablets I'd still wake up in the night sweating, sick with anxiety. It wasn't the busy side of things that freaked me out. I'd asked for that. It was the thought that if I was going to be on telly, I really didn't want to look like a lump. Which diet would I turn to this time?

* * *

I'm a great rubbisher of things. I'm quick to say, 'I'll never do that. It's rubbish.' This goes way back. I remember Jason, when he started eating seeds, what most people would've called Trill back in those days, after a brand of birdseed. We certainly did. 'Look at Jay pecking at his Trill,' and just thinking he was mad. We once all gave him a big industrial juicer as a birthday present because he really wanted one like a kid really wants the latest Lego. It was expensive and weighed more than a small Fiesta, but he seemed pleased.

Jay had taken these two girls on to cook for him on the *Progress* promo tour of Europe in 2010. We were in Milan. All the girlfriends were off shopping.

Someone wondered about the weather. 'Don't think it rains in Prada.'

I'd pounded the gym and was there, eating cornflakes with skimmed milk, drinking black coffee, cracking on with the usual miserable breakfast. Meanwhile, Jay was eating like a king. He had eggs, avocado and, blimey, was that a sausage? Jason had been using these two cooks, Jasmine and Melissa Hemsley, on the road now for a while. They always cooked if he had dinners round at his house and when we travelled they'd brief the hotel chefs on how to cook for him.

Being the great rubbisher, I called the two girls Mel 'n' Kim. 'That sausage is not health food. Where's your seeds?' We all ribbed him a bit; since he'd starting working with these two extremely attractive women, he always reeked of garlic.

For New Year's Eve, 2010, a family flew us all out to entertain their house party in Barbados. I took my Mum and Emily with me. Jason brought out Mel and Kim. Given they were meant to be health chefs, the Rubbisher clocked that they drank a lot that New Year's Eve, which made me like them even more.

I was interested in these girls. I was sounding them out; very quietly, obviously. Outwardly I rubbished away as normal. 'Ey up, here come Mel and Kim.'

We were all staying in a house together and these two were telling the chef what to cook. There was a lot of chat about butter. They weren't like any health gurus I'd ever met before.

I knew I was going to be doing *The X Factor* so I was going to be on telly all the time. I was ready for the next step because I wasn't solving it on my own. I wasn't putting weight on but I wasn't losing it either, despite all the working out. Telly is cruel. There's nowhere to hide. There's no airbrushing.

I mentioned to Dawn that I was considering getting Jason's mates, Mel and Kim, to take over my food.

'And what does that entail, exactly?' she wondered.

'Oh, just that they will deliver every single thing I eat. It's going to be a busy year, makes sense.'

'Great,' Dawn said, rolling her eyeballs.

Another fad diet from the man who's the bloody king of 'em.

★　★　★

On 16 February 2011 I interviewed two people. First, a new PA, Elisa. At the end of the interview I asked her, 'What is it that you want from your career?'

She said, 'I want to be working with the good people in this industry.'

'That's us.' I hired her on the spot and she started the next day. 'Come and work for the good guys, Elisa.'

Next up Jasmine Hemsley.

I've got to be fairer to Mel and Kim; they were actually Hemsley + Hemsley, a food delivery service who aimed to educate their clients about eating well while they fed them. The fashion crowd had got into them first, then music. Jay was early to the game, and, relatively, so was I. They were still just starting out, really. Usually they delivered food for a week or so. They might come into people's houses and show them how to cook, go through their cupboards. I was wondering whether their service couldn't kill two birds with one stone for me. One, they'd feed me while I travelled and worked like a dog over the coming year. Two, perhaps they were the silver bullet. Perhaps they held the secret to losing the extra weight I so hated.

Jasmine sat down opposite me one day, looked me in the eye and gave me her pitch. She's young, can't be much older than 25, and has deep dimples in her cheeks, which make her look even younger.

I could relate to Jasmine. She was a working model who'd had nightmares with bloating and constipation and had worked out how to deal with her health problems by changing her diet and her lifestyle. She understood the pressure of being in a business that expects you to look nothing less than perfect, all the time. She had no qualifications, just experience she said, very confidently. I loved that. I'd seen plenty of experts and they all had a narrow focus on one subject, gave me conflicting advice and left me confused.

'Gary. Losing weight is your life. It doesn't have to be.' She recalled watching me eat my breakfast in Milan and seeing the sadness in my soul as I looked down at the watery cornflakes. 'I can help you. This is not a diet. It's a lifestyle.'

Before our meeting she had asked me to fill out a food diary, which she read there and then, sitting opposite me in my office at the studio. Salmon, salad, chicken breast, Canderel. She read it out loud. 'I don't think you're telling me the truth. You wouldn't be coming to me if this was all you ate.'

So I told her the real story. The nineteen cups of coffee with Canderel, skip breakfast, baked potatoes and low-fat marge, tuna and pasta, sacks of fruit, low-fat fruit yoghurt, trays of sushi, rice cakes, sachets of low-calorie soup, gallons of Diet Coke, a skinny ladies' lunch and a massive restaurant dinner, or nothing, with a sleeping pill to take the edge off it all…

'I'm watching calories, I eat low fat, I train like a beast, but nothing ever changes. There's something wrong here.'

'Yes. All of it,' she said.

She spent some time talking to me about not just my diet, but my liver, my hormones, stress. When she mentioned something about cortisol, I said, 'But I don't eat that.'

'And you exercise too much. Stop all the training. You need to give your body a rest. You look tired.'

It all sounded bonkers. I listened intently, while not really listening. Could she really be right? Have I been getting it *all* wrong? I simply couldn't believe it. I'd give her a go but there was absolutely no way I was giving the training a break. I'd get fat. 'Okay, Jasmine. I'll try to give the training a break.'

'Let's put you on a diet of easily digested foods and a few days off some of the harder foods for your body to process.' She listed them all: alcohol, coffee, tea, gluten, sugar, dairy, meat, eggs. These foods would be reintroduced later, she explained, but for now I'd be eating a light diet of mostly vegetables.

While the coffee and the meat would come back, 'Artificial and processed foods, factory-made stuff, that's over for you now. Cut it out of your diet forever. That means the sweeteners have to go. No more Diet Coke.'

That was a major blow. Anyone on a diet knows this sweet, refreshing, bubbly, black drink is a gift handed to us chubby mortals from the diet gods. A guilt-free treat, to be used at any time.

Jasmine, like pretty much every health expert (except Derek), was very anti-artificial sweeteners. 'You don't need food designed in a chemistry lab. You need whole foods from nature.'

We would start on the Hemsley food in a week. 'Until then, please,' her tone was genuinely imploring, 'go off and use this transition time, eat regularly and not massive meals, relax, get lots of sleep, drink lots of water, and I would strongly recommend reducing the coffee, too.'

That night back at home I explained to Dawn what was coming with whacko diet number 1,563. She has a lot of patience but it's wearing thin. 'They want me to cut out the coffee,' I told her.

'Oh, no. No way,' she said. We were due to go to Oxford for the kids' half-term that week. 'No, Gary. I'm not having you coming off coffee and moody all week. We hardly ever see you. Don't do that to us.'

I figured I'd cut down a bit and go cold turkey on the first day. I'd be fine.

By the end of half-term I was already down from nineteen to ten coffees a day. Does that get me a sticker?

The day before I started on their food was a Sunday and the younger sister, Melissa, came over with my first three days' food. She started unpacking all these little brown paper pots and flasks full of soup. It was exciting, like Christmas. My day was broken down into three meals and three snacks – including the Rubbisher's favourite comedy material: seeds. It all looked good apart from the sauerkraut and kefir. 'Not sure about that,' I said, having a sniff. They start talking about the effect of fermented foods and their good bacteria on a healthy gut. More of my nodding and listening intently, while I'm not actually listening at all. 'Oh, I see, very interesting. I won't be eating that.'

Monday morning after half-term my PA Elisa came in and found me already at work and in high spirits. The first day of a new diet always gave me a brief surge of hope. 'Right! The Hemsley diet now. Peppermint tea please, Elisa?'

13

COLD TURKEY AND
A DINNER PARTY

'For the battles we have won,
for the day we reach the sun'

By midday I'm starting to feel a bit rough. As each minute grinds by I feel worse and worse. I have a headache; it feels like someone has stuck a screwdriver through the side of my head. I just can't get rid of it. I have to leave the studio, which I never do. I go to my bed and stay there. The next day, the headache is still there, but worse. I feel like someone has covered my ears. Shit! My hearing's going, my livelihood. I try to get up, it feels like I'm walking on marshmallows.

Why is the ground all spongy? Then the blindness starts. I can't see. I have terrible tunnel vision. I want to cry. What is happening?

What do you do in that situation? Dawn has no sympathy. I ring my new PA using the nearest of my two phones.

I'm a bit embarrassed. I'm a Northerner, I'm a Barlow. Even though I'm in the foetal position with the curtains drawn, lying at a junction between life and death, I'm trying to keep it light.

'I can't see, Elisa.'

She laughs, nervously.

'I can't fucking see, I'm blind, I feel blind, I'm blind.'

The poor woman's only worked for me for five days. There's a problem with our communication here. I don't know how to cope with suffering without resorting to humour. So my delivery must have a sort of comedy sketch quality because she keeps on with this nervous laughter but I actually think I might be dying here, even if I'm saying it like a punchline. 'I'm not joking. I feel like I can't, honestly, my eyes are glazing over. I feel terrible.'

'What is it you need, Gary?' she says. 'Is it support, is it an ambulance?'

'I don't know.'

I realise I am starting to scare her and tell her I'll be fine. I'm not. I lie there sweating bullets, palms wet, sick, scared and going deaf and blind for about thirty-six hours.

Turns out all I'd needed was a coffee with five sugars. I'd never given up caffeine *and* sugar before. Bad, isn't it? I'd gone cold turkey.

Of course I came out the other side. And hungry. That first week's food was very simple, and initially didn't taste of much because my tastebuds were knackered. Every day it got tastier, though.

At the end of the week I stood on the scales and, *holy shit*, I'd lost 18 pounds – over a stone. Although I'd been hungry, I didn't feel like I did on most other diets with that ravenous, deranged, tear-your-face-off feeling – this was hungry but cool with it. I wasn't climbing the walls. Add to this the fact that I'd had a lot of things removed from my diet that my two days in the foetal position had taught me were physically addictive. I had been eating very lightly, simply. My body has had a bit of a rest. Coming out the other side I felt euphoric. And I'd lost over a stone. And not done a minute's exercise.

I am pleased with that.

Right, I think, I'll lose myself even more next week because, whatever those girls say, I'm getting back to training.

When I went for my weekly meeting with Jasmine in tennis gear, I was proudly swinging a luminous sugar-free blue sports drink for her to admire.

First off, she was cross about the training. 'You're meant to be giving your body a rest.'

Better not tell her I'd done a weights session before the tennis. I told her how ecstatic I was about losing 18 pounds.

'Forget that. How do you feel? This isn't a weight loss service – this is about re-educating you into a new way of healthy eating so you feel really well.'

I was disappointed with that. The whole concept of healthy eating for me, the health for health's sake like Jason and Dawn were into, was completely unfathomable. Everything was about being smaller.

Instead of a pat on the back, she looked at my sports drink like I was swinging a dead rat. 'What the hell's that? That's got to stop.'

Don't worry, it's Powerade Zero, sugar-free, Jas. 'But full of sweetener. No more sweetener. Whole real foods only!'

The education had started because I remember glugging that stuff down on court later and thinking how synthetic and weirdly bitter the drink was. It didn't used to taste like this. These flashes of insight were the building blocks to a new me.

The next week, they started to introduce really good food, so good I rang up. 'Can I eat this?' Chestnut flour pancakes with Greek yoghurt. Can I really eat this? Beef stew. Unbelievable!

* * *

Jasmine became my main point of contact, and every week she'd try and teach me a little bit more. The most basic thing was to eat food in its most unadulterated form, eat as much as you want, whenever you want, because with real food the body will tell you when it's had enough.

You could put two apples, a pineapple and some carrots into a juicer and drink that in twenty seconds. Getting that lot down you in their unjuiced whole food form is a different story.

Toast? Toast. I could eat toast for hours. I remember sitting in a restaurant with a good breakfast ordering round after round of toast. It makes me so happy to eat toast but once you stop, it's all downhill from there. You give me a box of chocolates, I'll eat them all. Those sorts of foods, there's no stop button, you can just keep going. When I started eating in this new way, I could have half a chicken, roasted in butter (*roasted in butter. BUTTER!*) with a nice salad with lots of avocado and olive oil, Dijon mustard and lemon juice, salt, pepper, a few fresh herbs. Eat the skin. (*Eat the delicious crispy skin!*) I could have all that. I was full. And it was delicious. In fact, just writing this I'm thinking it'll make a good lunch for Dawn and me tomorrow. It's simple: eat food that hasn't been mucked around with.

I'm not hungry. I'm worried because if I'm not hungry, then I'm not losing weight. I ring Jasmine. The next day, I'm still not hungry. The next day's food includes pâté. As you know, pâté and pies are probably my two favourite foods. Normally, desperate Gaz, I only allow myself pâté on my birthday but here in my cardboard pot is chicken liver pâté. The next week I only lost four pounds but I'd already turned a bit of a corner. *I'm eating pâté!*

The Hemsleys opened the door to another world. My body is being fed food that is intensely nourishing. And I am happy. I feel alive for the first time in years. I'm more than happy, I'm euphoric. It's like a religious experience, this. For a moment there I can see the entire universe.

Once I started eating like this I couldn't believe I'd been led down this fat-free diet road for so long. To not be eating fat free any more felt like anarchy. For years when it came to food, I just shovelled it in, not considering that what I put in my body would affect me in one way or another. I thought of myself as a clean-living, wholesome guy, yet I'd been shovelling crap into my body for years. Is this any different from people coming off drink and drugs?

What's shit? I'll tell you what's shit. It's shit feeling guilty every time you put a fork with food on it into your mouth. It's shit constantly weighing yourself. It's shit not being able to eat what you want to eat.

I'm almost glad I tried all those diets, because I know none of them worked. All these diet books are peddling strange, disordered, confusing and most importantly unsustainable unhealthy systems that make a person feel like crap. Also, the stats ain't great. Did you know that 90 per cent of people on a diet will put the weight on again?

At this point I started to feel cheated and I started to feel pissed off because I've spent hundreds of pounds on books, thousands on dieticians and trainers and all these other people who were meant to know best. When I do my job, I do it properly. How had so many of these people been so bad at their jobs? All those years of thinking I was eating well, you know, with my Tracker bars. Now I wanted to sue them. Orangina, wanted to sue them too. Sunny D, I'll see you in court. Diet Coke, and all the ways that tons of sweetener were poured down my ignorant neck. I thought it was good for me because it had the word diet on it. These people are telling us bare-faced lies about being healthy. Processed food is junk. And that garbage is all I ate.

Then you've got an epidemic of obesity, even in little kids, and now the whole size-acceptance thing cranks up. It's a mess. You've got fat people suffering from malnutrition because the food out there has shedloads of calories, but it doesn't have enough nutrients to keep a human body healthy. Just consider that for a moment, the concept: malnourished fat people. Overfed and undernourished. Been there, done it. Burned the XXL T-shirt.

Now my food is every colour of the rainbow. My habits are changing. I start the day not with coffee now, but warm water and fresh lemon juice; I squeeze lemon on everything, in fact, it brings out flavours in the same magic way that salt and pepper do.

After a few weeks I was told I had to food shop for myself. The girls had given me a list and I took my sliver of free time off down Kensington High Street. Buckwheat flour. Where am I going to get that? Tried Tesco, tried Waitrose... In the end I found it in Whole Foods. Mung beans? I thought you only used them in jokes about hippies. Kefir. Ke-what? Kombucha. Bless you, do you need a tissue? I'm enjoying this. What an adventure.

The best in all of this is back at home. There's a new dad in the house and he's not on the sofa dozing or in the car waving his fist at the traffic, he's in the garden playing football. The afternoon sleeps are a thing of the past. Dawn could not have been happier about this.

Now I just needed to get her to eat with me.

'Have a try of this.' I'd offer her a forkful of sauerkraut.

'Shite.'

'Kefir, babe?'

'Filth.'

'Chia pudding?'

'Frog spawn.'

It was a beef stew that did it. I was sitting in the kitchen tucking into my latest delivery, and a fork appeared over my shoulder. 'What's that then? Smells good. Ooh, that's amazing. I like the rice.'

'Oh that's not rice, it's cauliflower.'

'Thought it was a bit tasteless. Not bad though…'

She was less excited about my offer for *The X Factor*, and for one major reason.

'Don't do it. The attention will be unbearable.'

'I've been on telly before; how much worse can it get?'

She was right about this. In the last few years we were going out to dinner less. I was missing a few more parents' evenings. As my face became more familiar, I was becoming more reclusive again. We were at the Oxford house one weekend and talking about this. I went, 'Don't be silly. It'll be fine.'

Dawn: 'It's already pretty bad, Gary. If you get more famous we'll never get you out of the house. You'll just want to stay in the whole time. You won't want to go anywhere or do anything because of the attention.'

Me: 'No, no, no. You're wrong. I don't mind going out. To prove it, we're all going shopping.'

We went to our local village. I took them all to the toy shop. I strolled confidently round the shop, I said a cheery 'Hello' to the staff. It was bravado on my part. Sure enough, a couple of people come up and want to have a little chat. Then some woman comes flying out of the estate agents. A few more come running over from Asda and before long it was chaos. Chaos. But I can't be wrong. So I'm working my way through the people acting dead normal as I disappear under a sea of arms. 'See, kids, it's fine. I'm all right.'

People are lovely wherever I go. I don't mind. My family struggle with it. Dan takes everything in his stride. The girls find it excruciating. Dawn and Emily hate it because it's intrusive and Daisy has been known to march over and say, 'Leave my Daddy alone!'

There's two ways to approach the problem. Say you're on holiday, staying in a hotel. One way is to keep your eye on everyone all the time, keep your sunglasses on the whole holiday, keep the shade on you all the time, hold the menu up in front of your face when anyone's got their phone out. You can do the whole week in a state of high alert. Or there's the right way. At the beginning of the week, you can go up, go, 'Hey, guys, how you doing? Do you want to have a quick picture? Do us a favour, when I'm with the family, don't take any pictures, but lovely to meet you, great stuff.'

* * *

I promised the family this new job would change nothing in our lives. Now I had to set about making sure that was true. It wasn't extra fame that was worrying me, it was what this shiny-floored juggernaut, *The X Factor*, really was. I've got a very healthy address book of TV professionals and I set about ringing every single one of them.

'*The X Factor*. What's it all about?'

To the last, they all said the same thing. 'The only thing anyone cares about in that building is *The X Factor*. They won't mind throwing you under the bus, using you to get a headline, feeding you a line that will end your career, as long as *The X Factor* gets a mention.'

This was terrifying. Is this the show I'd watched and enjoyed for all these years? 'Yup,' came the response, 'You don't go in there alone, you need back-up.'

It was Dawn who suggested Eliot. 'He's not only going to be great with the singers, he can be your eyes and ears too.'

'Perfect.'

I phoned James Corden. 'I'm going to be on *The X Factor*. I need someone watching my back who understands telly and will spot all their little producer games they play. Just someone with a TV head to go, 'Listen. The ratings are down this week so they're going to be looking to create a stir.' Someone to just warn me of things before they happen.'

'I've got the guy.'

He introduced me to Ben Winston, who is now his producer on *The Late Late Show*. One of the best things about *The X Factor* was meeting Ben.

Armed with Team GB, I was excited by the challenge and it would certainly keep me busy. My diet might have changed, but I haven't slowed down one bit. If anything, the new-found energy is helping me work harder…

The X Factor was announced in spring 2011. For the first time in a decade, the promo pictures they put out with the statement didn't make me want to jump out of the window. I looked like the me I wanted to be. The food bag became an extra team member. When I started on *The X Factor*, my pots and flasks followed me everywhere. My fellow judges were the singer Tulisa Contostavlos, who was best known then for being in the garage act, N-Dubz; Louis Walsh, the old manager of Boyzone and Westlife; and the singer Kelly Rowland, who was also in Destiny's Child.

I loved Kelly; she lived and looked like an athlete. Americans can embrace insane levels of healthiness, I reckon as a response to the fact that they live alongside some of the most poisonous junk that man has ever called food. As we lived and worked together on set, it was Kelly's nose that would be in everything I was eating.

'Oooh. What's that?'

'Oh, it's butternut squash curry and this is a buckwheat chapati.'

'Oh, Gary, is that risotto?'

'Oh no, kid, it's amaranth and sea kelp with cashew parmesan.'

'You're one lucky dude.'

There's no other word, she was jealous. Sitting to my right on the judges' table, she never stopped moaning about the food on the set and understandably so, it was crap.

A little further down, however, sat Tulisa. 'What's them seeds?' A rubbisher fortunately too young to remember Trill. Tulisa took the piss out of my little food pots, just like we all did to Jason. I didn't care.

It's pretty hard to abuse the sort of whole foods I'm eating now. But I found a way. Of course, I took it too far. Obsession created a pop star out of a nerdy teenage kid locked away in his bedroom in Frodsham. Obsession filled houses and barns and storage units with synths. And obsession got me into sample-size Dior, designed for the pipe-cleaner boy models on the catwalk.

I worked out that by eating this good food, and by staying always on the edge of hunger, I could drop a lot of weight.

* * *

In the autumn I did *The Jonathan Ross Show*. By now I've lost three stone. I'm in the dressing room and Lizzie, lovely Lizzie, who does Take That's grooming and always makes me feel so good about myself, is standing behind me working on the pop star hair. In the mirror she looked me in the eye, over the top of my head and said, 'I don't know how to say this but I think you've lost too much weight.' Well, I glowed inside at that, didn't I, even though she said it not as a compliment but a genuine worry.

Was I worried? Was I fuck. Life was grand.

As we travelled round the country doing auditions, I was shocked at the lack of talent out there. When we did unearth some, I was appalled at how little they were prepared to work. Not Little Mix – those girls were cracking, they were totally professional and dying to learn. They were determined to make it work from day one. El worked with them at the boot camp stage and immediately called Kelly and me to say we had something special. The next day they did an impromptu show for the judges in the hotel. They were brilliant.

Kelly and I went to the house quite a lot, and we were always there early on filming day for rehearsals with our artists.

It was around the time I was starting to get seriously evangelical about the food. I became a major pain in the arse with it, like the reformed smoker or the self-righteous non-drinker. I used to put stickers on the side of people's Diet Coke, saying things like 'POISON!' and 'tut-tut'. I became a complete nightmare. Bear in mind, as well, I'd ignored Dawn quietly telling me that artificial sweetener is carcinogenic for a decade and now I was a complete know-it-all. One of our Take That security guys since way back in the day is called James. He got a few stickers on his Diet Coke because I'm a pain in the arse, you know, but also because these are people I love and I want them to be well. I don't want any of them poisoned by Diet Coke or any other crap food. I evangelised to people around me thinking they'd love this, too. (Though I do like annoying people as well.)

It's all quite a turnaround from the man too embarrassed to say 'no thanks' to onion rings. Now I'm pointing at my plate going, 'Yup, you might want to see what I'm having.' I've turned into a zealot and a nag. 'Are you kidding me? You cannot eat this! Do you not want to see fifty? I thought you wanted a big party. Instead you'll be in hospital with your first heart attack.'

I started on the guys at *The X Factor*. I was hard on Tulisa. She comes in with her chicken nuggets and fries and I'm on her. 'See that spot on your chin? That's the work of Ronald McDonald.'

I was a complete nightmare.

By the time we went to the live shows, between our whole Team GB in the dressing room – El, Ben, Luke, Lizzie, Elisa, James – we developed a bad case of showbiz paranoia. Was the dressing room bugged? They always seemed to know what was being talked about behind closed doors, and eaten, too. Whatever happened in that building always found its way to the press.

I hate all that manipulative nonsense but the viewers love it, they lap it up. Most of the 'beef' on the show was a load of tabloid-friendly bollocks. About half an hour before the show goes live, the producers would come in and they'd go, 'Oh my God. That Misha. She's a bully. Can't believe it. She is such a bully. In fact, you know what? You should say it. You should say it on air. She's just bullied everyone all week.'

'Oh dear, is she a terrible bully?' I'd say, 'I can't believe it. How awful.'

They leave the room. Ben: 'Do not say that.'

Later, Misha comes on, and we're all sitting in the judges' chairs.

Tulisa: 'I think you're a bully.'

She said it!

Louis: 'I think you're a bully.'

He said it, too.

It's all gonna kick off now; that'll be three days on the tabloid front pages.

My turn. 'Whoa. I've not seen any of this. I'm not commenting. We're only here to talk about what's in front of us on the show.' I went the other way, completely. Thank you, Ben. Knowing he had my back let me get on and enjoy the job. I loved it; it's a brilliant show to be a part of.

The best place in the *X Factor* building was my dressing room. Most of the other judges were in there often enough. I'd sit there, with my old friend, El, and my new friend, Ben, and brainstorm.

Ben had a whole other thing going on. He was making a One Direction documentary at the time. He'd done all their videos. I was desperate to do something with him away from *The X Factor*. I mentioned one night that I had agreed to do the Jubilee song and had found a partner, Andrew Lloyd Webber.

This caught our imagination and for the next hour we were like over-excited schoolboys. 'Wouldn't it be great if...'

'You interviewed the entire royal family about the Queen's favourite music.'

'And pulled together a choir from the whole Commonwealth for the song.'

'No! *Travel* the whole Commonwealth.'

'Make the record on the move.'

'That'd make a great documentary; I could pitch that to the BBC,' said Ben.

'And at the end, we play the song to the Queen.'

'Don't be daft. She doesn't do telly.'

It all sounded proper exciting, and completely unrealistic.

Isn't that what creativity is all about?

Remember the show-off? Well, he's back. I wanted to share the secret.

I pulled out some ridiculously expensive old Bordeaux and got Jas and Mel in to cook. Kelly, Dermot and Tulisa were there. They'd all been teasing me saying they were going for KFC before they came round to my house for tiny portions of rabbit food out of a cardboard pot. As the girls brought out the courses, they'd explain what the food was all about. Tulisa wasn't into some of it. 'Sauerkraut? I'm not eating that.'

Kelly, however, couldn't get enough of it. Cauliflower mash and osso bucco – they loved that.

As I popped in and out of the kitchen, Jasmine told me to get Kelly to slow down on the sauerkraut. The girl was mad for it.

After dinner I stood with Jas and her boyfriend, Nick, drinking one more glass. I told Jas, 'Dawn says I'm a nicer person. Not snapping at the kids. Thanks for all this.'

Jas was briefly touched by this compliment and then she started talking about Kelly and the sauerkraut again. 'I'm a bit concerned. I've never seen anyone eat so much sauerkraut.'

In the morning she texted me to check everything was okay, saying she hadn't slept a wink because there was no way Kelly Rowland's digestive system could cope with that much friendly bacteria. Sure enough, Kelly wasn't well the next day. Turns out you can have too much of a good thing.

That dinner would make a great *Star Stories*.

14

FIVE MEN, ONE GIANT, HALF AN APPLE

'It wasn't good'

'**M**ake it stop, Jamesy boy!' I'm laughing despite myself. Is this the ride of my life or the end of it? Either way, it's bumpy up here. How my security guy, James, is going to 'make it stop!' I don't know, but it's at times like this you cry out for Mummy or your bodyguard. The fuselage bucks and rattles like a drum. Our arses are out of their seats more than in them as our plane climbs to 5,000 feet and then immediately descends back down. Elisa is sunk under her coat, saying prayers. There's no droll announcements from the pilot about cruising at 30,000 feet when you take an eleven-minute flight across London.

I have to get from shooting *The X Factor* auditions at the O2 to Wembley Stadium where the Progress Tour has landed for eight nights. The show that combines the new four-man Take That, Robbie Williams, and the old five-man Take That, will be on stage in thirty minutes; I need to be there fast. It's a distance of maybe six miles as the crow flies, but to drive will take hours. So we fly from City Airport in the east to RAF Northolt in the west.

Nothing like a light aircraft to remind you of your mortality.

I was 40 that year on 20 January. With excitement in her voice, Dawn asked me how I'd like to celebrate.

I didn't need to think about that too long. 'With a gig, I think, don't you?'

'Bloody hell, it's all about you, isn't it.'

'I'm forty, yes it is, thanks.'

Cue the great Dawn Barlow eye-rolls. She's not danced for a few years but those eye-rolls are still en pointe.

I hired Shepherd's Bush Empire, the sort of cool, iconic venue which is far too small for Take That to play. I love these atmospheric theatres that sound amazing to a musician's ear. This wasn't work, it was a birthday treat. The last time I was here was at a War Child benefit after the Brits in 2009, when I was part of a wannabe boy band Chris Martin put together: him, Bono, Brandon Flowers and me. Shame there was no Instagram back then.

As with everything I'm involved in, it couldn't just be an intimate bash among friends. This birthday gig grew and grew. Radio 2 broadcast it live, with Jo Whiley doing links from the side of the stage. We sold tickets and gave all the money to the family of Chris Dagley, who had tragically been killed on his motorbike. Chris was an old drummer who played with us in the nineties, and it meant the world to us that we could do this.

The guest performances piled up: Chris Martin, Ellie Goulding, Midge Ure, Stuart Price and of course Mark, Jay and Howard. I finished with 'Never Forget' and looked up to see Daniel and Emily with their arms in the air. And there's Dawn, too; all arms, no eye-rolls.

After the gig I went and joined all my friends and family on the second level and got on the cake and champers. I look around and there's Claudia Schiffer and Gwyneth Paltrow talking to my kids.

It's 2011. Welcome to my world.

Seven minutes into the flight we pass over Wembley. It's already full. The band I pored over in my teenage bedroom, the Pet Shop Boys, are on stage: our support act. I can see Om, the 60-ft-high robot who slowly rises up throughout the show until he is standing over us, Christ-like, with his eyes blazing. Om came to life in our production rehearsals on an RAF base where they built Zeppelins in World War I. Here, at Cardington, we watched 'Metal Mickey' rise to his full height for the first time.

It was Mark and Jason's idea, the whole progress of man concept to the album we called *Progress*.

These links between music, visual and live shows were becoming increasingly instinctual to us with every record we made. We love being on a bus going somewhere talking about how you make a show big enough to fill a stadium like Wembley; how you make it your own for the night. We were on a coach in Amsterdam when Mark said, 'I can see a giant man, a robot, spiritual figure to aspire to, this evolution of man… It should feel like Christ the Redeemer that looks over Rio, towering over us all in the middle of the stadium.'

Now the image is in our heads, we have to chase it, however mad it might have been. We knew it had never been done before. The idea was turned down by three companies who said it wasn't possible. Finally we found a team of people genius – and mad – enough to take this on.

That tour was so ambitious, it's gone down in industry history. Not long after it ended, our production manager was poached to do Beyoncé's Mrs Carter Tour. We had used the most sophisticated engineers in the business and, even then, we were pushing at the boundaries of what is possible in a live show. We pushed and pushed for things that would amaze audiences.

He was christened 'Om', the Sanskrit word for mantra, which is meant to be the sound of god. This sixth member of Take That was stupendous. And complicated. Om had hundreds of thousands of parts of mechanical hardware; basically, the Christ-like centrepiece of this 15 million quid show just hated the rain. He was incredibly human, too. He had good days.

And bad days.

Opening night. Sunderland. 'Why's Om not moving?'

A few days later. Glasgow. I'm taking a bow and looking at this thing and crying into the radio mic, 'He's moving, but in the wrong direction.'

By now, Om is less respectfully known by me, the great Rubbisher, as 'Tom'.

Wembley Stadium. 'Oh God, no! Tom's stuck in the shitting position again.'

We took it personally. The truth is, his failures felt like ours. We weren't used to things going wrong on a nightly basis. One or two events per tour, not per night.

One night in Manchester, Tom broke down, leaving Howard and Mark having to climb down off his giant hands on rusty ladders. Another night, Howard had to be rescued in a cherry picker, those platforms they use to fix street lights. The next song in the set was 'Never Forget'. Still stuck in Tom's palm, Howard started to sing.

'We've come a long way. But we're not sure how we are gonna get down.'

Classic Howard.

What's next? Every night we went on stage wondering if Tom would be taking a sit-down strike again.

Rain is a problem only stadium bands will understand. The weather had worked for us on The Circus Tour, to the point where the setting sun was built into our lighting programme.

On Progress, I can't tell you the amount of time spent on our phones checking the weather apps, praying for change. The first thing you think of is the poor audience getting wet. But why worry? The audience love it when it rains. Especially when you get wet, too. What you think is the end of the world actually makes the night. (But not for Tom.)

Mother Nature clearly wasn't an original Take That fan. You'd put money on it raining through the British summer but, even when we played San Siro Stadium in Italy, it rained on us and the 90,000 people in the audience.

We started to clock a feature in these Progress audiences that packed the football grounds. There was a home and an away crowd: TT fans vs Robbie fans. So present was this, Robbie asked a miserable-looking audience member one night: 'Are you a Take That fundamentalist?' Another night Robbie stopped the show. The band stopped playing. He pointed to a girl in the audience: 'What's with the face like a slapped arse? If Gary can forgive me, so can you.'

When we were sitting in that studio in New York in September 2009, I was already problem-solving like mad in my head. How are we going to do this with two management companies, two road managers, two tour managers, two bands, two record labels, two stylists, two of everything?

There was only one way to do it; we had to lead by example.

How we were going to make this crazy plan work was a regular conversation throughout the recording of *Progress*. And it served as a reminder of how far we had all come. From five very pretty boys who did exactly what they were told, to now calling the shots. Big shots, at that.

* * *

We got everyone together. 'Listen, I don't know how the hell you're going to do this but you have to make it work. If you can't, just bugger off now. Look at us, we've been friends, enemies, brothers, it's only one album and one tour. Get on with it. We don't want to deal with any drama.'

I am very proud of Progress. But I can't pretend the show didn't have a complicated energy, especially in contrast to the warmth and the fun of The Circus.

Creatively, structurally, emotionally... mechanically, Progress was a tough nut to crack. Not least, how would the show run? Us five decided, let's open with four-piece Take That – years 2006 to 2009, then Rob can do his solo stuff and then in the last hour we all come out and do this latest album together and cover original repertoire from the nineties. Simple, yeah?

Kim was sceptical. He always saw songs like 'Angels' and 'Rule The World' as big closing numbers. Us five overruled him. We were sure we had it right.

We finish our segment with 'Shine'. The place is going crazy. We come off. The baton passes to Rob. The next thirty minutes are his.

This is where we shoot ourselves in the foot.

The thing with performing is that it's not just about warming the audience up. *You've* warmed up, *you're* in a flow that has abruptly stopped, and suddenly you're sitting backstage in a sweaty little marquee being offered a cup of tea. It was like a dentist's waiting room back there; it's showbiz purgatory this tent where I sat for half an hour listening to a madness that you're not even part of.

I'd come off night after night feeling unfulfilled. But what could we do? The only alternative was to put Rob through the same. One of us had to go through it. It ended up being us. That tour was an experiment on an epic scale. Could it be done? Yes. Was it a moment? Yes. Did we get stuff wrong? Definitely.

And the lesson we learned? Once you're on, you stay on. Pop music has no intervals.

I didn't fly seven miles across London every night. One day we drove. And we paid the price for our cowardice. We were at a standstill in the Blackwall Tunnel and a chauffeur-driven motorbike had to meet us in the jam. I was bundled out of the door and onto the back of this bike while Elisa followed on by Tube with the food bag. This black and grey padded cooler bag with the day's food was permanently near me during this time. If it wasn't, I panicked. At this time, the food bag is the latest fifth Beatle, it's my crutch, it's my safe place.

Now I have seen the light. I feel light. I am light. I am often hungry but not in the way I was back in the bad old dieting days. This new kind of hunger is a bit of a buzz, and it almost feeds me energy; it's different from the roller-coastering of the sugar and caffeine years. I'm very aware of my body; it feels strong, lean and full of life. I'm slim and it is awesome.

There was so much about this show and the whole situation that was totally out of my hands. It's not a comfortable place for me, that. When I lose control in one area, I grab it back in another. The easiest place to start is food. Food is one thing we think we can control when everything around us is uncontrollable.

Being around Rob was great for all of us. It was a constant celebration. But it brought out some insecurities in me. Watching Rob spring onto the stage with virtually no rehearsal, having just put out his last fag, and then proceeding to slay the audience, was, frankly, annoying.

That's not me. We are both performers to our bones but our approach to getting a great performance could not be more different. I'll do six weeks of rehearsals. I'll know what I'm singing and where I'm standing for every moment of the show. I depend on preparation. Rob just rocks on there. You can't help but feel like he's better.

On that tour, it was absolutely inevitable that I would end up competitive dieting with Robbie.

Forget anthems, record sales, tickets sold, houses and all the other status symbols. The battle between Rob and Gaz would be fought over apples.

Rob and I were both on sparkly leotard form, we were top peacocks and we felt good. It was all a load of fun, but I particularly remember him eating an apple and I watched him eat the whole thing before making sure he was watching me as I made a point of cutting my own apple in two. 'Think I'll just have half.'

* * *

Simon Moran rang me the morning after one of the final Wembley dates. 'Did you hear? Last night?'

'What?'

'The whole stadium sang "Rule The World" after you'd gone off.' He's not one for big emotional statements, but Simon made the hair on the back of my neck stand up.

Progress was the biggest we've ever been. None of us will ever play eight nights at Wembley Stadium again. It was the pinnacle of us as a band. Seven years later, in 2018, it's still the biggest selling British tour ever and The Circus is the third; some fella called Ed Sheeran nudged us off the number two spot. I'm very proud of that.

So there we are. Rob popped back for a bit, we all shared a bit of our magic with each other, and he popped off again. That's Progress.

What next? A little break, before the next storm arrives.

Our favourite holidays are when we go away with Jason and Ange Donovan. Our kids all went to school together, they're all the same age and they get on great. Jason and I made friends at the gates back in the noughties while we were on the school run – him on his skateboard, me in the Range Rover. We went to France with them after Progress and I got myself ready for *The X Factor* live shows. Together, Jason and I become an act. The girls sit and talk about us right in our faces, our harshest critics. They're like the two old dudes in *The Muppets*, up in the royal box, passing comment, mostly on how immature we are.

Jason and I like to assume celebrities' identities when we're on holiday. One year we spoke in Michael Caine's voice for the whole holiday. Another year, Cliff Richard. Gordon Ramsay's always a good one if we run out of ideas. This year, the villa enjoyed – if 'enjoyed' is the right word – me and Jason as David Attenborough. We were narrating every move as if it was a nature documentary.

'And the female moves to the nest well ahead of the male to escape the inevitable holiday mating ritual.'

'Once again we see the female ignoring an elaborate mating dance from the male.'

'And the female is using the offspring as an excuse for rejecting the male's advances…'

* * *

The summer of Attenborough was spliced up with Bruce Forsyth because Jason was going on *Strictly*. 'I'm going to start practising early,' he says, as he's dancing round the swimming pool for two hours a day with a mop over his shoulder.

We all sat and judged him. He's terrible. Everyone's watching from behind their hands.

'Jason,' says Bruce Forsyth (me), 'you're my favourite.'

Those are the words you don't want to hear from Bruce. When Brucie said that it meant you were shit, like Ann Widdecombe or Andy Murray's mum.

'Jason. You're definitely my favourite.'

Day by day he's not getting any better. Us two would get up and make a proper entrance every morning. Samba into breakfast singing the *Strictly* theme. Charleston to the coffee machine. Waltz round the pool. Tripping down any stairway sideways, arms held wide, like Fred Astaire.

'Jason! You're my favourite.'

We're just stupid together. Dawn and Ange are there, all tuts, eye-rolls and side glances. Sometimes they're hamming it up because you can see them trying not to laugh; sometimes they hide it so well you'd almost think they didn't find it funny at all.

We do this whole thing with the kids. 'Hey, kids, imagine if we were the sort of dads who wear suits, the sort where you came into our office for a meeting, for a formal talk about important things. You know, "Now then, young Daniel, we need to discuss whether you are going to Oxford or Cambridge."'

They're all groaning in unison, 'I *wish* I had a dad like that. Then we wouldn't have to put up with *you*.'

We were just two silly showbiz dads gearing up for an exciting winter of big Saturday night TV.

15

ONE PIG AND FIFTY CROCODILES

'Hear a thousand voices shouting love'

Prince Harry had advised me on his grandmother's musical tastes. She'd love something that 'spans cultures' and 'nothing loud and modern – follow your instinct, you'll be fine'.

We literally made that record on the road with a laptop, a 'Zoom' handheld digital recorder and a mic. On and off for four months we racked up the air miles to Jamaica, Australia, Kenya, South Africa and the Solomon Islands.

Ben got this documentary *On Her Majesty's Service* commissioned in February 2012. He rings to tell me, then an hour later, calls back. 'We're going to be going to five countries. How are you going to deal with all these bags of food you need? I've got to produce this documentary. How am I going to travel with you?'

'Easy. I'll strap it to my body with gaffer tape and if anyone tries to take it off me I'll kill them with my bare hands. And then eat them.'

Keeping me fed while I toured Progress was already like a military operation. Now the operation's gone global. And there would be no Elisa, making the impossible happen in time for my 3pm snack. Jamaica one week, Africa the next. Sometimes I'd need to travel with up to a week's worth of food. I won't eat anything unless it's Daddy's Special Food. Mariah Carey's got nothing on me.

Jamaica was brilliant. I took Mum with me. Since Dad died she joined me more and more. She is brilliant to travel with, incredibly curious and unlike me, patient. Nearly 70 and nothing fazed her. Throughout these trips there's so much time to kill, and nothing fills a void like a quiz or a word game. In Jamaica we played a word game where you had to give a book title and an author that was related. You know that game: *Central Heating* by Ray Diator.

⋆ ⋆ ⋆

Our first visit was to percussionists in a Rastafarian community. I ate my cinnamon almond porridge on the way in the car. We all set off up to their mountaintop community. Mum shot off like a racing snake, she's so fit. As we neared these Rasta musicians I caught up. 'Isn't this good, Mum? We don't do this every day.'

'I know,' she said, 'isn't it lovely? And doesn't it smell lovely?'

It may have only been 8am but the air was already thick with the herbal aroma of burning marijuana.

I was thirsty and wondered if there was anything I'd be able to drink up here. The top Rasta guy starts doling out these bottles of home-made kombucha. I couldn't believe it. I was like, 'Get in!' I struggled to find kombucha in the Royal Borough of Kensington and Chelsea back then, and here it was, probiotic nirvana, 1,500ft above sea level in Jamaica. Result!

I let Mum try it first. She took a sip. 'No thanks. Not for me.' From there, we recorded the great reggae and jazz guitarist, Ernest Ranglin at Geejam Studio, which is in a gorgeous part of the island called Port Antonio. I was impressed because Jon Baker, the owner of Geejam, knew Banksy and there was evidence of this everywhere. The day we were leaving, Mum was looking at all the Banksy rats, going, 'Look at all these lovely mice on the wall.'

One of the reasons for hitting Jamaica was we could get time with Prince Harry. By time I mean ten minutes. When we'd done our first interview about the project with Prince Charles, he'd said, 'Speak to the family. They'll tell you what she wants.'

I wanted Harry to play tambourine on 'Sing'. We collared him on a visit to a school in Jamaica and, two days later, in Montego Bay, we were given ten minutes to interview him and get the essential tambourine strike on tape. El handed me this little handheld recorder we'd been using to record music all over the Commonwealth.

Ben needs me to ask him a few questions on camera while recording the tambourine bit for the song. 'Right, you've got to ask him this, this, this.'

El said, 'Make sure when you record him, the red light is solidly on, and hold it close.'

The royal team around him kept reminding me, 'You've got ten minutes.'

There was press everywhere, this huge junket that follows the royals wherever they go like a plague of locusts. The air was thick with them. I'm a pretty calm guy. The trials of Tom on Progress was nothing compared to getting this Prince Harry. I was starting to sweat with the pressure.

Suddenly, Harry appears, he just pops his head round the corner and says, 'Hello.'

Right, ten minutes, let's go. I feel a need to entertain him, be polite, make him laugh. 'Hello there, Your Highness. Nice weather, eh? Do you think nature created this Sandals resort or some humans? This won't take long. You must get sick of all this nonsense, I know I do. Loving the flip-flops, by the way, very Jamaica.'

Ten minutes is now three minutes, two, one... I finally get round to asking the questions about his grandmother's music tastes. The red light's flashing away and we record the key 'Bash!' We've got Harry's tambourine contribution in the bag. I breathe for the first time in ten minutes.

Harry says, 'This is not going to be on it, I don't believe it.'

'It will, oh it will,' I say.

Harry leaves and El looks at me. 'He's right you know, Gaz. You've not recorded a thing, you fucking idiot. The light was flashing red: standby. It's solid red on record.'

A few hours later, at the end of another long day, Mark the sound guy came over and gave us a present. 'There it is. Merry Christmas.'

His boom mic had picked up Harry's big moment and it sounded perfect. Obviously it's the tambourine that made the record.

* * *

While we were on the road making 'Sing', I kept to my strict regime. Everyone else was having the hotel breakfasts, trying the local cuisine and there's me with my Hemsley menu of little pots of bean stew, bone broth, flaxseed buns, spirulina shots, quinoa porridge and a tower of Paradise bars – the clean eaters' answer to a red Bounty. As the crew enjoyed a cold beer at the end of a long day shooting, I'd be joining in with a refreshing strawberry and mint cooler.

After Africa, on to Sydney. We filmed a blind Aboriginal guitar player, Gurrumul, in the Blue Mountains. I had booked a hotel room with a kitchen, and was making up my Hemsley food in the morning and taking it with me for filming.

As we leave Sydney for the Solomon Islands, and with a few days more filming to get in the can, my food runs out. What a disaster.

Added to that, there's a hurricane coming. We were due to film with musicians in a village called Oterama in the coastal rainforest of Malaita, an island about fifty miles east from the capital island of Honiara. Normally, this would be a thirty-minute plane ride. Easy! With a hurricane, however, it's a nine-hour journey by boat. The only one fit for the voyage in this storm is the coastguard's, which immediately begs the question, who rescues the coastguard?

There are 900 islands in the Solomons, Australia is 1,500 miles to the west, next stop to the east is Peru, 9,000 miles away. The nearest Paradise Bar is 10,000 miles north in London. I'd never been anywhere so remote. I was glad I had friends around me. Being this far away from home could've felt very isolated.

There was no way for me to whip up some of Daddy's Special Food in the Solomons, and I was in a mild panic about that. The things I do for Queen and country. Honestly! I set off for a long two days' filming to this island with just a bag of fruit.

After an uneventful nine hours at sea, the hurricane seemed to have passed us by. We landed on Malaita and the tribe we were filming came to pick us up in dug-out canoes. They paddled us inland for an hour under a thick canopy of vines and trees. Even in daylight, it was dark, cool and green. The guys from the tribe were in full regalia, teeth round their necks, shells on their little loincloths, the jewellery and painted faces. This was special, something else.

There was a huge welcoming party on the shore as we arrived and we had to dance our way into the village as they sang and chanted what were, hopefully, friendly words. This was thrilling and for a moment, in all the endless smiling and handshaking and nodding, I forgot we were there to work.

I looked across to see Ben tapping his watch. The hurricane did not pass us by, it was following us. We've got about three hours to rehearse and record these guys playing their flutes and pan pipes before we have to leave. However, the leader of the village announces with a flourish, 'First, we invite you to lunch.'

I'm having a proper wig-out inside. Serious panic. Not about the hurricane, mind. No, I'm scared about the food. 'Wonderful. What is it?'

'We killed a pig,' he says. 'It's been hung all week. We cooked it last night and, stuffed it all in bamboo and buried it to keep it warm.'

I took a moment to think about this. 'So, you reared the pig yourself?'

He nods.

I shuffled through Jasmine's rules: no processed food; know your provenance; is it organic? With every question I asked myself about this food, the more interested I was in eating it. We were sitting in the middle of their vegetable garden. This is it. I've found the holy grail. This is what these foodies dream of.

I grabbed a piece of bamboo and smashed my way through to the meat which was lightly spiced. My teeth just sank in and some of the juice tried to escape down my face but, don't worry, my tongue got it. Delicious. God. It was the best pork I've ever tasted in my life.

'Dessert, anyone?' Mr Sugar Free My Body Is a Temple starts sweating again. A guy shimmies up the tree and throws a papaya down. It hasn't even got a little sticker on it. More 'best I've ever tasted' moments followed.

We got straight on with recording which was super-fast because they were great; they had rehearsed like a Barlow. We had it in the can and Ben was chasing us down the mountain back to the dug-out canoes. The wind was picking up, the storm was on its way, as was dusk, which lasts two minutes on the equator before pitch-black descends.

It was like someone just turned out the lights. Everyone was starting to lose their cool; you could hear the panic. 'It's getting too late. We're going to get stuck here.'

Before we set off on our little wooden boat, all the villagers were sitting with their legs dangling over the side. Someone pulled out a flashlight and shone it on our exit route. There, looking at us, were fifty pairs of eyes. Crocodiles. The villagers whipped their legs back in and we set off. 'Boom, boom, boom' through the water with the crocodiles knocking against the boat as we plough through them. 'Boom, boom, boom.'

It was horrible and I was awful worried about El and Ben in the boat behind me. I could hear Eliot's voice behind me fading as the distance between us grew: 'Gaz. Gaaaaz!'

'We've had it here,' I thought, thudding downstream through the crocs, 'and I haven't even sorted the lead vocals yet.'

I only really took a deep breath once everyone was safely back on the boat for the return journey to Honiara. We'd made it.

The ship glided out of the lagoon and straight into the hurricane's sidewind, which hit us with such an unbelievable force. The rain came down like hammers. From here on in, for nine hours, huge wave after huge wave hit us. It was relentless. Miserable. It was like being repeatedly thrown over Niagara Falls in a barrel. I sat in the captain's chair watching the horizon the entire way home, willing us back to land.

I was waiting on the deck as we came into port. I leapt off that moving boat and started running. I ran all the way back to our hotel. For the first time in years I carried my own bag.

Every time I got home from those Commonwealth trips, I'd regale the kids with my stories of Prince Harry, the vastness of the Kibera slum, fighting ten-foot waves on a rescue boat and men wearing necklaces of human teeth.

'And?' They were very unimpressed. 'When are you going away again?'

* * *

I feel a bit sorry for the royal family. My experience of fame is that it isn't nice. It's one hundred per cent not healthy. It's a pain. That I can go on the stage is great, I love it, but walking down the street and being grabbed and stared at? That's not good. That's probably why there's so much protocol around touching the royals.

Having spent a bit of time around 'The Firm', I do feel for them. They are the original celebrities and they do a magnificent job for our country. Charity, diplomacy, tourism, trade: I think the list of what's good about them is a long one. It's a hell of a service they do.

You only get one life. Just the one. And theirs is given over to this country. Prince Charles, bless him. All he wants to do is his gardening and he gets dragged away from talking to his plants to these charity things or diplomatic tours or trade stuff where you've got to talk to people. He's constantly having to watch himself. He often gets criticised for having political views and for writing letters to the government. You're not allowed to think when you're a royal.

Sure, they get to live in big houses but it's not a better life they have in all those stately homes and castles. In the end, the Queen lives in a few cosy rooms, a bit like Dawn and I were at Delamere. All the palaces in the world wouldn't make me want to swap with them.

I've seen them in action. They're respectful and polite. They have everyone lined up and they have someone pointing out who they've got to speak to. When Charles met Our Ian, he had a really good chat with him. He already knew Ian was a builder, but I didn't tell him; someone had done their homework, and he was really pretty up with it all. You'd be lucky if a pop star doing a meet 'n' greet could be bothered with all that. And just as most other people his age are slowing down and going on cruises, his job's just hotting up.

Doing the Diamond Jubilee concert was not without its tensions.

According to the BBC, that June was the wettest since records began in 1910. Some magnificent British weather for this magnificent year. The concert was on Monday, 4 June, a special bank holiday. On the Sunday the flotilla on the river had been a washout. Reminded me of the Solomon Islands.

In the afternoon there were genuine concerns that the Queen would not turn up. The morning of the gig, the Duke of Edinburgh had gone into hospital. Standing in the rain the day before had done the poor guy in. We were prepared for every scenario. The man's 92, and everyone's bracing themselves for bad news. Is the Queen coming? Is she not?

★   ★   ★

For us artists, the work had started early in the day. The artists' village in Green Park was busy by mid-afternoon. There were TV and radio interviews, last-minute rehearsals, stylists and make-up artists pulling giant wheelie suitcases, the inevitable golf buggies ferrying musicians back and forth to the stage. Two years of emailing came alive before my eyes. It hit me for the first time; this was really happening. It's only then I realised it was a seriously important event.

The show started and I took my producer's hat off and put on my sparkly shirt. Now, I'm just another turn in the show. We heard the roar of the Red Arrows overhead and I watched their fly-past on my screen in the dressing room. I'd said early on we must have the Red Arrows; I'd always loved them since I was a kid. Goosebumps guaranteed and the perfect warning something big's about to happen.

The line-up was just ridiculous, a show where everyone's top of the bill. Robbie opened it with a bang. Jessie blew me away. That girl's technically one of the best singers in the world. Cheryl Cole and I met stage left before we went on. She, like most people, seemed a bit nervous but I just felt the atmosphere was so warm and supportive. I felt no nerves at all.

Fast-forward halfway through the show. I'm side of stage and things are going like a dream, clockwork. Just then Grace Jones walks past me in a black body suit with a shiny red breastplate. She has this huge red helmet sculpture thing on and a hula hoop spinning round her middle. She is humming 'Slave To The Rhythm'.

Grace kept up the hula-hooping throughout her whole performance and didn't miss a beat. She looked unbelievable and behaved like an angel, an Amazonian angel. She's a one-off, she is. I love her. Of course, she absolutely killed it. She came off the way she went on, hula-hooping, and every time I saw her, she was still at it. Maybe she is still, to this day, hula-hooping.

The first half of the show was us young upstarts, all just happy to be there. Grace ushered in the elder statesmen: Stevie, Sir Tom, Sir Elton, Sir Paul, Dame Shirley. The real big guns. They were all in and out of each other's dressing rooms all day. They've known each other a lifetime, seen the world change and survived it. Vinyl, cassettes, 8-tracks, LaserDiscs, MiniDiscs, Betamax, VHS, CDs, streaming: dominated the lot. I can't help but be impressed by the lot of them. They're mega.

The show came to an end far too soon for me. Did it really happen? I've never watched any of the footage, only what I saw in my dressing room and from backstage. That was my show and the one I'm always going to remember.

* * *

The Queen did show up. Two songs before the end of the show, as scheduled, I walked down the steps behind the stage and a massive

Range Rover pulls up. I said to the footman, 'Are you gonna help her out?'

'Oh no, sir. Don't touch the Queen, sir.'

'I've got the exact same Range Rover and it's a helluva drop out of that back seat.' She's nearly 90, for God's sake.

The footman opens the door and stands back. I go over to her, 'Your Majesty, do you mind if I help you down?'

'Why, that would be most kind.'

I took her weight and successfully put her feet on terra firma. This was stage one, successfully completed.

Next we have to get her up the fifteen steep steps to the stage. From there to the front of the stage is about 30 feet covered in a tangled mass of cables.

I remember Dan saying once, 'Why do people always want to come backstage, Dad? All there is is cables.'

He was right, especially tonight. It was like an assault course that we had to navigate on camera, beaming our every move across the world on live TV.

I couldn't believe that protocol dictated this 86-year-old lady can't have any help.

'Your Majesty, I'm going to hold your arm because I don't want you to fall.'

'Lovely, lovely,' she said.

I held her arm all the way to the front of the stage. My entire thinking at this time is: 'Please let the Queen get to the front of the stage without falling over.'

We get her there and she takes her place in the middle of the night's entertainment. Every artist had stayed and, believe me, most of them are the first to shoot off to a waiting limo, myself included. It was historic, and even the real royals of the pop world wanted to be there and be part of this historic moment. Prince Charles' speech was perfect, it struck the right centre ground between statesmanlike and personal, from a son to his mother.

Now we just had to get her back.

The Queen wanted to be introduced to all the artists so I took her to meet them all, one by one. The line-up ends and the footman signals her exit point back down the steep stairs to the gigantic Range Rover. We were now alone, just us two. Once again, 'Your Majesty, may I please ask you to take my arm down these stairs?'

'Oh, that would be most kind,' she says as we navigate the final stages of the backstage assault course.

When I got her to the bottom of those steps, I breathed a sigh of relief. And as the Range Rover pulled away, I thought to myself, 'What do these footmen do? Not much.'

My duties were done. Jubilee concert: tick.

'Right, the party! Are you coming?' Someone said Elton had already headed there with Stevie Wonder.

'Not for me, folks, I've got *The X Factor* in Manchester tomorrow morning. I need to hit the road.'

People were stunned. 'You're not going to the Palace for even one drink?'

To thank the artists, Her Majesty had invited them for what I liked to think of as an 'all back to mine' at Buckingham Palace. I had constant messages through the night from artists saying, 'William and Harry are looking for you. Where are you?'

Elton rang me the next night and said, 'I'm so proud of you. You did a brilliant job. But where were you?'

When I told him I had left to do *The X Factor*, I could feel his disapproval and disappointment. Not only had I left the Jubilee, the fact that I was doing *The X Factor* at all.

The amount of times I've kicked myself for leaving so dutifully. I regret that. I should have stayed and lapped it all up. I'm not a regretful person; always look forward is my thinking. My only regrets are always based around not properly celebrating my achievements, and not going to the Palace for a congratulatory shandy, and letting everyone pat me on the back for that. But instead I ran away from it. In hindsight I realise how special it was, and how everyone on the show had gone. The fact that Sir P and El went says it all.

That's who I was back then; a worker bee, there by royal appointment one day and off to ITV the next.

* * *

The other big story of Summer 2012 is the Olympics. Kim Gavin wanted us to sing 'Rule The World' at the close of the ceremony as a very literal message about music here in the UK.

There were some changes afoot at home, too. I'd given up the Hemsley deliveries. I took a doggy bag full of that incredible pork off those tribesmen. As I was sitting in first class on Singapore Airlines with my pork, papayas and a big glass of red, I made a decision. From now on I'm going to make my own food. It had been brewing that whole trip. Driving home from filming the Kibera Slum Drummers in Nairobi, Kenya, I opened up a little pot of tahini bliss balls in the back of the bus. It just didn't feel right after being in a slum. As we travelled around some of these places where people made so much of so little, I was already starting to feel ashamed of my special food, and a bit silly too.

Bigger than any of this, though, is that back at home we're expecting another Barlow. It had been such bliss with Daisy; we got greedy, we wanted another one. We all decided it was going to be a boy. It's going to be James. James is coming! James is coming! Dan's talking about how he's going to wrestle his new baby brother.

Dawn had found out the sex in the Easter holidays while I was in South Africa with the older kids. After making the Commonwealth doc, I was keen to get them out to Africa. They'd never been on safari before and they were the right age for sitting on those trucks all day, bouncing around and watching all the elephants and lions.

Dawn calls, 'I know the sex of the baby…'

We're all going, 'Yeah! James is coming!'

'...it's a girl.'

'Oh, where's James?'

They moped for ages. 'Come on, at least with a girl we know what to do. We're total pros at girls now. World class I'd say. I can't wait to meet her.'

It wasn't long before they were cheering their new sister, 'Yay! It's a girl!' We hit the bumpy roads of Kruger National Park again.

Dawn and I decided to call her Poppy. There was so much to look forward to in 2012 but this was the big one, becoming a dad again.

16

POPPY AND THE LIGHT

'Why bring me flowers?'

We only had one gig that summer, and that was it, closing the Olympics. Everyone was so focused: we had only one song to perform and it had to be amazing. It was everything.

And then it was nothing.

Ten days before the closing ceremony our daughter Poppy died. She was stillborn at full term. The Olympics ceased to exist, it just left my mind. Instead we were consumed by the worst thing that had ever happened to us.

We were at our house in Oxford and Dawn had felt rotten all day. She thought it was just one of those pregnant days. So the next day she says, 'I'm going to go and see the doctor.'

She didn't want to take Daisy, so the little one stayed with me at the house in Oxford while Dawn went to London, to the doctor's. She took Dan with her. He would have been about eleven at the time.

When the phone call came I could tell in the silence that something had happened. I could tell as soon as I picked the phone up, something was wrong. Then she just came out with it. 'The baby's dead.'

My reaction was similar to when Mum called me and said, 'Your dad's died.' There is something that makes you – makes me – go, 'Right everybody, let's get the bags. Come on, we're off to London.'

I made myself a cup of tea for the car and went into coping overdrive. I didn't give myself a moment to think or feel. It was just: pack the car, get everyone in, drive.

I was in denial and I kept thinking there was something we could do. You start thinking, the doctors are wrong, I'm dreaming it all. Dawn said she kept feeling Poppy move that day. Apparently the waters move and it feels like the baby is alive in there. For a few moments you have these false hopes that she is alive.

I called the doctor when I got back to the London house and we arranged to have the birth induced the following morning. We had a nanny at the time, helping out. We rang and asked her, 'Can you come in and look after the children while we're at the hospital?' She stayed at home with Dan, Emily and Daisy. Dawn and I would stay overnight after the birth. It was the same hospital and doctor we had for Daisy. Hammersmith Hospital. It looks out over Wormwood Scrubs prison.

We had decisions to make. Practical stuff. They talk you through what happens during the birth and the fact that you can have two hours with your baby. They tell you that they will do footprints and handprints, that you can take a lock of hair. They talk you through what's going to happen when they induce her. They were trying to be reassuring that there would be no physical pain. The emotional toll, however, was incomprehensible.

I was filled with dread for what Dawn had to go through. I couldn't bear the thought of the suffering ahead for this woman who is my heart, my soul, my best friend, my wife, the mother of my kids, beautiful, gentle, patient, *so patient*, this loving, constant, unchanging rock of a woman. I have to see her going through this. The prospect of it all felt like going to the gallows.

All through this, I don't remember thinking about anything except Dawn. I didn't want anything to happen to her. I just wanted to look after my wife. The mum. I don't need to explain it any more than that.

What she has lost doesn't need explaining.

Dawn was in the most awful place. It's the worst thing that could happen.

There's a helplessness as a dad. I'm in control of everything in my life but with this I felt just utterly helpless. Where is my usefulness here? It's stripped off you and you're just this person offering another tissue and desperate to be useful. Towel, towel anyone? Helpless. Hopeless.

* * *

Poppy Barlow was born in the evening on Saturday, 4 August, just before nine o'clock.

When she was born it was like a light came into the room; it was amazing; it wasn't bad at all. It was lovely, it was gorgeous, we both took turns cuddling her, and we took pictures. It was one of the best hours of my life I've ever experienced in the midst of the hardest time of my life. It was very powerful, that hour was. Poppy looked perfect and for an hour she was alive to us. She's in your arms, this beautiful little daughter of ours, a sister to our three other children.

Then the reality comes rushing into the room and all the air leaves your lungs. It felt like someone had a hand held tight at my throat. The nurses start hovering and they want to take her away.

What we experienced and saw over those 24 hours no one should have to see or have to go through. There's no sadder sight than seeing a mum with her dead baby in her arms, willing it back to life with all her being.

What's left to us now are the logistics of death that follow an event like this. They feel so pointless and mundane. I can't go and meet a vicar now; I'm not even religious. I can't bear it. How can I navigate these people and process them as quickly as possible? Now we've got to look for a funeral director and look at their selection of coffins for kids. Choose one. Which one do you like?

Which one do you like? Which coffin for a newborn baby *do you like?* What a question.

Now I have to choose some music for the funeral. What? There's music?

How do we choose a church? A church where there's not going to be loads of people because I don't want anyone wanting a selfie with me right before the funeral of my baby.

More questions. Do we drive ourselves? Do we get a big hearse? Do we travel through the streets of where we live in London behind a big black car with a tiny coffin in the back?

It's a real kick after something so awful has happened. All this 'shopping'. The practical considerations are as grotesque as they are absurd.

And then there's these three at home, our other children. Dan, Emily and Daisy. What do we do with the kids as we go to their sister's funeral? With the kids we probably got it all wrong. Everyone said, 'Involve the kids' but we just couldn't do it. We didn't want to subject them to the funeral. We did it alone, just us two.

Kids dying is a strange one. What do you say? There is nothing. So no one spoke to us.

People just sent flowers. They started arriving and never seemed to stop. Every time the doorbell went I dreaded another delivery of lilies. Oh look, more flowers. More death. Oh look, there's death over there. Let's go in this room. Oh, there are more flowers. More death.

I was gathering them all up and going down to the bottom of the garden and just slinging them over the fence. The Hemsleys sent over a couple of stews. This was more useful than white flowers.

I've gone public with this before. It's been all over my songs for years. But in the whole time I've been in the public eye, it's been the hardest thing to talk about because there's no angle, no way of dressing it up; there's no glitter you can sprinkle on it, it's just cold, awful, brutish reality.

All I want is to make people happy with my music all the time, so it's a big deal to share this. I think people look up at me on stage and I don't want to taint their escapist experience.

More than that, though, is do I even want to? This chapter has been in and out of this book since I started writing it. I have wondered about the value and purpose in sharing something so private and harrowing.

After Poppy died, over sixty people wrote to me telling me their stories about suffering the same awful experience. I knew quite a few of them, some of them were famous strangers, others normal folk; what so many of them shared, though, was that they had kept so much about their experience locked away in secrecy.

I'd have been denying our daughter her legacy not to write this. Perhaps by sharing our story, we can help others to talk about theirs.

17

WE BUILD A WALL

'You can measure the strength of a human
by the weight of the love around them'

I don't know where to find the words to express how devastating it was for us all. I can't. I don't want to.

Trying to take care of my wife, son and two daughters while everyone is consumed by grief. The sound of crying in the house all the time. It's beyond words. We retreated into our family bubble and I found it impossible to connect with anything outside it. We all decamped to Oxford and just built a wall.

I know now that Kim Gavin was beside himself, not wanting to call and ask me if I'd be at the stadium on 12 August. Despite all the worry, anxiety and grasping for strength, I knew I had to be there for the Olympics closing. I think everyone thought I'd not turn up. But I knew the others were excited, especially as we were the ones finishing the whole thing. I did it for the boys, for my brothers. I couldn't do that to them. I rang Kim and said, 'I won't make rehearsals; we've done "Rule The World" a thousand times. But I'll be there.'

Meeting them on that day was plain awkward. There were hugs, of course, but no one knew what to say. It didn't matter. I wasn't present in the stadium anyway; my whole being was at home with Dawn and the kids.

Once my 'in ears' were on, I didn't feel like I was there at all. There was this complete dislocation from the world that was like being underwater. There's one thing I remember from that day. It's always stayed with me. It was right before we went on and we're all huddled up in this artists' area with about forty performers, every face a familiar one. Everyone's in the zone, waiting for their turn. I was standing looking down into the stadium at all these tens of thousands of people, and Liam Gallagher came over. He put his hand on my back and said, 'I'm really sorry about your daughter.' I was touched by that. Apart from the band and my team, no one else said anything. It's ironic, isn't it, that in your darkest hour no one really knows what to do with you.

'You light the skies...' My voice wobbled and I grasped to find the opening notes in my throat, '...up above me.' And then I went into autopilot. 'A star, so bright, you blind me.'

Showbiz Gary did his job while husband and father Gary spent every second wanting to get home. The car picked me up from the house in Oxford to take me to London. I spent twenty minutes in the stadium and about three minutes on stage. I came off, stood there while they took off all my mics and the ears. And I was gone. I went straight back to the car and within a few hours I was back again at my front door in Oxford, back at the house with the big dark shadow over it.

Then, there, I started to cook.

I couldn't bring Poppy back to life. I couldn't mend Dawn's broken heart. Dawn was in a really bad place. It was one or two o'clock in the afternoon before she could get out of bed most days. There were years of healing ahead of us. It was actually too difficult to contemplate the future because I could see no end to this grief.

What could I do? How could I grapple back some control over the happiness of my family? I wanted and I needed to react. And so I went to the heart of the home, the kitchen table.

This is the place for a dad; this is where you get to be useful. I started playing around in the kitchen, flicking through the cookery books, and the more I did, the more I thought, 'Hang on, I can cook.'

All those years of living on my own in the early days of Take That came back to me. 'Gently cook chopped carrots, celery and onion'; oh yeah, I know that one. That's what the French call a *mirepoix* – it's the flavour base of loads of dishes like stews, soups, sauces and roasts. I might not have known it was a *mirepoix* back then, but I used it loads in the early nineties when I lived on my own in my first bungalow in Knutsford. I never saw that house much, as I was away almost constantly on the road with the band. When I got home to that house after eating on the road for months, all I wanted, physically craved in fact, was a plate of home-made food.

I'm going to give you a little heads-up. Here comes the new single, folks, time to put the kettle on. I'm about to start talking about cooking *a lot*. This is the truth of my life; this is what I go home and do.

* * *

There are no private chefs at home. We cook. We cook a lot. Behind the pantomime, this is my life.

It keeps us real, and it kept us sane, and it keeps us alive and together.

Cooking joined all the dots for me. I was doing it first and foremost for the family, but I had learned a lot over the years from those advisers – good and bad – and all that knowledge came through. I was cooking instinctively. I'm not a private chef kind of guy and that summer, letting anyone inside the walls was unthinkable. I could take any recipe and modify it to suit the way we ate now, post the Hemsleys, in this enlightened space.

The uncomfortable truth is, if you want to get a grip on your weight and your health, then you are going to have to cook. Cooking real food, whole food, fresh, from scratch, is the key to it all. Cooking is about something bigger than that now. It's not just me and my stupid diets. It's about finding the strength to battle through our private nightmare.

When Poppy died, something happened to me: I went into coping mode. As I've said, when I left the closing ceremony of the Olympics in east London, I went straight home. There, we shut out the world and made a nest where we could be safe, love each other and grieve. Food was such a massive part of that process. I was driven to do anything in my power to get us all through this. And cooking, not some massive telly, is the real heart of a family.

I went out and did a huge shop at the big Waitrose by the station in Oxford. Two trolleys, packed, with stuff skidding off the top onto the floor. All the spices, mountains of fresh veg; just the fats, there was coconut oil, ghee, several pounds of butter, olive oil for dressings, olive oil for cooking. With the kitchen stocked up, I pulled every cookbook off the shelf. Like most middle-aged people, we had shelves and shelves of glossy pictured food porn that we never looked at. They're ornaments, aren't they, cookbooks? I set about clattering away with my pots and pans. This wasn't about me timidly boiling a few lentils or baking the odd clean-eating biscuit, I was cooking everything: fish, meat, bread... The Food Channel was on in the kitchen every hour of the day and I was cooking every meal as if it was our last: breakfast, elevenses, lunch, dinner, snacks, tea. The Hemsleys Paradise Bars were stacked up in the Tupperware box. It was like a factory in that kitchen.

Dawn loved being looked after and I loved looking after her. It was filling a big hole because, other than that, we felt shit. Food was the crack where the light came in that dark summer. She says all she remembers of that summer is me making pizza dough – for the kids – and her and me sitting in the garden shelling broad beans.

The day would start the night before, when I'd stick something in the cool oven of the Aga to cook while we slept. Often it was a big leg of lamb in there with wine and stock that I'd whack in for a twelve-hour slow cook. Can you imagine what that tastes like? We'd wake up to this gorgeous smell throughout the house. Breakfast was eggs and bacon, big bowls of porridge; there was always a big wedge of frittata and smoothies of blitzed fruit and yoghurt. The lamb would be ready by lunchtime. Should we have it with a freshly podded broad bean salad and lettuce from the garden, or go large with a few roasted sweet potatoes? Sod it, let's have both. Oh, and Yorkshires. Dan likes them with everything – even breakfast.

There's a saying: 'The family that eats together, stays together,' and there's a lot of truth in that; despite losing my way for all those days on the road eating like a pop star, and then those daft, long and frustrating diet years. I had always had a role model. She was right under my nose. Mum always cooked and we always ate at the table;

we never ate in front of the telly. Even if we had chips for a treat, we always had it on a plate at the table, even if we were arguing. I'd always watched my mum cook, and I know she enjoyed it. Both Mum and Dad worked bloody hard, but I was never fed a Findus crispy pancake or a supermarket pizza.

There's only really family that don't feel uncomfortable with you when something so awful has happened. I spoke to Mum every day. We never spoke about what I was going through, what we were all going through. Instead, we talked about cooking.

Mum had also come to cooking in horrible, sad circumstances.

She was never a fast food person, Mum. Even going on an aeroplane, she'd take a packed lunch. My grandad, her dad, was a cook in the Merchant Navy. When she was eleven, her dad had to go to hospital and she had to have school dinners for a while, which she hated.

My mum was only just eleven when her dad died. My nana was the breadwinner because grandad came out of the war with TB. His ship was wrecked in the tropics somewhere and apparently it's a fact that you can catch TB in warm water. He never worked again after World War II so my nana had to be the wage earner. She worked for Littlewoods Pools in Liverpool. When he died, the mother of my mum's friend Rita looked after Mum and she's never forgotten her for it. Rita's mum said, 'Would Marjorie like to come home with Rita and have her dinners with her?'

So my mum would walk home with her friend Rita to her house and she introduced her to beetroot and corned beef sandwiches. She still loves one today. On another day, Rita's mum would go to a decent bakers and get the girls a meat pie, which (as you know) is my favourite food. Poor Mum; she lost her dad, but she always talks about how lucky she was. Mum says, 'I think Rita's mum, she did literally save my life. I couldn't have eaten a school dinner.'

With her dad gone, eleven-year-old Marjorie realised her mum and her little brother, my uncle John, needed to come home to a meal at night because she'd worked all day. It breaks my heart thinking about this, but my mum, just a little girl, really, went round to the two sisters that lived next door and asked them, 'How do I boil a potato?'

So little Marj, just lost her dad, kind of became like my nana's wife, almost. Preparing the food, making sure her mum was fed.

That's the only way she could eat. It must have been so tough for Mum. It upsets me to think about it. In this day and age she'd have been rushed to a therapist. But back then you coped. Mum, she's stoic and she's passed that down to me and my brother.

*　*　*

Don't think I'm trying to present us as some perfect family straight out of the adverts, sitting round the table all smiling and eating up our broccoli. Far from it. Our kids don't always eat like us. As Dawn says, 'You've got a fight on your hands convincing a sixteen-year-old to eat cauliflower rice.'

The kids might not be all over the lentils and sauerkraut, but they know what's healthy because they watch us cooking and discussing food among ourselves. My eldest might be Mr Pot Noodles right now, but if you gave him an exam on healthy eating, he'd ace it. If parents don't teach kids how to eat healthily, then who will?

There's a lot of evidence that eating together has loads of benefits, including the fact that you're far less likely to be overweight. I don't want to over-romanticise the whole thing. You know the score with term-time tea, that's hard work. Dawn says it's the worst time of the day when the kids get in after school; it's five o'clock, they want to eat, they're hungry, they're moody. You're just dishing up food at a moving target. That summer in Oxford was different. I took the summer off work and they were all on holiday; we were just loving each other and looking after each other.

The kids were incredible; in their instinctive way they were looking after us, too. What children do, especially our little one, is that they make it real.

We were all sitting in the garden one warm summer night and Daisy said, 'Oh, look, I can see Poppy in the sky. I can see Poppy in the stars.'

Some days I'd think I won't bring her up today in conversation because I don't want to upset anyone and I don't feel strong enough to talk about it. Then the little one, she's not even four yet, will go, 'Ah, Poppy was in there, wasn't she, in your tummy, Mummy?'

That openness hurt but it was a kind of therapy. It helped.

Yeah, the kids did a proper job of taking care of us. I'd often come in and find Dan curled up around Dawn on the sofa, this twelve-year-old lad just holding his mum.

They just make you so proud. I couldn't ask for better kids. They're all amazing.

Me? I'm a pain in the arse because of what I do and how much I want it to be right and, I dunno, I'm just a pain. It was time for me to step up and put the work away for a while. That summer was about me taking control of the most basic of family needs.

I'm not being all 'jumpers for goalposts', harking back to old times when women spent their lives toiling in the kitchen. It's easy to cook. I can challenge anyone on the busy front. What? You've got no time to crack an egg into a pan and fry a bit of bacon. Too busy for that? Rubbish. The enjoyment of eating something you've cooked at home outweighs any effort. It's not *MasterChef*, feeding the family. We're talking egg on toast, stew, a big bowl of dahl or even a fat butcher's sausage and sliced up tomato in a sandwich with a thick layer of butter and Dijon. It's all healthier than anything that comes in a plastic wrapper.

That *mirepoix* I mentioned earlier, the chopped carrots, onion and celery? Add some lumps of meat, a blob of tomato puree and half wine and half water to it, some salt and some pepper, and it'll take all of ten minutes. It won't look like much but you slowcook it at a low heat for a few hours, by which I mean five, six, twelve, even twenty-four hours, and you will feel like a magician. 'Slow cooking' generally involves only a short preparation time. So once the food is in the oven, and however long it takes to cook, you can do whatever you want. 'Low cook / slow cook' needs no watching.

Tom Adams, the chef of a barbecue restaurant called Pitt Cue, gave me the most incredible recipe because this one makes you look like a mad genius. People are nearly kneeling at your feet when you deliver it. Three ribs of beef, put in the oven for 24 hours at precisely 60 degrees centigrade (not 50, not 70, and definitely not 100). That. Is. It. No oil, no salt, no pepper, just all that flavour released from slow cooking just one ingredient.

I got this recipe off Tom that Christmas. I'd eaten at Pitt Cue a few times and thought the meat was insanely good. So I'd rung him and asked him to send over a selection of meat for the hols. Pigeon, duck, pork chops arrived and then this massive three rib of beef. Looked like something a T. Rex had picked out of its teeth.

'What the hell do I do with that? Feed it to the sharks?'

Tom told me this simple method. I said, 'You've got this wrong, this is going to be all wrong.'

What a bloody waste. I pulled a stew out of the freezer just in case. This thing when I took it out of the oven after a day in there, I swear it was pitch-black, like a lump of charcoal. Right, I thought, the guy's conned me. Bloody chefs. Never trust 'em. It looks like something tossed out of a volcano.

There was only Dawn, me and this black lump. We had circled it for a moment. Dawn said, 'Good thing I like it well done.'

Then I cut it.

Oh, we were groaning: it was red, perfectly red, cooked through but still red. There was no juice on the tray, it was all perfectly sealed inside the beast. It managed to be both well-done and rare at the same time. I'm going to have to stop writing about this because I'm drooling on the laptop. Damn it was good.

* * *

Me, I'm an instinctive cook, the sort who feels his way by trial and error. I love it when Dawn comes home with a bag full of stuff. I go, 'Ooh, look at that. I could do a such-and-such with that.' Remember *Ready Steady Cook*? That's me. I'll look in the cupboard and the fridge, use up all the odds and sods and stuff that could have gone to waste. I get a little thrill from using things up. Like, Daisy loves pasta and parmesan and I take those annoying nubbins left at the end of the cheese and whack it in a slow-cook stew and it just melts away into nothing, adding a bit of extra savoury deliciousness. If we've got none of them, another way I pump up the tasty volume in stew is to stir in a massive dollop of Dijon mustard at the end of cooking.

Dawn is the complete opposite, a right Mrs Logic with her scales and spoons. She always cooks methodically from a recipe. When I've got to start measuring, I just lose interest. (Yeah, yeah, I know, 'For a man who wrote a song about it…')

I felt complete dread about leaving our Oxford family bubble that summer. It wasn't like a holiday where you feel great after two weeks' rest. The grief is exhausting and it has only just begun. Just the thought of dealing with the real world and all the people in it made me tired. I didn't want to come back out.

Going into the autumn of 2012, I had to do the next series of *The X Factor*. I hated leaving Dawn alone for the first time. The kids went back to school and I had to go back to the shiny floors of showbiz. It felt like we were leaving her. And I knew things were going to get worse before they got better. It was hard work to leave her. But it wasn't hard going back to work. In fact, it made everything easier. I didn't give a shit. I always thought that our business, our world, was a load of bollocks. I knew it for certain now.

Sometimes on a set or in a meeting, I'd just sit there smiling, thinking what a load of shit this is. Honestly, it's not important. The job isn't the problem. I love the work, it's fantastic. Cut me and I bleed sparkly shirts and piano solos. It's the surroundings, the world, some of the people, all the drama and the nonsense.

Someone would come rushing in, screaming, 'Oh my God, the viewing figures are down to 12 million.'

How were we meant to react? Would jumping off a bridge be a good solution?

'You said in the auditions that so-and-so was a bad singer, and now they're through to the semi-finals. How do you feel about that?'

I couldn't care less.

'Dermot got more likes on Instagram for his outfit this week. Are you gonna sack the stylist?'

Sack him? I'm gonna kill him with my bare hands live on *The Xtra Factor*; perhaps that'll get the ratings up. Two birds, one stone.

I had a bit of anger. Even less patience. And somehow made it to the end of that season without killing anyone with my bare hands, or jumping off any bridges.

Most of all, I had clarity about what is important in this world. The train's late. Oh well, I'll sit on Instagram for a bit. There's a queue an hour long. That's all right, I'll listen to the new album by Birdie. London's at gridlock? I'm going to be an hour late. Time to catch up with people on the phone.

Nothing's important. It just gives you a default of knowing that is the worst it can get. It's the worst I've ever experienced, the lowest place I've ever been in my life. When you've gone through something like that, nothing matters except love.

18

SOLO, SECOND TIME

'I've made my peace with what may happen'

Without question, I used work as a very effective painkiller. The year after Poppy died my diary was insane. My iCal diary had three different colours defining each area of my life: Take That, solo, personal. From a distance it looked like a game of Tetris. I barely had a minute between appointments: making documentaries, promo stuff, meeting heads of TV channels, planning radio specials, charity gigs, school sports day, and, religiously, weekly date nights with my wife.

Not happy with being on *The X Factor* every Saturday and Sunday, one week I flew to Afghanistan for six days to make a documentary about the troops out there and returned to the judges' panel with sand in my ears.

If I wasn't exhausted at the end of each day, I felt disappointed. For good and bad, *The X Factor* just gobbled up time. I had very mixed feelings about the show. The model judge I was in the first season was less evident in the second (and had gone completely AWOL by the third).

Ben would watch the show back with me afterwards and critique my chat. 'You're a bit hard there. You didn't need to be like that.'

When I told Tulisa on air her breath reeked of fags, and she, in turn, came back with the fact that my breath stank of wine, that was a bit of a low point. I went backstage in the ad break afterwards going, 'Oh, no, I've gone too far there. I shouldn't drink during the show.'

The days in TV are long. I'd come back to my dressing room to where my team were – Elisa, Luke, Ben, Lizzie, friends or family – and usually a few other judges, too. By evening time I'd be straight into a big glass of Bordeaux. 'What's going on, kids? This is where it's all happening.' I'd glug half a glass of red and go back on.

Talent shows like *The X Factor* are an odd way to find talent. The problem is not a lack of talent, but that a TV show requires someone who will be good on TV – and that isn't a great indicator of a real artist. Imagine Bob Dylan and Kate Bush being asked what they think about the judges' comments. It's the stuff of comedy, isn't it? And that's the problem I had. For every good person that came through, there was the certain knowledge that another ten were sitting at home and wouldn't dream of putting themselves through the six-chair challenge.

James Arthur is a brilliant artist. He's a great writer and an amazing singer. And he won *The X Factor* in 2012. That doesn't make him the lesser artist.

The more I did it the more depressing it was, sitting through watching thousands of people with no talent at all performing in front of us just to make good TV. Sometimes we'd do all the cities, and you'd go, 'Have we got anything? *Anything*?'

There was one night where they'd play you the final contestants and all I could think is, 'We've got ten weekends on TV and not one person that's any good.'

God, I sound a grouch, don't I? I loved them all because you get to know these artists and you fall in love with them as people.

I was getting an education on *The X Factor*. I was learning to be the person off stage, the watcher not the watched. You learn to trust your instinct and make fast, effective decisions about what works and what doesn't. Sitting in that judge's chair, I liked it. I realised that I enjoyed nurturing, supporting, encouraging young talent.

What I hated about being in that seat was the bullshit. The classic *X Factor* line, 'You're the dark horse in this competition, the one to watch,' was a safe line. Literal translation: 'I can't think of anything to say. How am I going to fill my fifteen seconds. Will this do?'

In a career where I've never known what makes a hit and what doesn't, the whole thing is a complete guessing game. Anyone who tells you 'I know' is a liar. Run and don't stop till you hit some kind of coastline.

The day we filmed 'The Flood' video we had an idea – let's shoot the cover to show the evolution of man. We posed it up to send to photographers. It took two beautiful days to shoot this video and what a beauty it was. Loads of time spent together, laughing and taking the 'P' out of one another.

This was taken at the Red Nose shoot we did. Back in the 'Do What You Like' gear. It was always going to be a moment. Look how happy we look.

Shooting a Carpool Karaoke with James was the highlight of 2017. He is an old mate and a proper old-school TT fan. We laughed and sang our way through three lovely hours in LA.

'These Days' video shoot was superb. It was also kind of new for us to shoot big clips of time. Lots of choreography and things to remember. As the day went on, the more ridiculous the ideas became. That's how Mark and me ended up with huge hair. I'm afraid to say we didn't need too much talking into this. We thought we looked great!

Now that's a crowd! Hyde Park 2016. What a
way to spend a Sunday evening. I could go as
far to say it was one of my favourite TT shows.

I loved those opening outfits for the III Tour. Cracking clobber is one of our favourite things on tour.

© Andrew Whitton

This was taken just before I did my first solo show at the London Palladium. It only took 35 years to get there!

The Wonderland Tour gave us every excuse to go crazy on costumes. Being in the round meant the back of the costume had to be awesome too. Enter G! What a get up!

The goal for me, the thrill for me, was to find real talent. Initially what everyone loved, and definitely what I loved about *The X Factor*, was that it wasn't just a TV show; it launched people and gave them a career. As years have gone by, these talent shows, they're all getting a bit dark. What we've seen over the years is people loving the humiliation. People getting humiliated, and the audience going, 'I love this, I love this.'

The industry needs talent. I speak to record companies and they worry that the pool of talent is getting smaller and smaller. Kids are picking a guitar up and if it doesn't work out for them in ten minutes, they throw it away. I never devalue any type of music because it's going to work for somebody, somewhere. But there's none of that 10,000 hours of practising and playing because it's too hard; where's the instant reward in that? Let's have a go on Garage Band – wow, that sounds great immediately. That's why there's not so many bands any more. Where's the new guitar bands? I know the record companies are worried, really worried.

At eleven, the way I tried to understand music was the same way a kid will take a clock apart. I wanted to know why does music work like that? I used to play other people's songs to learn about how a song is made. Why do I like that chord? Oh, look, it's because it's in a major key. What makes that song sound so sad? Oh, it's in a minor key.

Thirty years on, when I'm around a lot of other musicians who haven't done that legwork, I see them struggle. I see their frustration. Other songwriters I worked with would say things like, 'I'm hearing this …' Whereas I could just write it down without even singing or playing. I thank God I did that, squirreled up in my bedroom for all those early years because of the time it saved me, the pain it saved me, the language it gave me. I don't need to even go to a piano. I can hear it and just write it.

I wouldn't have done the second season of *The X Factor* if the band had decided to do a follow-up to *Progress*. Should we do another album? We all met down at Coworth Park in Berkshire for a band meeting and, no questions asked, the consensus was, 'We don't want to.' If the band want to work, they always come first. I'll drop everything to make a Take That album. After doing the biggest tour in UK history and having our biggest selling album, we weren't left with much ambition to work with. It took a massive effort to get *Progress* off the ground. We'd done it. No one was in a rush to try and follow *Progress*. And I got that, big time.

So back to *The X Factor* I went. Round two, ding ding...

* * *

It was a weird season; there wasn't a great energy there. Tulisa was driving everyone nuts. The show weren't happy with her because she was just turning up late for everything and all of us were left waiting at call time. Everyone was starting to get a bit cross with her. It was no fake 'beef' set up by the producers this time. That was us all getting a bit tired of the young one not showing up. The other judge was Nicole Scherzinger, and she is a serious pro. She hits all the marks. Turns up for a filming on the dot and does more than she's meant to do.

I did like Tulisa, I don't want anyone to think I didn't. She could be infuriating but I cared for her. I think she'd had a tough life and now she's in this industry, where girls have to fight for everything, and they exist under a microscope that men can't even start to imagine. Thank God I joined the business in the nineties. There's so much more criticism now. It's not in a pompous music journalist's review tucked away on page 40, it's in your hand and constantly streaming, and absolutely vile.

Back in the day, if I read someone describe our latest single as throwaway pop, I felt suicidal. God knows how young pop artists cope in this vicious social media age.

Tulisa would sit there in between takes saying, 'Do you wanna see my Twi'er?'

I'd be holding up her phone, wincing. And I'm not making this up.

'Die now, you bitch. I'll fucking burn you.'

I was horrified, genuinely shocked. 'Block them, why don't you? Report them. Report them. Call the police!'

'No point, babes. I'll be here all day.'

'What! Is there more?' And she'd scroll down a screen full of horrible stuff, some of which she actually read. Bless her, she'd feed the trolls the odd 'Fuck off'.

I watch my kids use social media on an hourly basis and realise it's not just the pop stars being subjected to abuse, comparing themselves to others and constantly trying to perfect every flaw. It's a problem for everyone. It's like a virus.

All in all, the world at this point felt like a horrible place. Life had been cruel to us at home. And every weekend I'm sitting on a TV show surrounded by cruelty.

The one place I could escape was into my own music.

It's very rare that I'll sit down at the piano, like they do in the movies, and start playing a few notes going, 'Oh, I feel a bit down,' tinkle tinkle tinkle, 'I think I'll write "A Million Love Songs" now.' That's very rare for me. In this way, I suppose I look like a bit of a machine. But it isn't robotic like that, it's that writing music is like breathing for me. I do it all the time. My release is through music. Rather than going to a therapist or having an argument, I write. Writing never feels like work. I know when I need to write: I head there and sit down and go into a trance for a few hours. Given what had happened in summer 2012, I knew I wanted to write for myself, for the good of my soul.

After all these achievements in recent years there was still one thing I was afraid to address. It was thirteen years since my last solo album and the memories were still raw. The last one, *12 Months, 11 Days*, had been the reason I was dropped back in 1999. I went to see David Joseph, the chairman of Universal. He's always been our champion and he's become a good mate of mine as well. I trust him. It was to him that I was hemming and hawing about the solo album.

'This is it. If you don't do it now, you're never going to do it. Stop thinking about it. Just make great music and put it out there, Gary.'

Most of the album I wrote in the studio at home in London, upstairs, opposite our bedroom, there in the early part of 2013. Very unlike me to do that; I usually need to get away and work with a clear head and no distractions, but I couldn't leave Dawn. I didn't want to leave her. She was looking like a ghost, and was constantly tired. Upstairs from the studio, in the room above my head, Poppy's bedroom was full of untouched baby clothes, her cot, the toys...

I don't think I've ever made an album before where I didn't give a toss about the things you usually think about when you're writing pop music. I'd lost all respect for what anyone wanted from me. I didn't consider how many seconds it was before the first chorus, if the intro was too short, the middle eight was too long. If it sounded good, I recorded it. For the first time in my life, I didn't think about other people's expectations or needs or rules before I wrote. I just wrote.

Partly, this was because of the tragedy of that whole time. But also my last solo album had been so not me, so transparent and so plastic that this time round I was winning by just turning up because I was already a far better man than the one on that last fateful solo album. It was a solo singer/songwriter's album, written and produced by a committee.

Never a good sign, that.

I emptied my heart into the piano key and wrote it on the page. I did it in a trance: one mind, one thought, one purpose. Some lyrics came early. Some songs happened in twenty minutes. The day I got 'Let Me Go' was exciting. People don't often notice that behind happy melodies and pop hooks there's often sad lyrics. Most of the lyrics on that album were sad and I consciously beefed up the music to brighten up the message. Every time I played people 'Let Me Go' I'd study their reaction. I played it to Ferdy, the head of Polydor, and his only reaction was, 'It's a hit.'

No mention of lyrical content or message. Perfect. There's nothing more satisfying for a writer than getting a powerful, often sad, lyric and partnering it with an uplifting and infectious pop melody. Let the listener dig deeper if they want to, or just whistle along if they don't.

The ultimate test for any song is the Daisy Test. On the days when I was writing at home, I'd lose track of time. The hours flew by and then this little figure would appear at the door. She stood there silent and listening intently. She immediately started jumping at the chorus to 'Let Me Go'. Always a good sign. For the next week, at the end of every day, she'd demand, 'Play the fly high song…'

I look out in the audience while singing these songs about the bleakest period in my life and see everyone jumping around, dancing, smiling, hands in the air. When I play live, that song makes the room burst into life. Upper circles bow under the weight of people jumping up and down. What a beautiful way of keeping Poppy's memory alive.

In that song, the album had a lead track: acoustic and up-tempo and it meant so much to me. Some I had written years before, but they had never found their time to bloom. The body of 'Dying Inside' came to me way back in 2004. Sometimes it feels like the writer in you knows what's going to happen in your life. The message only emerged to me in that writing period in the studio opposite our bedroom at home.

I'm dying inside
Who knows what I'm thinking
What I'm trying to hide
Yeah, I'm dying all night
I'm breathing but I can't feel life
I'm smiling but I'm dying inside

I didn't want to make a downbeat record. Getting real content in a lyric without ramming human suffering in people's ears is pop's singular magic. 'Since I Saw You Last' was effortless to make, really, as I was writing in the moment. Creating in the moment is all any artist looks for. There was no thinking of playlists or radio stations like there had been for the last three Take That albums. Everyone, including me, was surprised by that album.

This album is for me. I thought, 'Let's just put it down and, even if just the most loyal core fans love it, I'm all right with that.' Albums. All they are, really, is just a diary of the couple of years when you make them. What's going on in your life is bound to be present.

Dawn took the album away to listen to it. She went off to a retreat in Glastonbury with it on her iTunes. When she got back she said she'd listened to it loads. She liked it. Poppy is in that album from start to finish.

*   *   *

While the album is full of my life, feelings and experience, I don't go to an emotional place particularly when I'm writing. Writing music is a discipline; rain or shine, happy or sad, you write. Lyrics are a different thing, though, because they seldom start a song. What starts a song for me is a great title, then the music takes over; eventually the message in the notes will lead to the lyrics last of all. I wish I just sat down at the piano and started singing, but the puzzle is more complex than that.

In my twenties I used to spend every day and every night in studios; I was insanely ambitious and that was how I got the results. The songs I wrote in the nineties were beautifully naive and lyrically, truthfully, they were a regurgitation of the pop music I listened to as a teenager.

The less time I spend in studios as a grown-up has given me more results. You have to live life to write about it. The true creation in being a songwriter comes from living life, love, loss, travel, watching the world, crying to music, being amazed by anything from the theatre to observing a woman sitting alone in a hotel bar. When I started appreciating music rather than competing with it, I became a more complete artist.

The problem with lyrics in a band is everyone needs to feel invested in them, otherwise it becomes 'your' song. Writing as a band, you need to tone down the really personal stuff. When you're doing your own record, it's like you can't get enough of it in.

I always play it down, what I do. 'I don't know what I'm doing, I'm just doing it. It's all a bit daft, isn't it?' I like to pretend I don't take it too seriously, but that's a solid lie. I take it really seriously. There is nothing more exciting, *nothing*, than that feeling when a song starts to reveal itself as you're writing and you realise it's a banger and your heart is zinging, your mind's on fire and you're just feeling, 'Oh, fuck, I want that song. I WANT THAT SONG. I can't wait for people to hear that.'

On the days I got good songs I'd run downstairs to the whole family, excited. 'Come on! Let's go out for dinner. Pizza? Sushi? Steak! We need to celebrate.'

I was like that the day I wrote 'Face To Face', which I sang with Elton John on the album. It was originally meant for Elton and Billy Joel as a duet – I grew up listening to them, worshipping them, and I think I know their voices better than anyone. We recorded and shot it in the same day. It was such a favour to me, a dream to have Elton sing a song I'd written. I didn't want to take up too much of his time.

As soon as we'd finished recording, he played me a few tracks off his new album. We're so similar, and we're both so proud of our own music. So we sat opposite each other on sofas at Abbey Road, him watching me intently. He loved Abbey Road; he worked there as a session player in the late sixties and always liked the way the cashier paid you in cash after every session as you left the building.

He's always called me Valerie Barlow. So we're sitting there. I'd compliment him. He'd beam. 'Thanks, Valerie.' I try so hard to hold it together and act as if it's just another day.

When I get home, I think, 'Did that just happen?'

Dad's home, he's been at work, at Abbey Road, recording, *with Elton John*. There's only ever gonna be one of him. And he's on my new album. I can't believe that day just happened to me.

No one gives a shit.

My family keeps me grounded. Dawn, especially, hates the whole pantomime around the work that I do. Once in a while, though, every few months, I love a good showbiz bash. We went to Lloyd Webber's birthday party and, as we were leaving, I said, 'What a brilliant night that w—'

'Worst night I've ever had,' says Dawn. I'm wondering if we went to different dos.

'You looked okay; I saw you talking away all night.'

'They only talked to me so they could get to you.'

So yeah, that's why Dawn and Ange Donovan are so tight. They've had a similar life, being the plus ones.

There were photographers at Lloyd Webber's do, but we didn't have our picture taken. We went in and out of the back door. There's always a back door, you know. I love spotting who does front and who does back door. It's amazing. It's not always the most successful who choose not to be seen. Some people like the fuss. The successful *like* the front door. Perhaps it's why they're successful. I'll never make it in that case.

All the lights flashing, people watching on the street and the calling and shouting, I find it embarrassing. I didn't lie in bed as a teenager dreaming of that bit; I just wanted to perform in front of an audience.

The reason I don't like it is that I get an audience when I sing. Actors, actresses, writers, painters, whatever, this is their audience and their crowd shouting out their support. Maybe that's why some people take the front door.

* * *

Back to the food and the obsessive side of me started to come through and, as usual, I had to take it to the absolute maximum. As with everything else with me, sourcing food had to become this big thing. That's the second stage in all this cooking. I was loving that process and was getting into ingredients. When you see where something comes from, it makes you so appreciative of even a simple lettuce or an egg.

Our chest freezer in the barn at Oxford slowly filled up with this fantastic produce, at first from local farms, then I got more adventurous. I found the only farm in the UK that reared Wagyu beef. They're in Norfolk. Now I'd eaten this beef in fancy restaurants all round the world. It's got a very special taste, more savoury than other meat and incredibly tender. It's the caviar of cows.

I rang the guy up and he was a bit taken aback. 'Bloody hell, we only supply to The Fat Duck, Le Manoir aux Quat'Saisons and Lidgate's, how did you find us?'

The farmer says he only kills a cow every two weeks so there's not much meat available. I'm on fire. 'Will you sell us a box of your steaks?'

The basic result was it helped to even more completely shift my focus away from bad food. Bad food is the enemy now. Yes, I think it's that bad. Food is also how I helped myself. Food is a small word, like war or love, that encompasses a billion possibilities. You can kill yourself with food, or you can use it to create a better you.

My focus has shifted to these beautiful raw ingredients now, food produced by real people and not some faceless corporation with all their strange processed, sugary, fatty, salty chemical poison. Food had gone from devil, to enemy, to friend. And now that I was cooking, it was more like a lover. That's some transformation.

19

THE ENEMY
IS SUGAR

'What makes us be the
people we've become'

Dawn kept saying to me, 'I'm so tired.'

Eight months on she is still in a bad way and she is looking thin, so thin. I can see her ribs, her breastbone; her skin is so pale, it's transparent. Something is wrong.

She went to the doctor's for a check-up and they did a blood test. The consultant rang her that night and said something weird: 'Your glucose levels are through the roof. It's as if you came in coated in sugar. Come back tomorrow. We need to check it's not a mistake.'

She was sent straight to the consultant endocrinologist who said, 'You're diabetic. You're Type 1 diabetic. We need to put you on insulin immediately.'

Right then and there, a diabetes nurse came down and showed her how to use the testing kits and inject herself.

'It looks like the trauma of losing your baby caused your body to turn on itself,' the doc says. 'Your immune system attacked the pancreas and now it is not producing insulin any more. It's as simple as that. You have an autoimmune disease and it is Type 1 diabetes. I'm very sorry.'

Dawn says, 'It's not possible, surely; you only get that as a kid.' Dawn's a dancer, she's healthy, she's never smoked, she is active, fit; she always ate well. The doctor says she has post-traumatic Type 1 diabetes. Apparently it happens to firefighters and police, people in war zones, people, basically, who have experienced distressing events. The emotional pain of losing Poppy had caused her physical damage. That's how her body dealt with it.

There is no turning back, no cure, it's not a question of exercising more or losing weight – for God's sake she looks like a ghost as it is;

it's absolutely heartbreaking. It's not like Type 2, which is down to lifestyle and overloading your body with glucose in your diet; with T1 diabetes your body totally stops producing insulin, the hormone that enables your body to take the sugars in all carbs – be it Toblerone, carrots, pasta or a saintly chia seed 'rice pudding' – and turn them into energy. Instead, the sugar hangs around in your bloodstream and causes all sorts of health problems, long term and short term.

The consultant referred her to this world-renowned specialist who describes how the blood sugars will react, not just to what she eats but to stress, jet lag, temperatures, when you're hot, when you're cold, so many different things. It's not just food that can cause your glucose levels to rise.

At the end of the day, she asks this expert to give us a bit of a hint. What does she eat to manage this? 'Go home, make a baked potato and some beans and have that for your dinner.'

Dawn's like, 'What? But baked beans have got sugar in them, and potatoes are high in carbohydrate.' It didn't compute. We are not an academic household, we do not pretend to be intellectuals, but we totally disagreed with this doctor's dietary advice.

Dawn says, 'I don't eat any of those things, so that's not going to happen. I don't see how it makes sense that someone with diabetes would put sugar into their body, especially if you've got too much of it anyway.'

'Well, that's what I tell all my patients,' she says, and sends her home.

At times like this you cling to medical advice, don't you. 'Well, they're the specialists.' We didn't take their advice, though. They were telling her to take masses of insulin. But Dawn doesn't eat cheap white bread or potatoes, we don't 'do' starchy carbs, and we eat next to nothing sugary. The amount of insulin they suggested was way, way too much and she would have what they call 'hypos'. It would frequently knock her off her feet. She would lie back on the sofa, groaning and feeling so ill and drained. The day's over for her now. Meanwhile, I'm hovering by the phone wondering if I should call an ambulance.

So, she started to study her own body. She wrote down everything that she ate, and everything that she did. If she did exercise, she'd test her glucose levels; if she had a crap day, test; tired, sad, happy, hungry… test, test, test. There were pages and pages of 'research' and patterns are forming. 'Okay, my levels were good then, so what had I done before it? And how much insulin had I taken?'

* * *

Through trial and error she just worked it out for herself and took charge of her insulin dose. It's a constant puzzle, but she armed herself with as many facts as possible.

We were bizarrely upbeat about the diagnosis at first. By now, both of us knew enough about the power of food to know how much we could manage this with really clever eating. Me, I did the only thing I knew to do when something went wildly outside of my control. I took over the food: 'Doctor, we're gonna sort this out; we're good with food in our house; we'll start working on it right away.'

The doctors had drugs. We had food. That was our weapon.

Dawn took it in her stride; it almost didn't bother her. My attitude was pretty predictable. Optimistic, organised, energetic. Clapping my hands together, saying, 'We'll get through this.'

The doctors warned us, if you don't manage this well your eyesight will suffer first. Sure enough, three months later, Dawn's being fitted with glasses. That's when it really started to sink in. She said, 'I've got this for life. I'm going to have to completely change everything. I've got to be on top of it. I've got to make sure I take snacks with me everywhere, and I've got to take my insulin everywhere. If I'm out, I have to plan what I'm going to eat or have to take glucose tablets in case I have a hypo.'

All of a sudden it felt very, *very* real. The kids were worried, of course they were.

We tried a different tack and went to an Indian Ayurvedic doctor. This guy seemed far more engaged in the whole food angle of things.

'Cut out all fruits, berries occasionally; no tomatoes, beetroot, carrot, far too sweet.'

We started to make radical changes to our diet. The kids ate what they wanted still, but I wanted to eat like my wife. Now, her treat is a slice of sourdough toast, sometimes. The only good thing about a hypo is when I hand her a bowl of berries, Greek yoghurt and raw honey generously poured over the top. (Raw honey is unpasteurised: it hasn't gone through a sterilising process that strips it of lots of its naturally occurring goodies like healthy bacteria and enzymes.) Other than that, we eat really low sugar and really clean. All meat is fine, though not processed meat because a lot of bacon has got sugar in, most smoked salmon too. They add sugar to so much processed food.

We go to a really good butcher where they don't need to fall back on sweetness to give their bacon flavour. We eat loads of salad and vegetables. This from a couple that back in the early 2000s at Delamere Manor kept a massive box of Cadbury's Heroes always open on the table.

Check the packaging next time you are shopping. Dawn and I have this thing: we'll taste something and go, 'Tastes too good. What's in it?' Or, 'Tastes good but not *that* good. Must be healthy.'

What's hilarious is that when Dan was little and I was as large as I've ever been, it was all about the mashed organic butternut squash for our blessed first-born. He didn't have chocolate till he was about two. Meanwhile, us two didn't eat veg until we were in our mid-thirties. Christ, if I could've cooked veg then like I cook it now we'd have eaten it.

But I thought vegetables meant plain, boiled, tasteless mush: carrots, frozen peas, steamed broccoli. Yawn.

I started cooking every day because if I don't cook Dawn never looks after herself. She says, 'I've lost interest.'

She feeds the kids with all their different demands and I cook for us. I cook as if our lives depend on it because, actually, now they do. So, learning to cook was doubly important because without home-made food we'd be stuck. Dawn can't buy anything pre-made from a shop because it's usually rubbish. This isn't from a dieter's perspective any more. It makes her ill.

When bad things happen they either pull you apart or bring you together. For us it's always been the latter. We approach life, and its challenges, as a team.

I always say to Dawn, 'There's only room for one star in this house' and she's happy with that. We work well together because she's as pathologically shy as I am an attention-seeker. Lately, though, I've had competition. Emily Barlow's coming through, don't you worry. When she was nine, in 2012, she did a stint as a munchkin in *The Wizard of Oz* on a West End stage. You could say she's a chip off the old block. I am biased, but she is a brilliant singer.

Emily says, 'I've got the best bits of Mummy and the worst bits of you.' What that means is, nice voice *but* she has no patience for anybody and knows it all.

I know I drive them all mad. I'll come in the kitchen in the morning with the enthusiasm of a Saturday night TV game show host. I can see the blanket of annoyance that settles on them all. It's a rainy Monday morning in November and I moonwalk into the kitchen backwards, waving and shouting, 'Hey kids!'

They'll glower, 'Can't you just walk into the kitchen like a normal person?'

I try to dial it down, drop the moonwalk perhaps and just jump in the room with two arms outstretched instead. Nope. It's never enough. 'You're not on stage. You don't have to announce yourself every time you come into the room.'

Even Dawn, who in our darkest hours I've never stopped having a laugh with, finds it infuriating. 'Can you just stop being so positive.'

And now there's a new check on Dad's ego and this one's on high alert every minute of the day. Our Em pulls me up on things every minute of the day. She's brutal. Yup. She's definitely a mini-me. It was a light switch with her; she was absolutely angelic till she was about ten and it was just like someone came in one day and flipped a switch and she was the devil child. It was all, 'Oh God, you stink' and 'I hate the way you eat.' And, 'Your manners!' When all that starts you know you've lost them for quite a few years. 'Don't kiss me!' It's a real thing to get a kiss now. Really hard work.

I've never really compared us to other families because we're not like other families. Underneath a lot of my time with the kids there is an area of guilt for me because of how much I work. I miss most of the football games and parents' evenings. I've sacrificed a lot, if I'm honest. Doesn't mean I don't miss them when I go away; I miss them like crazy.

If I'm performing, touring, and Daisy has a cough, I can't go home. I've got to get out of there. I can't risk getting ill. Being away from her is torture. Daisy's still in that gorgeous stage where she just loves everything you do. She'll listen to music I've been making that day. 'Oh, I like that one, Daddy; I can dance to this one.'

She's curious and interested. Jasmine had got me into tongue scraping. Tongue. Scraping. Yeah, I know. Sounds weird. But I can't face the world without scraping all the crap and fur off my tongue before I've cleaned my teeth. I don't feel quite right till I've got rid of that. Little Daisy stood watching the end of that routine one morning.

'What *are* you doing?'

'Getting rid of all the rubbish on my tongue,' I explained.

'Where's all that come from?' she shrieked.

'It's all the dust and pollution in the air.'

'Yuk!' said Daisy.

'Exactly,' says Daddy. 'I don't want that in my belly.'

I can just imagine Em's reaction. 'Urgh, you're so disgusting.'

Dan probably wouldn't notice. Boys are different. Dan's chilled, he wants the easiest life. Is that not men in general? They want the easiest route from A to B. But the girls are killers. They know where to aim. When Em starts on me I just ignore it; I don't know how else you deal with it.

The times I miss the family most is when I'm by myself, far away, somewhere like LA. I'm there in one of the most beautiful states in America, one of the most ideal places in the world, and I'm just depressed being away from my family. I get on FaceTime. Kids live in the present. You're in the way. You've rung in the morning and they're on their way home from school, hungry and tired. You're a pain. You're delaying them. You're 6,000 miles away just aching and desperate for a bit of time with them and you're just an inconvenience. If you're not going to be here with us, Dad, don't bother getting in our way. That's the reality of it. It's punishing.

I do fight for time with Daisy now. I'm around more than I used to be. Daisy's probably had more of me than the other two have just because when it all kicked off again with Take That it was such a lifeline for me. I put my heart and soul into it and a huge amount of my time. I missed a lot of Emily's early years because of it.

Dawn's diabetes diagnosis came as I was writing 'Since I Saw You Last', and gearing up for my last season on *The X Factor*. The writing is a dream; it's my happy place. Three years in, the long, long hours spent on primetime TV feel the opposite. I feel overexposed and over it.

Having said that, the final season was a blast. The best thing about that third series was working with Sharon Osbourne. I love Sharon Oz. Whatever you see on telly, that's her. It's no act. She's larger than life, up on everything. Every film, every hot new artist, she knows everyone – and everything about them. As soon as we met I gave her a fat piece of juicy gossip about a past *X Factor* judge and we were inseparable ever after. Just hilarious levels of gossip and bitching. It's all harmless. It's kept behind closed doors. It's extremely entertaining – until it's you. Oh yeah, I bet I've featured somewhere along the line.

You aren't anyone until you've been the subject of Sharon O's gossip.

I would imagine that I have. 'Have you seen that fat bastard?'

Sharon is Elton and Elton is Sharon. That's why they get on so well, those two. They've known each other for a lifetime. I'd met Sharon through him before. He was our mutual friend. We bonded over talking about how much we love him. I first met Elton in 1993. Paula Yates brought him to one of our Wembley Arena shows. The following night we went to Elton's house in Windsor for dinner. This was a big night for me. The eyes of this 22-year-old Frodsham lad were open wide.

This was success on a level I couldn't imagine, then. There was a butler, and a butler in charge of the butler. In fact, there were staff everywhere. There were miles of heavy drapes, museum grade antiques and thick silk carpets. My mouth dropped open as I came through the door and it didn't shut for two hours. I caught Nigel's eye as we sat at this dining table that just disappeared off into the distance. He was obviously as dazzled as we were.

What was lovely was we sat down to a really traditional meal we knew all about: roast beef and Yorkshires. Pudding came: apple crumble and custard. Elton said, 'Don't worry about dessert, it's got no sugar in it, only sweetener.' Of course I was shovelling it in. 'Food for nowt!'

After dinner he got on the grand piano in the living room and played 'Your Song'. The penny dropped. If I'd had a beard, I'd have scratched. The mouth closed. All this. From that.

I had been so influenced by countless record industry people saying, 'I know.' They were trying to make me less traditional. What you need to do is: new jack swing/write to beats/use less chords/listen to the charts... Seeing Elton, I knew what I needed to do next. Go back to the piano.

It's a significant place sitting at a piano. It's changed the course of my life on so many occasions. It's where I've written my most memorable songs. It's a place to turn when things have gone wrong, when times are bad. It's a place I go when times are good. Two weeks after I met Dawn, I went to my piano and wrote 'Forever Love'. In finding our place in the charts, I realised that night that I'd been thrown off course. Seeing Elton play that night made everything clear. Go back to the piano. Not long after, I wrote 'Back For Good'.

On a less noble note, Elton's gaff gave me major aspiration issues. Guess I needed to go off and make some money. The seeds of a big pop star mansion in Cheshire had been sown.

For all my grumbling about *The X Factor*, that last season was a lot of fun. I had a great gang around me and week after week my dressing room became the place for the unofficial after-party. It'd always been a bit like that. We'd put some fabulous wines on my rider. Margaux, Pauillac, St Emilion. Sometimes I'd bring in rare reds from my cellar at home while Mrs O. brought in the vintage champagne. We'd order in from Nobu to Nando's. Yup, we ate dirty some weeks. Everyone swung by that dressing room.

Sharon Oz would lean across between acts, sometimes while they were singing: 'Let me know when that Nobu's arriving, I'll be straight in.'

Everyone would pile in. My gang are all great fun: Lizzie, Elisa, Luke, Danielle – Luke's assistant. Ben would be there. Showbiz pals would drop by: Keith Lemon, Harry Hill, James Corden, usually a footballer or two; they love a bit of *The X Factor*. Let's just say there were definite end-of-term vibes. People got to hear about this party. Peter Fincham, the Head of ITV, always popped by: 'Good show. Ooh! Nobu?'

'Come on in. You a left-bank Bordeaux guy,' I'd say, holding up the Paulliac, and then the St Emilion in the other hand, 'or right-bank?'

I never worried about my rider on ITV. They looked after everyone on that show, except the contestants.

The BBC? Different story. On the BBC you bring your own rider. If I ask for anything it might be some water and some nuts.

On a Sunday night we'd get the results done as quickly as we could and then one judge would take their turn to take us all to dinner somewhere. I took us to the Arts Club in Mayfair, Nicole took us to Nobu Berkeley round the corner, Mrs O. took us to the Dorchester on Park Lane and only went and got a stripper in. Louis took us to Mr Chow's in Knightsbridge. We'd take others with us but it was strictly invitation only. 'Shall we invite ITV this week or the production company?'

Getting an invite to the judges' after-party became a bit of a thing. On Dermot's week he took us to Pitt Cue in Soho. We've got toilets in our house bigger than this room, but, damn, it's good. Best meat ever. Place is packed, and Sharon's passing her little Pomeranian round. Dawn's there, giving me those eyes; not the rolling ones, the I-want-a-puppy ones.

You could not have met a more different judge from the one who was constantly hanging round the contestants' house in Season One, working overtime trying to nurture talent. I wasn't just like Tulisa by that third and final season – I was worse. By that 2013 X *Factor* it was 'Come back, Tulisa, all is forgiven.'

Funnily enough, I saw Tulisa not long ago. We gave each other some big showbiz hugs. 'It's great to see you, girl.'

She stands back from me and goes, 'Guess what? I do yoga and I'm gluten-free.'

'What, after you took the piss out of me for two years?'

She looked great. 'Yup. I'm loving it.'

One more rubbisher converted.

*   *   *

After Christmas, on our wedding anniversary, Dawn nipped off up the M6 and found Hugo the Pomeranian, the runt of the litter, who looked like a tiny fluffy black sheep and behaved like a massive pain in the arse. Pedigree Hugo joined Cookie, our mongrel who'd been a peaceful, biddable and loving member of our family for a few years. That little Cookie, if she could talk... the secrets I've told her coming in after a few wines on a Saturday night. She's adorable. Unlike Hugo. It took three years to house-train the little bastard and he's never stopped yapping to this day. He arrived and it seemed like a good time to head off and do an arena tour of Since I Saw You Last.

I wanted to do this tour without the safety net of Take That. And without all the bits that I feel like, sometimes, we put there because we think we're not good enough. Going on stage by myself with no 20-foot screens, none of the neon rain, pyrotechnics, dancers and elephants of

Take That was a new challenge. I needed to look back to when I was in the social clubs, to the purest kind of stagecraft that I learned when I was 17. It wasn't easy winning those audiences over back then. They'd see this kid with dyed blond hair come out and be thinking, 'Oh, Jesus, this is gonna be shite.' If you don't grab them in the first four minutes, you've lost them and you'll never win them back.

In the clubs I'd win them over with my voice. I'd start with something big like 'Phantom Of The Opera' to show my voice off. 'Hang on. He's quite good, isn't he.' Then a little gag. 'I'd better be quick because I've got to get back to the children's home before eleven.' Cheesy, which would tell all these old folks that, yes, you knew you were young but didn't take yourself too seriously.

They're tough those clubs. People don't come out for the acts. They come out for the bingo. You're second fiddle to the bingo. I've been on before when you're one song away from the end of your first spot and the entertainments secretary of the club will click the mic on and announce, 'Bingo. Bingo cards being sold now,' as you're belting out 'Love On The Rocks'. Nothing's ever been as hard as a working men's club gig, if I'm honest.

As I introduce my last song, every chair leg in the whole bloody room is scraping the floor as the audience is up and off to buy their bingo cards. Your closing note is to a sea of backs in their Saturday best.

After the bingo you come on to do your second set of the night: the dance spot. This is where you play classics like 'The Final Countdown', 'Celebration' and 'September' by Earth, Wind & Fire. This is the easier spot. Only the lazy bastards don't want to get up and dance to Kool and the Gang. Three songs before the end of the set, that mic clicks on again. There's only one thing in these clubs that trumps bingo. 'Piesavarriv—'. Yup, you're singing to an empty room again.

On a solo tour the chat is key. As soon as the audience feel like they're your friend, you've got them. Back then I would start with, 'Good evening, Sunderland,' then I might tell them they all look gorgeous. Then, I'd do the whole, 'In 1991, Take That started.' Yay!

They all cheer. 'In 1996, they split up.' You get the boos. Bit of a pause. Then, 'Go on, who called the helplines?' You've got 'em. 'You should be ashamed of yourself.'

We're all friends. Now let's have some fun.

As a performer, I'm so lucky. I can do a Take That show, and it's massive; it's all arms in the air and rocking out with 80,000 people. And I can do these solo shows, which reflect where I started and require a totally different kind of confidence. A solo show is very exposing in the most thrilling way. There is nowhere to hide.

I love these contrasts in my work. And I love it when it's hard; I love fighting for anything. It's very rarely easy in music. When it's not a battle, I get bored. The artists that come out of those clubs are a very particular breed. Competing with other singers? Easy! Try going up against bingo and pies. There's only a few that make it. And there's the haunting reality that we leave this world as we enter it. We may always go back there again.

20

AMERICA NOW AND THEN

'The tension is high
and the silence is loud'

I'm in Aberdeen, in the dressing room, doing a few stretches and vocal warm-ups, getting my body ready for the next two hours on stage.

Elisa comes in with the phone, her hand over the mouthpiece. 'You've got to take a call.'

I wasn't too friendly about this. 'I'm going on in ten minutes.'

'Take the call, Gary. It's Harvey Weinstein.'

I'd heard his name a bit. I didn't really know quite what it meant back then.

She obviously did. 'Trust me. Take it.'

I talk to this Weinstein. He wants me to write one song for his musical, *Finding Neverland*, which is based on his movie starring Kate Winslet and Johnny Depp. He's just premiered in Leicester for four nights (it's a testing ground for new musicals apparently). He invited friends, who had told him it's missing one great song. One song, that's all.

I did the Aberdeen show.

The next morning I called Eliot. 'El, who's Harvey Weinst—'

'Whatever he wants, tell him yes, we'll do it. Because whatever he's doing, it'll be big.'

El and I started working together on a few songs at my place. He'd play a little something on the piano and I'd listen a while before sitting down next to him: 'Budge up, I think we've got something here.'

We send this song over. They like it. One song turns to two, to five. Then Weinstein says he wants us to come to New York to meet some woman called Diane Paulus. They want us to do the whole score.

It's a big, *big* meeting. Weinstein, all the big guns are there, and we pretty much apologise our way through it in a 'We're from

England; we've never done this before; we're the little pop guys' kind of way.

We're introduced to all the Broadway types at various meetings in New York. All these theatre-types start imparting their knowledge from a great height down on us, the newbies. El and I suck this up, but a couple of them are starting to rub us up the wrong way and are driving me nuts.

So by the time we're back in the UK, I say, 'El, I'm not having this, mate.' Didn't they know who I used to be? No, they didn't. Being Americans they didn't even know who I was now.

We'd walk out of these meetings feeling patronised by their 'Remember, it's the law of Sondheim' chat.

'I'm not having this, lad. We need to get our heads together. We've got to get one step ahead of this bunch. We've got to work out why our music should be in this show.'

The one thing El and I noticed about the score was that it mirrored the setting, 1900s London. We'd never dreamed of being Rodgers and Hammerstein. This felt like old theatre. We sat there and thought about it. Did that really make sense? J.M. Barrie was a visionary. He was creatively a radical of his time. If he was standing in that theatre in 1904, he wouldn't have been hearing classical music. He'd have been hearing pop music. The music that we write. That's why we're doing this show. He wouldn't be harking back another hundred years.

'By Jove, I think he's got it. That's the bit they don't understand; that's the bit they can't do,' says El. 'That's us.'

* * *

That conversation changed everything. We've got a job to do here and that's to write pop music, and by that I mean great music. Great melodies that tell the story and it ain't gonna be traditional.

'Some woman called Diane Paulus' turned out to be amazing, an incredible woman. One of *Time Magazine*'s hundred most influential people in the world and a great Broadway musical director. As our director, she totally embraced that ethos. We never heard Sondheim's name again. Once they realised the great Diane Paulus was behind us and they heard the songs... they'd got our backs.

From pretty much that day forward, we stopped being passengers and started driving. That's when it got exciting. We started delivering song after song, 'Believe', 'Feet Don't Touch The Ground', 'Stronger'... Diane was loving it. 'This is kicking off.' She was so excited.

Once we gave ourselves permission, it all fell into place extremely quickly. (It's usually the way; there's a lesson in there somewhere.)

Finding Neverland opened at the American Repertory Theater, which is right on the Harvard campus near Boston. I loved my time in Boston. The total anonymity was heaven; to know you're just another bloke in the coffee shop and there's no one in here peering at you.

Boston, Chicago, Philadelphia. If a show is successful in those cities it transfers to Broadway. We broke box office records with *Finding Neverland*. I don't know which records, but it sounds good. Fact is, it was sold out every night. They're a pretty educated theatre crowd in Boston; this is a new audience for me.

The theatre would empty and we'd stand at the door asking, 'What have you just watched?' 'Was the music good?'

I couldn't do that in the UK. People would just say, 'Oh look, it's that pop group bloke off the telly. He's not very tall, is he.'

Finding Neverland was one of a new generation of Broadway musicals, like *Hamilton* and *Something Rotten!*, with very contemporary scores.

I had joked at the time to the *New York Post* that Harvey would make a great Hook because he was 'the best baddie of all', but as time went on we realised it really wasn't a laughing matter. I've got to say up front, he was always fine with us but you could see he was horrible to his staff. And there was other stuff going on that was kind of worrying. The very day the show opened on Broadway, an Italian model accused him of groping her and he was taken in by the NYPD.

I remember thinking, 'Well, at least he won't be around on our opening night.' But there he was that night, with his wife.

The overriding feeling was of excitement and the team we worked with on Broadway was incredible. Every day I'd be pinching myself as I'd walk down the street to the space we rehearsed in for a month on 46th and Broadway. Broadway! From Frodsham to Broadway, sounds like a great idea for a show.

We opened in March 2015 and to date we've had 1,200 performances. We opened at the same time as ten other shows on Broadway. Within two weeks, there were seven left. Within a month, three. Six months later, there's only two of us left. We'd run our course after eighteen months; only *Something Rotten!* stayed on for another three months after. Broadway likes new, and it has a fast turnover. (The West End doesn't take risks in the same way, as I was about to find out, but let's not get ahead of ourselves.)

Finding Neverland was a genuinely successful show and that was a huge deal for me. At last, I could say that I had achieved something over there. Other than 'Back For Good', which I still hear on American radio, I've never had success in the US. And that's not for the want of trying, I can tell you...

I'd had success this time round. Flashback to the late nineties and the story is very different for me. It's painful to remember but I can pinpoint the start of my demise in the nineties. It was the meetings with Clive Davis, the head of Arista in the US. He'd signed Take That in the US on the strength of 'Back For Good' in 1995. On signing us, he told the American industry paper, *Billboard*, 'This group has a great songwriter in Gary Barlow,' and compared me to Elton and George Michael. So far, so good.

When the band broke up, Clive signed me as a solo artist. He started taking a big personal interest in my solo career and sculpting me into what he thought would be a successful artist stateside. He insisted that I do lots of co-writing, following trends, writing to beats/fewer chords... you know the score. All my proven skills were irrelevant to Clive.

But how could I argue? He knew. 'I know,' he told me. And if anyone did, it was definitely him. He knows. He *knows*. Clive is another word for God in the music industry at this time. He knows.

But does he?

I had two options. Follow my gut and the voice in my head that was saying, 'Fly home, lock yourself in a studio for six months and write great songs.' Or do what 'God' wants. Change my direction and be a pop puppet and don't risk your opportunity to break America.

For those early meetings, I arrived packing bags of confidence and an ego to match. A sequence of gatekeeper receptionists would just wave me through like a big star. 'Go right up, go right in... this way, Mr Barlow.' But over the course of about twenty meetings with 'God' at 30 Rockefeller Plaza, he steadily chipped away at my confidence. I started out swaggering into that building and practically floating up to his big corner office. As time went on, I was feeling on edge before I even entered the building. '30 Rock' is an imposing seventy-storey Art Deco skyscraper. Clive's office had pictures of all the greats he'd worked with: Aretha Franklin, Bruce Springsteen, Whitney Houston, Janis Joplin. He had this great big desk across one corner of the room and behind him a ridiculously massive hi-fi system – of course he did, he's Clive Davis. He's the one who calls up David Letterman and shouts, 'Put my band on the show, Dave!'

He had a 'turner up and downer' who controlled the volume and put the music on. There were always three or four staff in the room hovering around: A&Rs, secretaries, his *people*... He works like a beast – in the morning he's always the first one in and the last to leave at night. Clive's a seriously important guy. You get the picture.

So by now these meetings with Clive Davis were crushing me. I was constantly taking him songs and he simply didn't like the direction I was going in. I'm writing mid-tempo piano-led acoustic guitar, folky British singer/songwriter music. Clive had different ideas and constantly quoted how successful urban music was in the charts. He was determined to make this part of my sound, whether I wanted it or not. Clive paired me off with Jermaine Dupri, who did all the Kris Kross stuff, and Montell Jordan: everyone knows 'This Is How We Do It'. I put my foot down after Montell. Clive's put me with R&B writers and producers, some of them immense talents, but it's just not my sound. We were musical chalk and cheese.

The closest match was a writing session with Babyface. The session was great, nice guy; song, not so much. I played Babyface some of my own music, and he loved it. He was as perplexed as I was about this whole new urban direction my music was being forced in.

It was a frustrating time. I was in a strange country, miles from home, no bandmates. No manager. I was alone.

By this point Nigel has gone. The job description for a manager is pretty clear. Manage me. This is a huge new pond we're swimming in and it's full of sharks. My family were completely out of their depth, so they couldn't help. No one in my life could manage this. Except a manager. Nigel's job. I've said before, don't expect too much from the artist. They're already flawed. Get them singing and songwriting, dancing if they can. Expect no more. They can't cope. I certainly couldn't. The whole situation was way too big for me. Unfortunately, it was way too big for Nigel, too. It was the reason we parted ways. He was no more able to stand his ground with Clive than I was. It was a mess.

My ego walked, which in and of itself was not a bad thing, except it took my confidence with it. Once that happens to any artist you should go and take a long career break. But I didn't. I carried on breaking America and myself at the same time. I knew my confidence was being chipped away at but there was a false hope. Clive Davis is God. He's going to make me big in the States. Just blindly follow, however bad it feels, break the US, break the US. It's every musician's holy grail.

Those meetings with Clive dented the one thing that needed protecting more than anything else. He trashed the one thing that should have been the crown jewels: my creative being. After that, when

I sat at the piano to write a song I didn't know if I was good enough. My confidence had gone. That whole situation did that to me.

When I started writing this book, I didn't want to say anything mean or weasely about anyone. That's not me, and I didn't want to write that kind of memoir. But there's no other way around it. It was Davis who started the beginning of the end for me at that time.

I never felt big in that corner office. I never felt tall. I always felt like everything was miles out of reach. Isn't hindsight amazing? Someone should have gone, 'Uh-oh. This isn't right. The music's not as good as it used to be. You're not the same person you used to be. Your ex-bandmate is doing awfully well out here, so unless you come up with something ten times better, don't do it! DON'T DO IT!'

*　*　*

One day in January 1997, Clive calls. 'I've got you on the next Concorde out of London. I'm flying you to perform "Love Won't Wait" at my pre-Grammy party.' I am flying across the Atlantic faster than the speed of sound, rehearsing the song all the way and thinking, 'I'm flying to America for my last bite at the American Dream.'

There's not many performances in your life where you feel like all roads lead to here. It isn't only a career-changing performance, it could prove to Clive that I can do it. This is my X Factor final. Every performance I've done since I was eleven has led up to this. These pre-Grammy parties have launched hundreds of great artists. It's centre stage for any new artist. There are three people on the bill tonight: Sean – 'Puffy' as he is at this time – Combs, 3T, Michael Jackson's nephews, and yours truly.

I'm marched straight through into Clive's office and he actually says, 'Welcome to America, Gary.'

'I'm there, Clive. I know the song back-to-front, word-for-word.'

'I've had Junior Vasquez do a remix,' he says.

This is the hottest DJ in New York at this time; he's remixed Madonna, Prince, Donna Summer. This new version has got to be ten minutes long and it isn't even a song. The verse is now where the chorus used to be and there are lines in the bridge that are from the intro. The whole thing is a patchwork quilt designed for the dancefloor at the Limelight, not for Gary Barlow.

What do I say? I try to assert myself. 'I don't think I can learn that in time, Clive; I'm on in three hours.'

'Great,' says Clive. 'Let's all head over to rehearse the song now.'

We march down Fifth Avenue and I'm struggling to keep up. No one listens to me as we march over to the venue. In a few hours the insanely opulent ballroom at the Plaza will be packed with 500 of the most powerful and talented people in the music industry – and I'm not ready.

'Clive, you know this, this version. I don't, I don't think we should do this tonight.'

He doesn't listen. He clears an act off the stage. 'Gary's on now.'

As I'm singing he's waving left, waving right, showing me how he wants me to move round the stage, 'Centre, centre, right...' while also shouting out instructions how to sing to this thudding house backing track. All I'm thinking is, I need to learn this, I have to learn this. I'm starting to panic, which is very unlike me. 'Clive, I don't think we can do this.'

Clive isn't listening. So I try his assistant, 'Look, we shouldn't be doing this tonight. We really...'

Another assistant grabs me, 'Gary, quick this way. We're going to do some interviews.'

We go through these double doors and outside there are 150 people in a pre-dinner reception. Full red carpet regalia, champagne. I walk into a wall of press interviews, CNN, MTV. All these people are saying, 'Hey we heard that single, "Back For Good", love it, love it.'

I'm going on in an hour and I still don't know the song. I turn to another assistant. 'Hey listen, guys, when are we gonna rehearse the song?'

'Hey Gary, we've got your suit...'

I'm in the middle of an interview and just walk away. I've never done that before. I'm tugging at the assistant, 'I need to rehearse, I need to talk to Clive.'

No one listens to me.

I'm not going to get out of this. 'Listen, no more interviews. I need to get my suit, which is still in the hotel. I need to get it and I need to learn this fucking song...'

Do I count these bars until I get to the bridge, which used to be where the verse was? Or, I think I could just walk away now and no one would ever know I was meant to have been on.

Clive appears. 'Gary, there's a full house!'

This is Clive Davis' pre-Grammy party. The first people I see are Whitney Houston and Bobby Brown. Clive's date for the night is Aretha Franklin. I spend the last ten minutes trying to learn the song while people are dressing me, fussing over me, doing my hair and make-up. It feels like I'm on death row.

And then I hear the words, 'Here's a guy from England...' My heart is pounding, my mouth is dry. All I've had all day is people, people, people, fussing and pushing me from one thing to another.

The last thing is these four people pushing me onto the stage and the music starting right away. It's so loud that I lose count of the bars. I can't hear where I'm due to come in and start singing. I miss the first chorus going on and then I start to forget the words to my own song because I'm thinking Clive said dance here, move over there. I look out and see Bobby Brown with his back to the stage. It is the longest ten minutes of my life.

I walk off that stage to the sound of my own footsteps and people talking amongst themselves. No applause. And the worst thing of all is that I come off and there's nobody there. It's like I am radioactive.

Puff Daddy goes on stage and people are going crazy. I walk out of the theatre and in front of the Plaza Hotel and it is empty. There's no one out there either. It's pouring with rain and I just walk ten blocks to the Royalton Hotel where I'm staying.

* * *

It was another year before I was dropped. But I knew it was over that night. That was it.

What a lesson I learned from that. The big man doesn't know better, after all. I should have turned round and gone home. I should have said, 'No, I don't think we should do this.' All those years in working men's clubs, I never let someone else tell me what's best for me. Pretty hard way to learn a lesson.

El loves that story. Tears rolling down his face, 'Tell it again, tell it again, tell it again,' he says, like a child. All my best stories revolve around the worst periods in my life. I've almost forgotten the truth because I've told that story so many times, tailored it to different audiences to be the funniest thing ever, but actually that was a painful, traumatic time. For any artist you truly get just one chance in the States. That pre-Grammy party was more than an unfortunate event. It was catastrophic.

Whenever I tell this story to another artist, they say, 'I feel sick.'

In this frame of mind, I go back home to make my second solo album. From any angle, it's not looking good.

What's that story really about? The biggest reason my career bombed at the end of the nineties is that I didn't follow my gut instinct – I didn't follow my intuition.

Now I live on sauerkraut and kefir and other rich sources of good bacteria, my gut is in such insanely good health. Perhaps if I'd eaten more sauerkraut back in 1997 I'd have made it in the States, or maybe not. Gut instinct is a powerful thing; we should trust ourselves.

Weinstein asked me to do his 2014 pre-Oscars party. El and I would sing songs from *Finding Neverland*. Coming through customs at LAX with El, that little story popped into my mind. I straightened my back, looked upwards and thought, 'Look out America, I'm back.' (I've got to say 'for good' now, haven't I?)

I wanted some familiar faces in the crowd so I invited Harry Styles and Nicole Scherzinger. Nicole wondered if she could bring a friend to the after-show party and I said, 'Sure.'

A text comes back. 'FYI, it's Prince.'

After the show, which went well this time, Prince strolled into the VIP section. He's got the cane and the shades on. Even in his Cuban heels, when he walks by he looks tiny, angelic and sweet. I only needed the merest signs. As he walks by, he tips his hat in my direction where I'm sitting with Eliot and Mrs O. The keyboard player in my band, Marcus, was there too.

I'm straight in there like a shot. 'How do you make music in the modern world? Do you use a computer or do you still have an SSL desk? Are you more Eventide H3000 or Lexicon 480L?'

There was a magazine I read when I was a teenager called *Sound on Sound* – it had a readership of about twenty. I'd seen a piece in it about Prince's studio, Paisley Park, when he first opened it in the early eighties. I had so many questions for the guy. Nerd to nerd.

I couldn't shut him up. This Prince fella loved his gear. He'd spent lots of time in East Germany buying outboard equipment and microphones that had been stuck behind that bloody Berlin Wall. He talked about all the Gefell microphones he'd bought there. I said I'd got two of them and he pretty much asked for the serial numbers. Prince was a gear geek of epic proportions.

It was a relief to hear how passionate he was about wires and knobs. We both felt the lack of romance with the music created digitally on a screen. We talked about the convenience of digital versus the quality of all that old equipment. You couldn't find a better person to talk to about it. This is a guy who would play the drums, bass, guitar, keyboards and about thirty other instruments on an album and then kick everyone out of the control room while he mixed the record. The talent is off the scale.

He left us and went and sat in this little booth with the curtain drawn. Fair enough, he's Prince. Sharon shrieked across the table, as only she could, 'All right, Prince, you snotty little cunt.' And Prince drew the curtain back again and smiled and everyone pissed themselves laughing.

Moments later, Marcus turned round and said in his Brummie accent, 'You know what, I can't remember if tomorrow is blue bin day or black bin day.' Keeping it real, thanks lad.

21

FROM FOUR TO THREE

'And we're left in the shadow of doubt'

I f we go back to the start and remind ourselves why we do all this, it's because we love showing people a good time. That's the reason we went to see Nigel as individuals, because we loved entertaining people. We'd done it well over the years. There's a comeback tour and a new record. Another great tour. It's the great awaited second album… everyone's happy again. Best tour ever with *Circus*.

Happiness delivered. Tick. How do we top that? Ah! Robbie's back. Everyone's crazy happy now, and we're gonna do a mega tour. Biggest tour ever. Happy's stock is rising again. It's been non-stop, steady happy for nearly a decade. Our last big gig had been a huge one. Hey! Let's close the Olympics. Yup! It's thumbs-up all round

Then 2014 happened to us.

In January, Jay said he'd probably not be going to do the next Take That album. The year's come in on wobbly wheels. By May they appear to be coming off.

Tax.

Take That are not a scandal band. There'd be the odd thing in the *News of the World*, the odd kiss and tell, but nothing really dirty like that. The tax thing, yes, it felt dirty.

When I agreed to write this book I made it clear I wouldn't be dwelling on the tax issue, but as I wrote I found I felt differently. All the feelings around the tax situation have been a part of my life these last few years. I've felt ashamed. I wanted to apologise for ever entering into such aggressive and risky financial transactions. I have to take the full blame – I signed the documents. I knew what the investments were designed to do and I simply didn't ask enough questions about them. I let it happen and it was definitely one of the most stupid things I've done.

The history of these decisions goes back to when I was 18. As soon as I joined the band I never had to think about finances again. I had money and everything was done for me. Bank accounts, tax returns, pensions, mortgages, expenses, inheritance planning, family trusts... they were all things that showed up in front of me, completed, and waiting for me to put a signature on them.

When it comes to finances I only understand things up to a point. But I pay someone, a lot of people, a lot of money to take care of these things and keep me out of trouble. It's easy to fall back on the defence that we just don't understand these things, let alone the danger of getting involved in them, but it appeared the accountants didn't either.

These Icebreaker things sat alongside SIPs, pensions, tax relief on charitable donations and ring-fencing inheritance. Solutions to rich people's problems, basically. I never worried about them or lost any sleep over them. Frankly, I gave them no thought whatsoever. I was told, 'These are just things you do to reduce your tax liability.'

In May, my lawyer got sent a story that would be appearing in a newspaper the next day accusing me of 'aggressive' tax avoidance. That sounded more like tax evasion and nothing like 'financial planning'. I read the story and you know what, I agreed with it. How can this kind of tax avoidance be legal? And if we shouldn't be doing it, why is it legal? And, Jesus Christ, how am I the face of it?

My first thought was, 'Am I going to jail?'

My second thought, 'Can I blame somebody for this?'

My third? 'How do I escape it?'

The truth is the story ran. And so did I. The guy who wants everyone to like him was suddenly the baddie. I disappeared from view. The only thing on my mind was sorting this mess out.

It was easy to sort the money side of the mess; I just paid it back. Getting rid of the smell of it, that was not so simple.

What I did next was a mistake. Instead of making a statement apologising straight away, I turned my phone off and ran off to

Oxford. It took me six months to make any kind of comment on the matter. And when I did, I cocked that up too. Taking other people's advice had got me into this situation so I thought I was wise to write the statement myself and tweet it directly.

What a stupid idea.

Whatever President Trump might think, grave situations are not best addressed by writing tweets. They were analysed and my apology deemed lacking. The more I dig, the deeper the hole.

This is in September. Two months later we have an album coming out. I feel weak.

It's at times like this I am even more grateful for the fans. I'll always be indebted to them for their support during this period. In the good times it's easy to be a fan; you come to a show, buy a record, you support a glowing career. I sometimes took this kind of support for granted in the nineties, and I assumed it would be there for ever. At times like these, that's when you really appreciate the fans. Having known me for as long as they had, they knew that I had messed up, but they also knew I would put it right.

* * *

I think we put our heads in the sand about Jason. There's a Take That album due this year. It's a case of, let's get in the studio and imagine us as a three. Can we do it? Yes, we can. And you never know, he might have a change of heart. Deep down, I knew he wasn't coming back.

So we started the process of being Take That. Hanging out together. Laughing, lots of talking. Writing. Recording. And it wasn't long before it felt all right. We'd call the album, simply, *III*.

One of the things that has always fuelled our ambition is feeling the need to prove the doubters wrong. Ambition's always fuelled by something and when that's gone, that's the day it's over. Finding the ambition with *III* was a situation we'd never been in before. We were making a record not knowing if it was going to be released. We knew we could cut it. But maybe, when the record company and the world discover we are Jay-less, they wouldn't want us.

In the back of my mind, I'm thinking it might not happen at all this album. Do I want to give six months of my life to something that may never be released?

Of course you go for it. And Mark was convinced he could talk Jay around. Mark and I, we're always ready to do a Take That record. For us it was business as usual.

There were complications with this album: a hangover from *Progress*. *Progress* had left us a slightly worse-off four-piece. Mark and I had really got a fantastic partnership going on, writing music together. We all wrote on *Beautiful World* and *The Circus* but Mark and I always led that process.

The seed of a Take That song is generally Mark and me sitting scratching our beards, staring into space and batting ideas back and forth. We're both good at lyrics, we're both good at melodies and we're like two excited kids when the two things collide. The reality is that on *Progress*, Robbie took that position next to me as a songwriter. I don't even know if this bothered Mark or not, but it was up there with all the other anxieties at that time. We needed to find our songwriting mojo again and then it would be business as usual.

There was a symmetry in Take That. Me and Mark. Jay and Howard. Howard has lost the most. The reality of being a three-piece hit him the hardest because the pressure was on him now to do the job of two people. With four or five, you can all take it in turns to hide a little bit. As Mark sang a song, I'd go and sit at the piano and take the weight off. Howard hates interviews, detests them, but we can carry him. Howard doesn't have a lot of confidence.

I worried for Howard. I wanted him to feel safe and happy as a three.

One of my best memories of that *III* period is watching Howard grow into this new role of not being a handsome bookend. He's tall, he looks better centre stage between us two. There's always good that comes of these things. Now we bookended him.

It's September now, and it's getting awfully late to make this next album. Is Jay in or not? We all agreed to meet at Jonathan Wild's house to finally settle it. Mark was still optimistic he could talk him round. Howard and I, less so.

It's a beautiful day in Notting Hill. We all go round to Jonathan Wild's townhouse. He makes us a cuppa and makes himself scarce.

It was obvious Jay was out. You could see it in him as he walked into the room. He'd made a decision and he clearly felt great about it. Jay was listening to his gut. I of all people could not argue with that. We had no choice but to say, 'Thanks for being here for the last three albums.'

We were so lucky to have him. We had all looked up to him and continue to do so to this day. Jason was the first of my bandmates I ever met at Nigel's office. Afterwards us two went for a Burger King. I seem to remember him not really eating the food; he certainly was not shovelling it down in the way I did. It's Jay I have to thank for the food epiphany. He was always telling me, as I rubbished away, 'When you know what I know, it's like a light being switched on.' He was dead right about that.

It was a sad day; we all felt pretty downhearted. However, you put four Northerners in a room, especially ones that know each other as well as we do, and there's not many things so sad that they won't turn it into an opportunity to take the piss. Yes, we reverted to how we deal with most things. Every time Jay would say something serious, Howard would crack a joke at the ridiculousness of it all.

'Sorry to disappoint all my fans…'

Howard would repeat after him, 'Sorry to… No you should change that, Jay. Sorry to disappoint my four fans.'

Howard groans, 'Oh, God, I'm not gonna be able to walk down the street without hearing, "Why've you left the band?"'

The papers are always mixing those two up. There'll be a picture in the paper of Howard with the caption, 'Jason Orange, walking through Manchester yesterday.'

This reminded me of when we all first got together in the nineties. Even though back then we were doing something astronomically life-changing for all of us, it constantly felt silly. It is silly, all this stuff.

We left Jonathan with our statement for the fans. 'Jason leaving is a huge loss both professionally and even more so personally. Jason's energy and belief in what this band could achieve has made it what it is today, and we'll forever be grateful for his enthusiasm, dedication and inspiration over the years.'

It's all true. So true.

Now he's gone. He's definitely gone. Would Take That have a future as a three?

* * *

Being in a band like ours is a bit like being in a football team. The fans are vocal. And when they speak, you listen. It was me that had the idea of sitting and watching our Twitter feed for the next few days to measure how the audience reacted. It needed to be a few days, so we could get beyond the devoted superfans. We needed to hear from the casual fan as well.

If it was a vote, then it was a landslide.

Social media said yes to us as a three. We decided to carry on and see this album and tour out, but in the certain knowledge that this tax stink and no Jay had sucked some of the magic out of the air.

With all this doubt and change, my did we need each other. Us three leaned on each other. We spent a lot of time together that year. We'd come in to write and spend most of the time moaning. We did more family dinners than usual with the girls. It was great; we were rebuilding our team. But there was no doubt, no matter how much of a positive spin I put on everything, it had rocked the boat. We were unsure.

We just crammed that album with content and made it as seductive and pop as possible. It was our mission to entertain *everyone*. We threw everything at it, like a divorced parent at Christmas.

With confidence low we did more co-writing than normal. There was one thing I was sure about. We had our killer single: 'These Days'. We also made the decision to make the most straightforwardly pop album we'd done since we came back. There was no directional change. No great creative story. If I call it safe, it is as a positive. It was us asking the world, 'We're only three, is this going to be all right?'

Looking on the bright side, though, the constant question of 'When's Robbie coming back?' was replaced now by 'When's Jason coming back?'

22

DRINKING SLOP

'It's all right it's okay,
I go through this every day'

Returning home to Cheshire at the end of 2014, I realised how much my eating habits had changed while watching my brother work his way through dinner. Honest to God, my brother's plate. As he took something off the top, something else would roll off the edge. There were sprouts tumbling this way and that. He'd finished his dinner before I'd finished my little girl's bird plate. Then the crash; he falls asleep because his organs are all shouting at one another, 'Quick! Emergency! We've got to break down seventeen roast potatoes and ten pigs in blankets before the Christmas pudding comes in.' The image that comes to mind is A&E on New Year's Eve.

Then he wakes up saying he's peckish. That used to be me.

I don't eat too much any more. I avoid the feeling of fullness because it takes me right back there. Takes me back to how I felt all day and all night in the wilderness years. Fullness makes me depressed. It makes me feel guilty when I've eaten a lot of food. It's gives me a pit-of-the-stomach dread. The feeling of fullness gives me a flashback and in my head I'm back on my knees in the studio at Delamere.

It's automatic, now. I know when to stop eating.

I'm still haunted by the whole thing. But maybe that's a good thing. Maybe that's healthy because it keeps me checking myself.

It's going to sound like I've got a food problem here now. I just keep food a bit more at arm's length. It can cause so much damage. But I also love food. I love it. I hate it as well. I went for dinner recently and they brought a plate of macaroons at the end. I didn't touch them. I didn't even notice them.

The person I was with asked me why. 'Those are the foods I'd have been eating back then. They're the foods that made me end up so fat I was stuck in my own bed.'

* * *

Come on, one won't hurt.

That's how I got into that state, by thinking one won't hurt. By going, 'Oh, sod it. Let's just have a plate of chips with that. In fact give us another one! Yeah, and let's have a macaroon or two while we're at it.'

I have to keep tight control. I never want to go back. It was a life lesson back then and I respect it. You've got to have your mind in gear all the time. Our human default is one of laziness and greediness. It takes no effort to be lazy or greedy. Making the right decisions requires effort and sometimes some soul-searching. It isn't easy.

Let's compare it with smoking. I officially stopped smoking the day Dan was born in 2000. However, I'm still a smoker. To mark an auspicious day once every couple of years – end of a tour, an Ivor Novello, an especially large cheque – I'll spark up a Marlboro Light.

Love a Marlboro Light.

I used to be a freak for smoking. In my nature there's an obsessiveness and the way I smoked, oh it was beautiful. I loved the ritual and the order of my daily smoking habit. It became everything. It was when I was first rattling around my big pop star mansion waiting for the label to drop me. That was the big smoking period. There was a real routine to it, which I enjoyed. I used to go to our local Esso garage at midnight so no one saw me, especially not my mum, and buy twenty Marlboro Lights and forty Silk Cut Ultra Lows.

The order was, I'd open them that night before I went to bed; I'd open both boxes and leave them in the studio. I'd wake up the next morning and because they'd dried a bit overnight, when you lit them, you got this satisfying crackle. It's such a lovely calming sound, the sound of the flame burning the paper and creeping up the strands of tobacco; it's like music this sound of smoking amplified in my ear. My dependency was sufficiently high to wake me in the night with cravings. Usually about 3am, I'd get out of bed and have to go downstairs to smoke some more.

I'd lay them out in threes. So I'd have two Silk Cut Ultra Lows and then a Marly Light for pudding. That was the cycle. And that's what I'd do all day. I got through nearly a box of Marlys a day, always Lights – obviously, not the reds, I'm not an addict, come on gimme a break. And a box or so of them Silk Cut Ultra Lows. There's a point where I couldn't be arsed with them at the end of the day. They barely hit the sides. It was just to make me feel better: smoke an Ultra Low – it's like a low fat cigarette that, isn't it. 'Healthier.'

That's what my day was then. Smoking was just another way to attack myself.

I loved that routine, it felt so... so, *gentlemanly*. When Dan came, I just put patches on my arms for six weeks, enjoyed that, too, then I stopped.

When I first met the Hemsleys, what they were saying was a much more forthright version of what ended up in their first book. There was real anarchy in their message: that we're all being conned and poisoned by this processed packaged crap.

Every time they spoke about food they were telling me the complete opposite to what I'd always known from reading the back of cereals, watching adverts, reading diet books, even talking to the professional dieticians. The anarchy in their message was brand new to me and it was thrilling to feel like we're little people fighting an industry.

I was so excited about their book; me and the whole team had been helping them test recipes, and we all felt so invested in their success. We all felt great, mincing around showing off our tiny bums having done no exercise or diets. It was such a surprise to then read through the book that made it to the shelves and see how much they had to sieve, filter and compromise their beliefs in order to appease a mass market unready for the truth. I always liked that Deliciously Ella girl too. She was early to the party with this whole thing of eating well and wise, or 'clean eating' as it came to be known. She was beaten up for it too.

I'm not saying, 'Hey everyone, be exactly like me.' It's just that I'd spent an adult lifetime never knowing how to eat well. Now all the Rubbishers were piling in on my mates who had changed my life for the better and telling everyone clean eating is rubbish, and what you wanna do is eat more pizza.

How about we rephrase clean eating as the slightly more clumsy, 'food you make yourself from scratch so that you know exactly what's in it'. Is that cool? Or shall we rubbish that too.

Ella and the Hemsleys have stopped using the word 'clean' now. They've stepped back from the health angle because they got a bashing from the media. Well, not from me.

You know what? I'll admit it. I read those Gwyneth Paltrow books. Love them. Kale. Yes. Turmeric. Yes. Tongue scraping. Yes. Yet the attitude is to do it down. Rubbish it. I don't care any more if people think my eating is cranky, or if people accuse me of having an eating disorder. Couldn't care less.

Why shouldn't we be interested in the food we eat? The Hemsleys just got me started. I'm on my own journey now. Sometimes I eat rib-eye steak. Other times it's a 'cauliflower steak'. Cauli-what? you say. I know, some of this stuff is ridiculous.

People say, 'Clean eating will make you obsessive about what you eat.'

Now that's true, it *is* true. Is it such a bad thing? We need to be on high alert, when so much of what's out there is rubbish. That 2000 period when I am overeating, puking and miserable, I was overfed and undernourished. Now, if there's such a thing, I'm underfed yet overnourished. I feel great. Make of that what you will.

You've got an eating disorder, says one person; you're my healthy eating role model says another.

Sometimes I go to places where there's nothing to eat. There's nothing on the menu I can eat. Sometimes in America, I meet people for breakfast and the menu will be all pancakes and fried bananas and maple syrup and just nothing I will eat. It doesn't bother me any more, I'll just say, 'Coffee for me.'

I can skip a meal now and again, anyway. Never worry about that. Love a bit of a fast, in fact. I like sticking to the rules of clean eating. Sugar. Don't go near it: no apple crumble, custard, ice creams… I see it as fanning a fire, that stuff. If I start on that, I can't stop. Hence, no macaroons.

We were doing a show in Hyde Park and beforehand we sat down for an interview with Jo Whiley. She's coming out with some summery banter, asking all the lads what their favourite ice cream is. Howard's mint choc or something, Mark likes strawberry, and then she turns to me and just says, 'And I can't imagine the last time you had an ice cream, Gary.'

And she's right. For me, the party is over forever. But, like with that occasional Marlboro, I will eat an ice cream, just the one – every year. I never feel like I'm on holiday until I've had an ice cream from this little place called the Creamery in Santa Monica.

I care about the fact that people are still harping on about how bad clean eating is while half the food we buy in this country isn't just processed, it's *ultra*-processed. (That's a statistic, by the way, it's not me exaggerating.) Our priorities are totally out of whack here. Stop shooting the messenger. Jamie Oliver is passionate about the effects of industrially produced 'big food' on our lives. And what do we do? Rubbish him and slag him off.

I'm not always saintly. I'll eat like a clean-eating princess for a while and then, of course, I start to lose my grip and have a glass of wine and then you feel a bit different the next morning, and then the next time you have two glasses of wine, then three. Then you're like, a few peanuts won't hurt with the wine. That's life, isn't it? Humans aren't robots. Bits of your old life come back. I might have coffee now and again, and that builds up and suddenly it's coffee every day. Peanut butter's coming back. Next thing you know I'll be on the Golden Grahams.

One way of resetting these habits is to go on a 'three-day green'. I never feel like I eat enough green stuff. So for three days, the only rule: eat anything, as long as it's green.

* * *

I was on a three-day green the first time Tim Firth and I got together to work on *Calendar Girls*.

I said to Tim, 'Listen, it's great that we're here but I just need to tell you, we're doing green only for three days.'

I used to have this thing called 'slop', which was whizzed up mint, spinach, coconut oil and coconut water. Mum walked out on cue with two glasses for us. Tim was both horrified and impressed; he had known me since long before Fat Day. 'What happened to the man with a giant tub of Quality Street? I've not seen chocolate in your vicinity for a decade.' Mum put down his glass of greenness. 'What's that? Fermented marsh grass?'

'That, Tim, is slop. Tuck in. I recommend you use a spoon.'

Mid-afternoon, Mum brought in a platter of broccoli with our tea – green tea, it goes without saying.

Tim said nothing, but his expression said, 'What, no Hobnobs?'

Not long after, he said he needed to go home to finish up some scripts and never came back in the next two green days.

Tim Firth and I both grew up in Frodsham. We didn't know each other as kids, he's a bit older than me, and he was headed to Cambridge University to study English while I'd spent what could have been my college years doing dance routines in red vinyl hot pants and taking private jets.

Over the years we'd been thrown together. When I won the BBC *Song for Christmas* aged 15, he was one of the judges. Way back in 2000 he had approached me with the idea of doing a musical. Nothing really came of it. In 2010 he'd asked me to come and see his play *Calendar Girls*. He'd had so much success with this story, he wanted to turn it into a musical. Was I game? He took me to see it in Milton Keynes with Lynda Bellingham in the lead role. *Calendar Girls* is about these middle-aged, outwardly ordinary British women, triumphing over personal adversity. It's based on a true story about a branch of the Women's Institute who made a topless calendar.

Going into the third telling of the tale, I had to give it my own spin. I wrote so much of it with my mum in mind, and a lot of those ideas came from watching her struggling with life without Dad. There's a character who loses her husband; she talks about how 'I'd love to climb Mount Kilimanjaro, but do you know what, going upstairs by myself, that's my version of it, it's as hard.'

Mum never said that to me but I saw it. I'd see things like that when I went round her hourse. But her spirit picked her up. Mum got a dog, Teddy, and she started to rebuild her life without my dad. She's part of every club; she sings in a choir, she goes to the theatre, she walks miles and miles every day. Amazing, absolutely amazing, her spirit is what's made her survive. She inspired me so much as I started to write with Tim.

The way Tim and I write is unique. We both had a keyboard and played and sang through the entire story at random writing sessions set around my mum's lounge table.

I'd asked him early on, 'What musicals do you want me to listen to?'

'God's sake, none,' he said. 'If you try to write what you think a musical should be it'll be a lie. There's no such thing as what a musical *should* be.'

He gave me my first shred of lyric to work with: 'So I've had a little work done...' Plastic surgery? Love it! That lyric is never going to crop up in a Take That or a Gary Barlow song. As a result, the melody I came back with was like nothing I'd ever written. New avenues. This always excites me.

That first song, 'Had a Little Work Done', made it into the show. After five years, Tim and I finally brought the story to the stage. I was excited to see it on opening night in November 2015 at the Grand Theatre in Leeds. Stress is like a meditation for me. The bigger the stakes, the calmer I get. We two writers, Tim and I, shared a box at the side of the theatre; I settled in, excited about seeing our show. Whatever it is they learn at Cambridge, it isn't how to chill the fuck out because Tim was a complete nightmare. Any lines that didn't work or moments that went awry he'd crumple up into this contorted ball of anxiety while I just watched in fascination, noting the changes needed for the following day.

I told the house that I really didn't care where I sat tomorrow, as long as I wasn't near him. To date, Tim and I have written two musicals together now, and are working on a third. But we've never, *ever* watched the show from the same place since.

23

"CHILL THE F*** OUT"

'You light the skies, up above me
Λ star, so bright, you blind me'

On 15 January 2016 I arrived in Los Angeles and collapsed on the bed in my hotel room. Something was wrong. I felt dreadful, I felt sick and my body was weak, bordering on paralysis. I rolled over to call down for help, but I couldn't get my shit together. The phone defeated me completely. I just lay there; it felt like I had flu. I was exhausted, but I also felt a terrible anxiety.

I'd nearly missed my Heathrow flight running from a recording session. I had a deadline. I worked on my laptop for the duration of the twelve-hour flight. My head was pounding. For the hour's drive from the airport to the hotel I'd been on the phone dealing with a major issue on a film soundtrack I was doing for Matthew Vaughn. My right ear was cooked. I'd planned to arrive in LA and have two days off. I had been so excited about just lying by a pool doing nothing.

I fell asleep and didn't wake up for seventeen hours. When I woke up I sat up in a fog of nausea. Stumbling into the bathroom, fumbling with the mini bar trying to get water. Everything was difficult. I went back to bed. It must be a virus. I didn't have the strength even to know what to do. I felt like I'd been awake for ten years.

Lying there, then, I had the first panic attack. I'm gasping for air, which doesn't seem to go in. I'm suffocating. Am I having a heart attack? I was scorching hot and then suddenly cold and shivering.

More worrying than the heart attack, I started crying. At first, proper convulsing sobs: shoulder heaving, stomach clenching. This calmed to weeping and a feeling of immense sadness. Nothing's happened, there's been no bad news. My world's all good. The sun's out. I'm in LA.

When the panic attack subsided, I went to sleep for another fourteen hours. When I woke up I cried until I fell asleep again.

I wasn't sure what day it was when I woke up. The curtains had blacked the room out completely, but I could see a sliver of sharp LA light leaking through. It must be daytime, but which day? I stumbled about getting my bearings. I was so dehydrated my pee looked like real ale.

I rang El, like I so often do, and he said, 'Let's just think about this, mate; let's just line up the shit that's happened in the last ten years. You walked off one of the trains on 7/7, two months later your band gets back together and it's been full on ever since. You haven't really stopped since then. Every day. On telly all the time. Stop for a while. Your dad. Poppy. Dawn. Gaz, you're not bulletproof.'

I couldn't do it myself. I couldn't stop. So my body did it for me. It was saying, 'Enough.'

This was burnout.

Eating oily fish and mung beans can only do so much. That just keeps me going, that just keeps me moving; what's going to sort my head out? My mind just exploded.

There were problems the food couldn't solve. I was hiding stuff, you know, hiding emotions, stuffing my feelings under appointments and jobs and busy, busy busyness. Putting sadness under the mattress. My body's spent years full of these feelings that I don't want to confront. El is right. I've tried so hard to be bulletproof, just like my mum was. I've adhered to that stoic attitude, like Mum. But all that pain has to go somewhere. Can we really escape grief?

Any fool could see a crash would come.

These kids know how to emote. Aged 16, Dan went out and got a tattoo of Poppy's initials. Two years on he got another. The men of his generation are educated to respect and listen to their feelings. When Dawn's stressed, she'll say, 'I need five minutes; I've got to get this off my chest because it's really bothering me.' Me, I don't know where it goes, I never deal with anything, I ignore it. I power on.

A lot has gone on in my life but over and above everything else I don't think I realised how devastating losing my daughter was. I had seen grief quite literally physically destroy my wife's body so that she was left with a chronic illness that she will never get better from. She has Type 1 diabetes now, for life. I couldn't tell you how much the worry of that, of seeing its effect on my wife, lived constantly in my own body.

But I didn't dare confront it. I just coped. And worked. And worked. As a dad of a lost child, your grief has to come later. The home is not made for everyone to give up.

I still don't know how I feel. I am still very angry. Anger isn't far along the road of grief. When I talk to the grief counsellor about it, when I say I still feel angry, she says, 'We're still there?'

'Yeah. We're still there,' I say. 'What's that all about? Why?'

'That's all about control,' she says.

Well, there's a surprise.

The grief I felt at losing Poppy, too often I tucked it away. The whole thing is fraught with questions: do I talk about it, or not? If I talk, will it really help me? Will it help other people? The truth is, the one reason I never accept those invitations to talk is because I can't draw any conclusions or analyse it. I'm nowhere near through it. The truth is, if I don't think about it or talk about it I can push it down, evade some of the pain. But the feelings are there. Is a fear of confronting them a reason why I landed on that bed in LA?

It's still hard to believe we've gone through that. Taking that phone call. It's hard to imagine yourself in that hospital room.

There's a different sort of coping too. It's how can we honour this short life that Poppy had, and the experience we had with her, as a part of our life story?

There was a long time without laughter in our house. And laughter is one of the defining things about mine and Dawn's relationship. We do silly voices, we take the piss out of each other. In a restaurant we'll pass the time making absurd comments. On the beach we give everyone around us names. If a bloke with a moustache gets up off his lounger, it's, 'Oh, Midge Ure's off to get an ice cream.' Bald guy walks past, 'Ey up. What's Duncan Goodhew doing here? I always wondered what he was up to these days.'

We keep each other amused with stupid stuff, all the time, with non-stop family in-jokes and constant nonsense.

That all stopped.

Dawn's light went out that night in 2012. It's the only way I know how to express it. I've watched Dawn since then and now, five years on, the light that came into the room when Poppy was born has passed to Dawn. She holds the light now. It's beautiful to see. She took it and every year it burns brighter.

It's very vivid still, and I don't want to forget the day that my daughter Poppy was born. You don't just grieve and things get a bit better and then it's over. When people ask me how many kids I have I want to say four, but I say three because to explain that Poppy died so young is to invite questions. Yet every time I say I've got three kids I feel guilty.

What people don't realise is that to lose a child in this way is no different from losing them at any age.

We've got other kids. I don't know if that makes it easier or not. It probably does.

The pain of losing Poppy is our connection to her. In some ways you don't want the agony to end because when it lets up for a while you feel guilty. You feel like you're forgetting her. You think, 'I'm not hurting as much today. I need to quickly remind myself... oh that's painful again,' the pain is back and she's back. 'Hello, Poppy.'

* * *

So, you might be wondering, how did I get off that bed?

On the second night the hotel got me a doctor. He came in with his stethoscope and did a load of tests. Then he asked the million-dollar question, 'Has anything significant happened to you in the last few years?'

I didn't know where to start.

Five minutes in he said, 'Stop. Welcome to the modern world. My most frequent patients are CEOs in charge of thousands of people, taking no time for themselves, slaves to their devices and burning the candle at both ends and in the middle, too.'

He tells me of all the false diagnoses he has to make so their board and shareholders don't realise these CEOs and big, important people have had a nervous breakdown or a burnout like mine.

'Half my patients are people like you,' he said.

He said he could prescribe all sorts of therapies or treatments but really, there was no medicine required, no pills, no need to come and see him next week at $500 an hour. His prescription was, 'Just chill the fuck out.' Just as the doctor ordered.

On the Friday after this I was flying to New York to meet Dawn. We were both booked into the Crosby Street Hotel. We'd go to see *Finding Neverland* on Broadway, eat in some hot restaurant, do some walking around Manhattan and focus on planning our lives.

Mother Nature had plans, too. On the Friday morning I woke up to 27 missed calls from Elisa: 'There's a storm heading to NY. Get your arse on the next plane. Dawn is already in the air.'

I turned on the telly and this huge snowstorm is all over the news. I ran to LAX and got on the first plane to JFK where I jumped in a cab. As I pulled up and took the case out of the boot, sure enough it started to snow.

I had only just made it and so had Dawn.

We sat in our hotel room with room service watching snow blanket the city. By the next morning it was so bad that Broadway was closed for the weekend. Broadway is run by a guy called Bob Wankel of the Shubert Organization. In an irony too delicious, he made the call to close Broadway from the Lowry Theatre, Salford, in the interval of a little new British musical called *Calendar Girls*.

This was a message from on high. Stay in bed with your wife. Chill the fuck out.

They shut the hotel, all the staff stayed over and they cooked for us and put movies on for us in the screening room in the evening. We had nothing to do all weekend. This was an auspicious start to the new mindset.

* * *

The ways I found to 'check out' were predictable. I discovered yoga, and did it badly. I'm used to going mental in the gym and the gains in yoga are barely noticeable for someone who wants everything, *now*.

Just when I was going to throw in the towel, the words of the doc came back. It took me a long time to get it. But I love yoga now.

I went back to reading. I was always reading in the nineties. In the last few years it had been nothing except my own lyrics and emails.

I'd pull on my magic anonymous beanie hat and take Cookie and Hugo for a walk round the park. Walking the dogs is a brilliant way to escape the world. You're gutted when you see someone you know and they come over to chat.

Less predictably, I went to Hugh Fearnley-Whittingstall's River Cottage cookery school for a few weekends. On one I learned how to make bread; on another I learned how to butcher a pig. When I look back on 2016, those two days were more fun than Christmas and Boxing Day combined. Butchering a pig is like building a raft. One of the most satisfying thing for me is finding things I enjoy that aren't related to music. Turns out cutting up pigs with sharp knives is one of them.

You know what else I got into? Just bumbling about. Pottering. It used to be that if I went to the toilet without my phone I'd be stressing. 'Gah, there's five minutes I'll never get back.' Christ, what a nutter I was.

I stopped thrashing myself in the gym. Very rarely now do I walk out of the gym with a face like a beetroot and soaked in sweat after pumping iron.

Something else I love is just the quiet. Even if I sat in silence before, there was a lot of noise in my head. What taste I've had of quiet has taught me the big goal now is meditation. You don't just decide, 'Oh, I'm going to be a great meditator now.' It takes practice. First of all, you need to grow a bushy beard. I've no time for growing a beard now. But I'm longing to really master this.

The best thing of all, though, was that in these moments to myself I started playing the piano for no other reason than I enjoy it, and not because I've got work to do. It was so good to come home to the place I loved without a deadline or a motive attached.

Obviously the one thing I didn't chill about was taking this goal of chilling out extremely seriously. If I was going to do it, then I was going to do it really well. I would be the best person at chilling out. This required a bit more than yoga, dog walking and pig butchering.

My friend Jeff Rothschild, John Shanks' old engineer, had left the perpetual dark of studio life and gone back to school. Now he is an expert – and you know I love one of them – and a good one at that. Jeff is a sports nutritionist to Olympians, a sleep doctor and a big proponent of fasting and meal timing. He really sorted out my sleep patterns. Before bed I wear big yellow Bono goggles, £15 on eBay, to protect my brain from overstimulation from computer and phone screens. Before I fly, I eat protein at specific times of the day. Jeff had me in bed by ten every night.

Taking time out and not working so much, sleeping properly and wearing Bono goggles had an immense impact on me. I was better at my job, a better dad, a better husband. Without a doubt, a better me. The changes in my life were now so vast, I could barely recognise the old me. What next? If this is what I could do with a little bit of down time, imagine where proper meditation would take me.

24

A NEW REALITY

'If you remember me
everyone else can forget'

G uy Freeman at the BBC had approached me way back, not long after I left *The X Factor*. 'How do we get you on the BBC?'

'It'd have to be my own show, my own idea, and the prize has to be incredible.' Off the top of my head, I had one idea. I mentioned it to him. 'There's going to be a Take That musical and obviously we'll need a band in it. How about we do a show to find the five lads?'

I was sure if we did a big enough sweep of the country we'd find that talent, but it was risky. It was a big ask. You need talent who can sing, dance, act and they've got to have the professionalism and stamina to do eight shows a week for eighteen months.

What I failed to add was that this risky proposition was literally an idea on the back of a fag packet at this time. We had no writer, no producer, no story, no anything. At that point I'm thinking it'll be something like *Jersey Boys*, a musical telling the story of Take That.

If there's one thing I know about the BBC it's that it is a red-tape jungle. Because of their diversity and inclusion policy, we couldn't put an age or gender restriction on who applied to play us. Theoretically, five *Calendar Girls* could show up and get the main parts.

The potential for cock-up was spectacular. But I always think things work out in the end, don't they? Anyway, we'd never get it. The spot they had in mind was the big Saturday night New Year slot to replace where *The Voice* used to be. Given these high stakes and the fact that every production company in Britain was pitching, what were the chances?

Three days later they commissioned it. Better get our skates on.

* * *

By now it's early 2016; the new show, *Let It Shine*, would air in January 2017. We started searching for talent straight away. We had two producers, David Pugh and Dafydd Rogers, who loved Take That enough to get involved with an idea that was, as I've said, not even in its infancy. We still had no writer and no story. We all agreed Tim was the man for the job.

Tim Firth had done a good job taking Madness songs and turning them into the musical *Our House*. I'd just spent five years doing *Calendar Girls* with him. I've got a huge amount of respect for the man's mind. Also, I really relate to Tim. We're very similar in some ways; we're both from Frodsham, we've both had long, stable marriages – which isn't too common in our business. We share a sense of humour. I strongly believe you can't write about the north unless you come from there. Tim understands the humour, he's got the northern touch. You know with Tim it's going to be warm, emotional and funny. Writing our story, it had to be Tim.

Problem. Tim was non-committal. I asked him four times and he kept saying, 'No, I haven't got any ideas.'

Once I got the BBC on board, I called him one last time. 'Tim, this is it mate. I'm about to book another writer here but obviously you are way above everyone else…'

I made out he was top candidate among many. The truth is as far as any musical about Take That went, it was Tim or nowt.

Dead nonchalantly, I told him about the big Saturday night slot.

'Okay. I'll go away for the weekend to have a think,' he said. 'I'll let you know on Monday.'

Monday he comes back with the whole thing sketched out. We went to David Pugh's office in Soho and we sat – Howard, Mark and me – while Tim gave us the old 'picture the scene' treatment.

'The show starts with a girl, Rachel, standing on stage in her teenage bedroom; there are band posters everywhere, her parents are fighting next door…'

The show's called *The Band* but Tim's idea was that it wasn't really about us. The whole show paid respect to a faithful audience. Not just Take That fans, anyone who loved a band as a child growing up. Aside from our music, we don't even figure; there's just a band, The Band, who bring these girls together as kids.

We all loved it. 'Let's do this!'

Things were starting to come together. One of the challenges with this TV show was keeping the two teams happy. Musical and TV production needed different things. All these guys are sitting there in auditions, often disagreeing on who should go through and who shouldn't. In the initial search stage they saw 12,000 people. No more than 120 people can get through to filming stage. Normally you'd audition 1,000 people for a part.

I left them to it, but the jeopardy had me in a panic. To be honest, the musical is looking bigger than the BBC show now. Is the BBC show going to end up a bit of a ball and chain? I know better than most that this TV format might stop us from finding anyone good.

New British musicals are thin on the ground. There's not been many successful Brit musicals in the last twenty years. Tim Minchin's *Matilda* did well, but that's about it.

Tim Firth's idea was a winner. Do we even need the BBC show? Howard and Mark would ask how it was going and as we got closer to the auditions I asked them to come in and help. It was all hands on deck. This was our musical and yet we were handing it over to the BBC team who at the end of the TV show would have nothing to do with it any more. It would be us left holding a baby that can't sing, can't act, can't dance but makes good telly.

While I was doing the singing auditions, Howard and Mark spent time with the actors, sounding them out. Risky, yes, but it was also exciting. It didn't take long to get immersed in the talent show dream. Jason Brock was the best audition. It was the best vocal I'd ever heard on a talent show. I remember Graham Norton running along the corridor at Manchester Studios, going, 'Oh my God! What just happened?'

We'd got Graham on board to host the show. He's the best. It felt like we were booking royalty, and I like him. Graham is funny, not nasty. In the middle of all this I've got *Calendar Girls* opening in the West End and we're writing our next album, *Wonderland*, while putting together ideas for the tour.

Looking at what I'm doing that year, you might wonder what has changed since my supposedly life-changing baby coma in LA. Where's Mr Chilled the Fuck Out?

He's here. The way I rolled had changed significantly.

Considering *Let It Shine* and *The Band* were without doubt the riskiest projects I'd ever done, I was remarkably chilled. The odds on a new British musical succeeding aren't good. Even if you only break even, you're considered a success. That's three and a half mill of David and Dafydd's investors' money in jeopardy. Plus, if I screw up a TV show, that's even more money. Worst-case scenario? They both go tits up. I look bad, they look bad, everyone looks bad.

Step forward Mr Chilled the Fuck Out.

Prior to the LA breakdown, my way of dealing with this project would have been to go to every single meeting and be on every email. I'd be dealing with vast quantities of correspondence going back and forth. On a normal day, I go to sleep with nothing in my inbox and wake up eight hours later to 250 emails.

The new me, he just left them to it. I had my own algorithm. When there's fifty missed calls instead of just ten, then that's the bat phone and it was time for me to get involved. What I'm saying is, I stepped back. I was hands off. And because of it, everyone did their jobs better without this annoying Rubbisher-in-Chief picking at their ideas all the time. Be involved only when it matters, that's my new mantra.

Another change was, I knew exactly what I was all about. I was adamant in those early meetings with the BBC about what I *didn't* want. First and foremost, I told them, 'I want only talent on that show. No one for TV's sake; no one for the audience's entertainment, just there to be laughed at. In brief, do not make it nasty. Any sign of nastiness and I'm walking. You can have your show back.'

When you are this brutally clear about what you want, people react well. It's refreshing for them.

My other mantra with *Let It Shine* was 'Find me talent, real talent. Let's find people real work and let's be decent about it.' And for that you've got to be nice to people. If you want to replicate how theatre works, no one's nasty in auditions. There's none of this humiliating people in theatre. I made these demands, not because I'm a nice guy (though obviously I think I am one); it's because I'm in the business where I've got a theatre show to put on, I need to find the best possible people and for that I need people to come to auditions. *Let It Shine* is not a stunt.

So we've got our writer, producers, we've got a pool of talent, and we've got this big shiny new show launching on BBC1. I know I'm always having massive moments, but this really could be a life-changer for me. If this format works, I could go global, do it all over the world. Launching the musical in every country.

The run-up to the first show was not a smooth ride. As if! I've already had Cowell on, trying to sue us over the format. Then Lloyd Webber's being quoted: 'It's the same as the one I did with finding Joseph.'

I told my lawyer, tell them all: don't spend any money on lawyers. Because it's not even me your suing, it's the BBC. This is a different beast.

Rather than being on the studio floor poking around in the auditions, I went off and did a little PR job ahead of the show launch and had dinner with most of the editors of British newspapers. Some old acquaintances, some new faces. I told them about my idea for this show that would find talent for a musical. I wasn't asking them to write nice things, just asking them to write. They all seemed interested.

Graham hosted a screening of the first episode for the press and a few other people for us. We did it at the Ham Yard Hotel in Soho. The BBC gave us all the difficult questions we'd be asked. The obvious comparisons with *The X Factor*. Do we need more talent shows on telly? No one asked any of them. It was quite unlike any launch I'd ever done for other TV shows. *The X Factor* press conferences were always a bloodbath of mean tabloid panto questions: 'Oi, Gary, when you gonna be fired?'

The response was good. They all loved the singers we featured. A couple of the female journalists even had tears in their eyes. I was waiting for the daggers and they never came. Everyone felt, I think, that this was something new. The time had come to celebrate talent without any sob stories.

I've got everyone in a good place. Everyone's calm. I entered that first weekend feeling calm and really confident about the show.

On the Monday morning we were all celebrating record figures for *Let It Shine*. The highest rated new format in eight years. We were all made up.

Then, ping. An email arrives with a little attachment. A story in *The Sun*. 'This show is too nice.'

* * *

Nigel! The one box you don't tick will be the one that catches you out. I was convinced I had covered all the bases. The one I hadn't thought of was dear old Nigel Martin-Smith.

Now people had a hook for the show. *Let It Shine*. It's not nasty enough.

Old Nigel's quote attached itself to us for the rest of the series. I've got 200 people, 200 lives, 200 careers working on the TV and the musical. Putting all their hours, all their effort in, and one throwaway comment could screw it all up. Every week the press wrote the same story because Nigel had put it in their heads. Why did he do it?

He's like a ghost, rattling his chains and reminding me of who I owe it all to. I can ignore most people but I can't ignore old Nige. That may have been his opinion but why did he have to say it? Is it because his name isn't anywhere in all this stuff, because he's not a part of it?

I felt so disappointed in him. We were getting on at the time and now this criticism from someone I considered a friend, a very old friend.

I hadn't really told Mum about this. Whenever I complained about Nigel she'd say, 'He's all right... he's got this lovely side to him.'

Nigel's still friends with all the Take That mums. He was always brilliant with them back in the day. Taking them to the Royal Variety Show, getting their hair done, making them feel special. We were all so young he couldn't have done it without the unqualified support of our parents. He took them all to one side and told them, 'I will make your sons' dreams come true.'

And he did that.

I was so upset about what happened with *Let It Shine*, I did something I never do: I moaned about it to Mum.

Mum said, 'I've spoken to Nigel, and he's explained it all. Apparently the journalist asked the question after the interview had ended. He didn't mean for it to get out.'

'That old chestnut! Mum! Please! Nigel taught me that one. He was the one that said, "Be careful, because after the interview they keep the tape running and that's when they'll ask you all the sneaky questions, when your guard's down." He'd told me that the best part of thirty years ago. Don't tell me he's forgotten his own lesson. Bollocks. I don't think so Mum.'

I was so angry with him. But the damage was done now.

When *Let It Shine* ended and we had our five band members, I disappeared off into the familiar safety of Take That world. It had never felt better to be there.

This new me was in evidence as we put together *Wonderland*, too. At one point, when we were rehearsing, I just lay there on the stage with my hands behind my head. I didn't tweet, or answer any emails; I didn't jot down song ideas. Or make a phone call. I just lay there. Kim Gavin looked at me. 'You all right?' I don't think he'd ever seen me do this chilling thing.

'Never been better, Kim.'

Going into a big tour is a good time to have a bit of a reset. Rehearsing Wonderland, I was doing a juice fast. Loads of us were.

People say, 'Oh, you mustn't juice, it's bad for you.'

No, heroin's bad for you. For God's sake, get a grip, people, it's just juice. After a few days juicing you start to get a real buzz and all this energy appears from nowhere. Mark joined me. Much of the Wonderland rehearsals were done hungry as we're all coming to work swinging our Juice Master bottles. Inevitably the juice fast becomes all we're talking about.

'What day are you on? How much longer are you going to do it?' I loved it. Mark's even madder for it than I am. We might even be in competition here.

'I'm going for seven days.'

'Yeah, thought I might push through for ten, actually…'

Howard thought we were both mad. We're all different.

There's a lot of the same conversations in the run-up to these big shows. Like, there's always a serious sit-down conversation with my team about the hair. For Wonderland we obsessed over Cara Delevingne's shade of blonde, which was nearly white-blonde at the time. Should I go the full Cara? If the hair's not the right shade of blond, I'm not on point. If the hair's not blond, I can't work. A pop star's got to have the pop star hair. Everyone knows that.

Sorting the hair was simple; the dancing was more complex.

* * *

I say everything was brilliant but my back was something else. I was still battling with an inflamed disc from back in 2009 when I climbed Kili. I'm not going to get through the show without painkillers so they put me on the Tramadol. It's a strong opiate, Tramadol. You get what they call 'tram rage' because they make you mental. I was off my head, if I'm honest, and not in a good way. I was fainting on a regular basis, once a week probably. I did *The One Show* one day and knew I was a heartbeat away from fainting on camera and, famously, walked off on air. The papers loved that. Every time Lizzie used to try and put make-up on my face, the physical contact made me burst into tears. The Tramadol made me flip out and cry, but if I didn't take them, I was in agony.

The tour's getting closer and closer and my back's not getting any better. I'm 46 at this point and I'm constantly going for X-rays, physio, massage. Is this my life from now on?

One week I decided to drop all that. Instead I just walked the dogs every day. The more I moved, the better it got. Less is more.

But I still wasn't up for some of the moves Mark and Howard were gunning for. They still love it. That's their means of expression. It's not mine. There's a constant pushing and pulling over what I will and won't do.

The world of Take That is in a state of change. Since 2006, and back in the nineties, nearly every song we release goes to number one. But the charts aren't working in our favour any more. It's based on streams, which our audience don't, as a rule, do. It's our fans' kids that stream. Our fans still buy CDs, they're a real old-school bunch. They're gonna stop making CDs soon. Yikes. What happens now?

In 2012 I remember Rob featured on a song with Dizzee Rascal. The video is brilliant. Rob and Dizzee roaming the streets with lots of old people on one of my favourite things, a mobility scooter. I've got no idea what that video's all about. If it was meant as a comment on life as an ageing artist, then it was bang on. Later in the year when a song we wrote together called 'Candy' came out, Rob told me, 'God. I'm not getting on Radio 1 with this one.'

Rob and I talked about it. He was gutted. To add insult to injury, Nick Grimshaw called him 'irrelevant'.

Rob cheered right up, though, when 'Candy' went to number one because then Radio 1 had to play it; they don't get a choice when it's in the Top 10.

I've known these days were coming for us for a long time. Since *III* especially I've been talking about this a lot. Writing something because you want it to get to number one has been a constant train of thought since I was a boy. Now it doesn't matter how good it is; you could put out the best thing you've ever done in your life and it's not gonna make a difference. Even before streaming, artists hit these walls at a certain point in their career. Even the great Elton John, Stevie Wonder, Sir Paul don't have regular hit singles any more.

We've all seen this day coming. It's a time everybody comes to. How do you move forward with your art after that? Do you ruthlessly target Radio 2, Heart, Magic? Are we screwed? Do we face the final curtain? Do we let ourselves be suffocated by a need to please people or do we just chill out and make music we love?

I went to the label, I went to management, and told them their expectations had to change. We'd just write without obsessing over the hit-seeking missile. From now on, we'd just go in the studio and make music we liked.

Any artist is constantly navigating changes in music. I guess it's just the start of a different era for us. I was just coming to terms with this when we were making *Wonderland*.

And then a song called 'Cry' comes at you out of nowhere.

One day an old Scouse mate of mine, Brian Rawlings, rings me and says, 'Hey, Gary, d'yer wanna curve ball?'

'Bri! You know I love a curve ball.'

He emails over the beginnings of this track, 'Cry'. I call him back, 'Love it.'

'Great, let's do a sesh.' So we have a little writing session, get the song finished and it's only then he tells me, 'It's a "featuring" gig, you know and you're featuring.'

'Oh, right, to who?'

He reels off ten artists: 'Let's ask them all, and first to come back gets the record.'

'No, Bri. Let's ask someone at Radio 1 who's the biggest of the lot and get them on it.'

Sigma came out top every time. 'They're our guys.'

At this stage, we weren't even looking for a single. We were just going to offer it with this jazz club vibe to someone for an album track. But as soon as those drum 'n' bass artists called Sigma got their hands on it they owned it.

That felt good for us and the audience. At gigs it goes down a storm. It's the song of the night, no question. I'm not tempted to start pimping us out to credible young artists in order to hang on to the Radio 1 audience. We're not going to get facelifts and try to forget how old we are. Take That aren't drum 'n' bass, that's Sigma. That's what they do. I loved it, but I think you only need to do it once. As a band, we'd grow old gracefully. Did that mean it was time we hung up our sparkly shirts, put away the Cuban heels?

Did it hell!

Wonderland comes out, we go on tour, it's brilliant. I think it's one of my most enjoyable tours. For the first time we perform in the round, in the centre of the venue. Being in the round means Wonderland needs some incredibly flamboyant costumes; the name demands it, too. This calls for sequins, lots of 'em. Luke the stylist really goes for it.

Our audience might be growing older with us, but there's no less love in the room. It's still overwhelming. The love never wanes. Out on the road nothing has changed.

It's stadiums all the way again in 2019 for our next Take That tour. The audience is going nowhere and neither are we. We love it. I can't believe my luck.

* * *

I was with my mum when I heard there had been an explosion at the Manchester Arena on 22 May 2017 as the audience left an Ariana Grande gig. It was about forty miles away from where we were playing in Liverpool, and only two nights before we'd played that very arena in a city that is one of my favourite places in the world to play. That's my home audience.

At this point in the evening they didn't know for sure what had happened, but we woke the next morning to the most terrible news. There were 22 dead, more than a hundred injured. It's just so close to home. Gigs aren't the place where things like that happen. Gigs are where we go to escape from the world.

That's our world now. I'm just a middle-aged bloke from Frodsham and I've had three brushes with bombs. My dad didn't have any his whole life.

On 7 July 2005 I had been in a Tube train that collided with an Underground train hit by the terrorist bomber at Edgware Road in London. The biggest memory of that day is the cries of other people and the screams and panic of very frightened passengers in a carriage full of dust and smoke. I will never forget the extraordinary deep and powerful chiming sound of the bomb going off probably no more than 30 feet from where I sat. The sound seemed to ring in my jaw.

In 2012 I heard that sound again when I went to Afghanistan to entertain the troops. At 3am on my second night there my bed moved underneath me and I heard and felt that sickeningly familiar sound again. I was told the next day that a small truck full of explosives had been detonated on a nearby highway.

And now this in the middle of Wonderland. The world doesn't feel as safe as it once was. For my children's generation it's normal. Like most kids mine love going to Westfield, but now they'll say, so nonchalantly, 'Oh, I don't go on a Saturday. Bombs.'

You know what. I think for a lot of people who bought tickets to those reunion shows in 2006, it wasn't just because they love us and our songs. I think, for some, for one night only, they wanted to escape into memories of far simpler and safer times. And they brought their kids with them.

Wonderland was a long tour; we did a lot of dates. It was a lovely show to do. When the tour ends, that's the point I'm racing on to: what's next?

This time, guess what? I went to a retreat. What would have happened previously is I'd have leapt out of one project and straight on to the other, possibly missing the after-party in the process. Not any more; rehearsals were well under way for *The Band*, which was opening in a couple of months.

The new me, Mr Chill, packs his bags and nips off to a retreat in Arizona. I tell you, after that I feel great and I am in the best shape of my life, without question. It's mad. I can't believe the body something as subtle as yoga has given me. Going to retreats is another way to reset my mind, like fasting, like doing nothing – these things just make me feel better and better.

I did some thinking while I was away.

We've got a *Greatest Hits* album and tour coming up in 2019. This is a line in the sand for me. We've followed this cycle of tours and albums every two years religiously. It's going to end.

It's not about the band splitting up. I can promise you, there will never be another Take That split announcement. I won't miss the after-party for Take That's Greatest Hits Tour. But in the future I'm up for pastures new. Don't know what they are, or where they are.

For once I am not planning ahead; for once I want the space for possibilities to be open for me instead of that game of Tetris called my diary. I'm 50 soon. It's time. I want to be excited by the unknown.

* * *

When I came off tour I told the BBC, 'It's a no to a second series of *Let It Shine*.'

It was meant to be celebratory, that show. It was about bringing real talent to the stage, teaching them the craft, giving them a proper job *and* putting on a kick-ass show in the process. As if that wasn't enough, the audience might even enjoy it. It was such an epic ambition. It had gone so well. Yet it felt like the whole thing had fallen flat.

If you Google that TV show, Nigel's quote's the first thing that pops up. 'Too nice.' My mantra had come back and bitten me on the bum. Mad, isn't it, that being nice seemed such a daring idea? That being nice would be our downfall? But there's still the musical and I was buzzing with excitement about that. Onwards!

The Band opened at Manchester Opera House on 8 September 2017. The three of us were determined not to take any of the shine away from the actors and actresses on the stage. So we didn't sit in the theatre. We set up in the box with the worst view of the stage and we all lay on the floor with James Security. We couldn't see much. We didn't need to. We just listened. The whoops, screams, applause, gasps and raucous, raucous laughter. This was a crowd having the night of their lives. We were all high and we weren't even on stage.

As we gathered at the side of the stage waiting to go on to perform the show's final medley, the reprise, Howard said, 'Ouch! They sound better than us, these guys.'

Even though it was a joke, that would have been unbearable to hear in a former life. But I had to agree; maybe they did. Or maybe they didn't. We entered the stage to the biggest roars of the night.

Jason's mum, Jenny, was there that night. All the mums were. Rob's mum, Jan went with Marj, mine. They all met up together as they arrived and were catching up on the gossip. It's hard to imagine as a parent what it must have been like for them watching that. If you think about it, who else can you share it with, your kid's bizarre life as a pop star?

Us boys get so desensitised to and blasé about these events and seeing the mums there reminds you how monumental the night was. A group who started down the road near the Arndale Centre – five teenagers who started out in the nightclubs with five plastic mics, £15 each from Tandy – and now there's a bloody musical about us. There's a tendency to see these nights as just work: the Olympics, Royal Variety shows, Wembley Stadium, this musical. The mums brought it all home.

My mum said, 'They've made a musical about you. Isn't that good.'

Yeah, it is. For a moment I let myself believe I was really amazing, that everyone loves me. Whatever making it is, I felt like I'd done it that night.

Then we ran off the stage straight into the back of a people carrier and swiftly got stuck in traffic. We were normal again.

I feel so safe inside this Take That bubble. Everyone who works with us is brilliant, half the crew are old friends, and being wedged between Howard and Mark feels like the safest place on earth.

Howard and I always have our Laurel and Hardy moments. In the middle of 'Hold Up A Light', Mark's holding court centre stage and me and Howard go to do one of our famous crossovers where we swap places on either side of him. We both raise our hands up to high five and completely miss. We might even add a little trip in there. We must have done this thousands of times in the last 25 years and we still find it absolutely hilarious.

Those *Wonderland* costumes were fit for Vegas (nope, haven't ruled that out either). Put me in a packed arena with those two lads, wearing a white suit covered in sequins, and there's one happy fella right there.

Before I get too puffy-chested here, let's not forget, I'm a star sometimes but I am always a dad. And Dad's reception at home doesn't always match the audience.

My two girls stopped by the dressing room before we went on at the O2 in London. I turned round with a big grin so Daisy could take in the rhinestone G on my white suit.

Her face lit up. 'Wow.'

Big sis is behind her with a hand over her mouth, 'God, Dad, are you not just really embarrassed wearing that?'

EPILOGUE

'STOP BEING SO HARD ON YOURSELF'

Today, I'm in the best place ever. I've changed my life. I'm going to be 50 in 2021 and before that comes I'm going to take a year off, grow that beard and really learn to meditate.

But the man who couldn't get out of bed in 2003 is still with me and he still frightens me. He's still in there, waiting for a big bowl of Golden Grahams.

I don't know if I could say I'm in a healthy place now. Just as I think I'm in control of everything, I feel for no reason, 'Help. I'm fat again.' It's a paranoia that I don't think I'm ever going to escape. I was at a dinner recently, a little Christmas party, where there were three things on the menu and one of them was pie. I've got a couple of reds in the tank. I love pie, as you know. 'I think I'll have the pie, thanks.'

The pie was delicious. I felt full.

Afterwards I went to the bathroom and there was a full-length mirror. I looked at it and thought, 'I've put weight on.'

Suddenly I couldn't wait to leave. I couldn't be gone fast enough. I said, 'Get the car, get the car now.'

I can't remember the last pie I had. Three years ago? Four years? Was it that one at Clarke's?

In all the fighting we do with ourselves, the unattainable goals, the picture we see is never the picture we're going to end up with. It never is. I'm never gonna get to the look I'm dreaming of, but I enjoy the challenge and the discipline of trying.

Make sure you enjoy the journey on the way to your destination because I guarantee there'll be another destination further up the road you'll start striving for. You'll never arrive. The journey is our story. (Christ, did I just say 'journey' twice in one paragraph? I am sorry.)

My point is, I don't think at any stage I can say, 'I've got all the answers here everyone.'

When Dad died I realised very quickly that I would be organising the funeral. Everyone had just checked out. It became my mission to find pictures and put beautiful poems in the order of service. There was a great picture of Dad on the front that, on the day, no one could even look at. In the end, though, that order of service is all you have left to remember of that day.

I was talking with the vicar before the service, talking about Dad. The one thing I remember he said is this very old-fashioned thing. 'He liked himself, your father. He was very happy being himself. He never wanted to be anyone else or have any other lifestyle.'

'He was happy with what he had.'

It stuck with me ever since, what the vicar said. In our world where we're all reaching and grasping and always wanting to change and be something different, we're never happy. And it's against everything I've fought for in this book, really. Dad was not at all a man that was down the gym; he called salad 'rabbit food'. He was a big fella all his life.

Among all this fine-tuning we do, at some point you've got to be at peace with who you are. I'm never going to run a marathon. I'm never going to look like Brad Pitt, or have a body like Howard. I'm never going to write 'Yesterday'.

I believe they call it 'practising acceptance'.

Dad never called it anything; he didn't have to say it, because you could see it in him and that was beautiful. It was a very big thing for me that, in the middle of something as sad as my father's funeral, of holding my mum who was just broken in two, it was the one big thing I hung on to throughout that time. Hung on to until now, in fact, nearly ten years later. I continue to hang on to it as tight as I can through all the madness. Like yourself.

ACKNOWLEDGEMENTS

Thanks to my gorgeous supportive Dawn, Dan, Emily, Daisy, Mum, Ian and family. My brilliant co-writer Kate. My personal team Elisa and Ryan. My bandmates Howard, Jason, Robbie and Mark. To everyone at James Grant – Eugenie, Chris, Emma, Martin and Neil. My friend and company leader David Joseph. My new publishing team: Natalie Jerome, Oliver Holden-Rea, Karen Browning, Lisa Hoare and all at Bonnier. All my close friends Eliot, Jason, Rossi, John, Ben, James, Jasmin and Melissa, Tim, David and Daf.